TERMINUS:
THE END IN LITERATURE, MEDIA AND CULTURE

Editors:
Brian Russell Graham and Robert W. Rix

Volume 5 in the book series *Interdisciplinære kulturstudier*

AALBORG UNIVERSITY PRESS

Terminus: The End in Literature, Media and Culture
Edited by Brian Russell Graham and Robert W. Rix

1. Edition

Volume 5 in the book series *Interdisciplinære kulturstudier*

Editors of the series:
Brian Russell Graham, Robert W. Rix, Kim Toft Hansen & Peder Kaj Pedersen

© Aalborg University Press, 2013

Graphics on frontcover: Ernst-Ullrich Pinkert
Layout: Hofdamerne ApS v/ Lea Rathnov & Cecilie von Haffner
ISBN: 978-87-7112-119-3
ISSN: 1904-898X

Printed in Denmark by Toptryk Grafisk ApS, 2013

Published by:
Aalborg University Press
Skjernvej 4A, 2nd floor
DK – 9220 Aalborg Ø
Phone: +45 99407140
aauf@forlag.aau.dk
forlag.aau.dk

This book is published with financial support from Department of Culture and Global Studies, Aalborg University.

Books in the series Interdisciplinære kulturstudier:

Jørgen Riber Christensen & Steen Ledet Christiansen (red.):
Monstrologi. Frygtens manifestationer, Aalborg Universitetsforlag, 2012

Steen Christiansen, Brian R. Graham, Louise Mønster, Peder Kaj Pedersen og Jan T. Schlosser (red.): *Spøgelser. Genfærdet som kulturel og æstetisk figur*, Aalborg Universitetsforlag, 2012

Steen Christiansen, Kim Toft Hansen, Peter Stein Larsen, Louise Mønster og Peder Kaj Pedersen (red.): *Kulturtrafik – æstetiske udtryk i en global verden*, 2011

Peter Stein Larsen, Peder Kaj Pedersen, Ernst-Ullrich Pinkert og Bent Sørensen (red.): *Interaktioner – om kunstarternes produktive mellemværender*, Aalborg Universitetsforlag, 2009

All rights reserved. No part of this book may be reprinted or reproduced or utilized in any form or by any electronic, mechanical, or other means, now known or hereafter invented, including photocopying and recording, or in any information storage or retrieval system, without permission in writing from the publishers, except for reviews and short excerpts in scholarly publications.

CONTENTS

5   A Note on *Terminus:* The End in Literature, Media and Culture.

7   *Terminus* as Cultural Epistemology – Introductory Reflections.
      Robert W. Rix and Brian Russell Graham

21   Fictions of Apocalypse: Taxonomy and Meaning.
      Brian Russell Graham

33   Genes, Germans and Genocide: The End of Celtic England?
      Robert W. Rix

55   *Terminus*: 'No vestige of a beginning – no prospect of an end'.
      Frances Carey

67   The Wheeling End: Tarot as Eschatological Text.
      Camelia Elias

81   Apocalypse and Anniversary: America's Bicentennial.
      Joe Goddard

107   Bob Dylan Sings the Apocalypse.
      Bent Sørensen

115   'It was a time for saying goodbye':
      Humphrey Jennings's *The Silent Village* and *A Diary for Timothy*.
      Jørgen Riber Christensen

137   The End and Ends of Walking with Special Reference to Will Self's Psychogeography.
      Jens Kirk

163   *Terminus*, Politics and the End of History: Some Thought Questions about Human Rights, History, the State of Global Culture and Political Ends.
      Ben Dorfman

185   Suburban Apocalypse: The Haunted House of Capitalism.
      Steen Christiansen

203   The End: Aesthetic and Ludic Topoi in Digital Entertainment.
      Alessandro Canossa and Gordon Calleja

213   About the Authors

A NOTE ON *TERMINUS: THE END IN LITERATURE, MEDIA AND CULTURE*

This is volume one of a two-volume collection of papers on the *Terminus: The End in Literature, Media and Culture*. The origin of the papers was – for the most part – presentations at the eponymous conference seminar held 2–3 May 2012, at the University of Aalborg, Denmark.

Volume two is the Danish section of papers. Together these volumes represent an attempt at collaboration between various fields of research in defining how 'the end' has significance in a wider spectrum of cultural forms. The conference/seminar offered representatives of many traditions the opportunity to learn from one another. This was effected through formal presentations and debates, as well as more casual discussions and debates.

The organisers chose 'the end' as a topic because endpoints are a central concern within almost all cultural epistemologies. The intensive interaction that this conference generated demonstrated with much clarity the value of gathering scholars from different traditions. The papers that participants were asked to prepare for this volume are the result of considering their own specific subject in the context of the general agreements and arguments elicited at the conference.

By way of a note on style, in the present volume, the editors have decided to maintain the individual author's choice of either British or American spelling.

We owe great thanks to Kasper Rueskov Guldberg, who has tirelessly gone through the articles with a fine-toothed comb, correcting mistakes and coming up with useful comments for improvements. His perspective on a number of issues has been invaluable to the editors.

TERMINUS AS CULTURAL EPISTEMOLOGY: INTRODUCTORY REFLECTIONS

The end has been with us from the beginning. Imaginations of the end are nearly universal in the religious literatures of the world. The oldest example appears on a single fragmentary tablet written in Sumerian cuneiform, from approximately the 17th century BC. It is the tale of a divine deluge sent to annihilate mankind, and how one man, Ziusudra, is told to build a boat. The motif of a Flood can be found again in the Babylonian epic of Gilgamesh, in which the survivor goes by the name of Utnapishtim. The Hebrews called him Noah; to the ancient Greeks he was known as Deucalion and so on. It is a common trait that the end is the beginning of something new. Radical change cannot come about through evolution but necessitates an end. The Flood was a past event that cleansed the old world in order for mankind to continue under a new dispensation.

Every society projects its own cultural fears and fantasies on to visions of the end. This is particularly prevalent in mytho-religious discourse. In the imagination of the old Scandinavians, cataclysmic tsunamis were replaced by a terrible frost. This was the *Fimbulwinter*, in which all living things would perish. But this is only the prelude to a greater event, *Ragnarök*, the final destiny of the old gods, followed by the rise of a new world. Cataclysmic ideas of the end are intrinsically connected with notions of return, repetition and new beginnings, as a number of the articles in this book show. The end is seldom finality. Rather, by invoking a sense of the end, we invigorate our awareness of the present, as well as raise our hopes for the future.

A crucial distinction suggests itself. 'The end' may be an episode in what is a linear sacred history, but in other settings, primarily Eastern religions, it may represent a phase of a cyclical history. When 'the end' is a phase of a historical cycle, it is naturally followed by a new beginning, as a matter of course. The finality is not always marked out as a cataclysmic event. In the Western world, however, where sacred history has been linear, the need for a conclusion leads to insistence on debacle, devastation, and world-shattering calamities as marking the end of times. But within that context, the end is not really finality either. Rather, it marks the point at which temporality is transcended: time runs its course and human life is separated into two worlds – heaven and hell. In order to make the transition to the new world beyond the present, many branches of Western Christianity insists on a Day of Reckoning, at which the life that is passing will be judged.

An important insight in dealing with 'the end' is that the final conclusion invariably intrudes upon the present. A good example of this can be found in relation to the Last Judgment scenario carved above church portals, painted on the walls of cloisters and shown on portals to cemeteries in the Middle Ages. These images taught that only good conduct would enable the individual believer to be numbered among the blessed and that backsliders could expect awful punishment should they fail to reform. Visions of the end are a projection of present misdeeds and serve to evaluate our actions here and now. This idea of judgment is also found in modern, secular versions of world cataclysms, and is something also accentuated in eco-disaster movies of recent years, such as *Waterworld, The Day after Tomorrow, Wall*E* and a number of others. Fears of the end, whether on a grand or more personal scale, are represented in a number of modern films, some of which are taken up for discussion in the present companion volumes.

When earlier versions of the papers in this collection were delivered at the conference/seminar in May 2012 at Aalborg University, it was an apt time to have a conference addressing *terminus* since 'the end' was imminent: the world would end on 21 December – at least if one believed the flurry of media attention that was given to an ancient Mayan prophecy. That a prophecy from an ancient culture was hyped in the media is evidence of our continued preoccupation with 'the end'. The background may be sketched briefly. When the great Mayan civilisation declined, large stone monuments with hieroglyphic writing were left behind. These monuments record a calendar that tells us that time will end after thirteen baktuns (a baktun is approximately 400 years). In 1966, Michael Coe of Yale University first linked this presumed end of the Mayan calendar to an end-of-the-world scenario. This idea was later amplified by Jose Argüelles in his best-selling book entitled *The Mayan Factor* (1987). Since then, articles, documentaries and websites have been teeming with 2012 apocalypse warnings. In fact, what is missing from the singular passage in the Mayan inscriptions on the 13th *baktun* is a notion of finality. No cataclysmic event is foretold, nor do we find any promise of a new and better world. Furthermore, the Mayans predicted other events far into the future well beyond 2012. In turn, the threat of annihilation has inspired the American disaster film directed by Roland Emmerich with the eponymous year in the title.

But it would be a mistake to lump all apocalyptic thinking together with the doom-and-gloom scenarios that attract headlines. Apocalyptic thinking plays a significant role in revolutionary movements. Social upheaval is dependent upon visions of a transfigured future, without which no revolutionary movement would be able to disengage from dominant orthodoxies. For example, various versions of apocalyptic thinking undergird the creation of class consciousness among 'lower orders' in England. This is the thesis that E. P. Thompson presents in his *locus classicus* of social studies *The Making of the English Working Class* (1963). Thompson's book concentrates on the formative years between 1780 and 1832, and discusses many of the millenarian movements that played a part in creating class consciousness in England.[1] But the connection between apocalypse and marginalised/disenfranchised groups finds parallels in many societies and at many time periods.

As revolutionary thinking was increasingly secularized, the distinction between linearity and cyclicality resurfaced. Modern history

---

1 The latest version available of this hugely influential monograph is a 2013 50th anniversary reprint from Penguin Books.

is on one level the result of a view of the end of a linear history. Karl Marx conceived of history as linear and, along with Friedrich Engels, advocated a socialist ending to history, completing a story which begins with feudalism and proceeds to capitalism, before its triumphant ending. But, from another point of view, the cyclical view of history, and the notion of the end tied in with it, produced an equally devastating effect on the modern world. Oswald Spengler, author of *The Decline of the West* (1918), produced a version of the end which (much to the shock of the author) was seized upon by German Nazis as indicative of the true nature of the situation faced by Europe in the first half of the twentieth century. Spengler's central argument, as Northrop Frye explains, is that all cultures go through the phases of 'rise, growth, decline, and fall'.[2] Elucidating the salient points of the cycle, Frye states:

> Spengler sees history as a series of quasi-organic developments or 'cultures', which are at first agricultural and feudal, then urban and oligarchic, and finally become industrial and totalitarian. The last stage is one of huge cities, nomadic population, profiteering and dictatorships, mass wars, the impoverishing of agriculture and the exhaustion of the arts, and the growth of technology.[3]

The diabolical logic of Nazism concludes that at such times in history one nation must place the world under martial law.

But Nazism, as a *grand récit*, showed itself incapable of giving rise to another *Reich*. Subsequently, the Cold war produced a dualistic world view with two competing blocs threatening each other with Armageddon. Today, however, a number of historians have discussed the present fall of ideological competition in terms that have affinity with the postmodern philosopher Jean-François Lyotard's pronouncement of a death sentence for all 'metanarratives'. This was how one can translate the American political economist Francis Fukuyama's ar-

---

2 Northrop Frye, *Northrop Frye on Modern Culture*, ed. Jan Gorak (Toronto: University of Toronto Press, 2003), 266.

3 Frye, *Northrop Frye on Modern Culture*, 248.

gument in *The End of History and the Last Man* (1992). In an earlier article (on which his book was an expansion), Fukyama writes:

> What we may be witnessing is not just the end of the Cold War, or the passing of a particular period of post war history, but the end of history as such: that is, the endpoint of mankind's ideological evolution and the universalization of Western liberal democracy as the final form of human government ...[4]

As sceptics – ranging from the Marxists like Perry Anderson to political theorists like Benjamin R. Barber – have noted, the resurgence of Russia and the rise of China compromise Fukyama's interpretation. Rejecting the notion of a contest altogether, the French philosopher Jean Baudrillard does not see the end of the Cold War as simply spelling the victory of one ideology over another; rather it marks the vanishing point of global utopian visions. As he argues in his book *The Illusion of the End* (1994), Marxist or liberalist hopes for a final goal of their ideologies are chimeras; there is no Hegelian motor controlling the course of history, and there is no end to be had.[5]

Most essays in this book deal with how literature and films reflect cultural anxieties. The inability to kill off the old world while a new fails to materialise has since the advent of Modernism been the focus of much literary endeavour. It is most memorably captured in T. S. Eliot's famous poem *The Waste Land* (1922). The epigraph Eliot selected for this *tour de force* refers to the Greek tale of the Cumaean Sybil, who had asked Apollo for eternal life. Apollo granted her the boon, but without the accompanying gift of eternal youth. In line with the traditional 'be careful what you wish for' *topos*, the Sybil became increasingly more crippled and shrunken with age, so that, after a millennium, only her voice was left. Eliot's epigram is taken from chapter 48 of Petronius's

---

4 Francis Fukuyama, 'The End of History', *National History* 16 (1989), 3-18, at 3.

5 Jean Baudrillard, *The Illusion of the End* (Stanford, Ca.: Stanford University Press, 1994).

Satyricon, in which the Sybil is reported to have been suspended in a basket by the uncaring people of Cumae. When the local boys teased her, asking 'Sybil, what do you want?', her reply was simple: 'I want to die'.

Literary critic Frank Kermode discusses Eliot as one of the writers who saw his own time as a *saeculum* between the death of the old order and the beginning of a new age. This was in a published series of lectures entitled *The Sense of an Ending* (1967, rev. ed. 2000). In these lectures Kermode seeks to establish a connection between fictions and apocalyptic modes of thought. The central point is that humans will 'impose form on time', punctuate the continuous lines that otherwise vanish into eternity. Kermode notes that having a firm idea of a finality towards which the clock is ticking has the greatest organising power of all. This he sees as an analogy with the processes of reading and writing fiction. Kermode expertly discusses our concept of time in order to gauge how every story structurally anticipates its own conclusion, and how the conclusion determines its opening. Events derive their significance from an imagined coherence, as in Kermode's example of Aeneas's journey, where 'the episodes are internally related; they all exist under the shadow of the end'.[6] In other words, the end is not something superimposed upon stories, but contained within as a guiding principle behind all its moves.

That literary 'endings' are significant for understanding how stories are narrated has been pointed out in a number of studies: Barbara Hernstein Smith's *Poetic Closure: A Study of How Poems End* (1968), David Richter's *Fable's End: Completeness and Closure in Rhetorical Fiction* (1974), Marianna Torgovnick's *Closure in the Novel* (1981), John Gerlach's *Towards the End: Closure and Structure in the American Short Story* (1985), Elizabeth MacArthur's *Extravagant Narratives: Closure and Dynamics in the Epistolary Form* (1990), and John Neupert's *The End: Narration and Closure in the Cinema* (1995) to mention just a few. As is clear, many of these studies were born out of a concern with formalist and structuralist concerns of past decades. An update on the epistemology

---

6 Frank Kermode, *The Sense of an Ending: Studies in the Theory of Fiction with a New Epilogue*, rev. ed. (Oxford: Oxford University Press, 2000), 5.

of 'the end' in various cultural forms and products with a broader remit is warranted. It is our hope that this collection of essays will make some headway in this respect.

On the marking out of the spatial lines, a few words should be said about the significance of the title given to the present collection of papers. In Roman religion, Terminus was an agrarian god who protected boundary markers. Stones were often used to provide an effective means for marking these boundaries, although a stump or a tree could also serve to demarcate adjacent properties. Descriptions of these boundary markers can be found in classical writers such as Ovid, Tibullus, Prudentius and Horace.[7] Siculus Flaccus, a writer on land surveying, also records the ritual by which landowners celebrated Terminus. These rituals involved sacrifices made at the boundary markers placed between estates. The Terminalia was an annual renewal of a contract. It was also celebrated as a public festival. One place where this was held is visited by many modern tourists: the transport hub Termini in the Italian capital of Rome (a place to which all roads lead). This was the god's ancient shrine on the Capitoline Hill, at which Terminus was worshipped as an aspect of Jupiter. The celebrations took place on 23 February, the last day of the year according to the old calendar.[8]

These Roman customs provide a good illustration of some of the core relationships discussed in this book. One such theme is the need for making sense of the spatial and the temporal by punctuating their potentially endless lines of continuation. Societies are forced to impose boundaries and to sanction them – sometimes through reference to divine or sacred forces. The boundary (or end) marker is a way to parcel out rights of disposition and regulate social space. A topic taken up in this and its Danish companion volume is how the possession of space is negotiated in a historical perspective. History is often an account of how the present is created as the end product of a series of past final-

---

7 Roger D. Woodard, *Indo-European Sacred Space: Vedic and Roman Cult* (Urbana: University of Illinois Press, 2006), 65-6.

8 Anthony Aveni, *Empires of Time: Calendars, Clocks, and Cultures* (London: Tauris Parke, 2000), 114.

ities. These are aspects of cultural epistemology that are addressed at several junctions in this collection.

One of the reasons that the notion of *terminus* or endings is of interest for extended discussion is because it is not only something to be observed objectively by discerning academics. In fact, academia thrives on making sense of the world, its history and its cultural forms by viewing it as a series of stops and starts. If one takes just a cursory glance at academic publishing over the past twenty years, it is clear that the sense of living after 'the end' of once dominant paradigms (spatial and temporal) serves as a guiding principle for discussing our fast-changing world. Studies such as *After the End: Representations of Post-Apocalypse, British Culture and the End of Empire, The End of Print, The End of Hardware: Augmented Reality and Beyond* and many similar titles have been published. If we way take this to be an expression of a particular 'postmodern condition', we hope these two volumes will contribute to how notions of 'ends' have always been important, if not central, in cultural discourses.

The papers are organised so that they reflect thematic, national and chronological perspectives. But the essays on widely different topics and periods also show that it is possible to identify several threads of continuity, as well as correspondences and similarities, in the way that 'the end' has been conceptualised.

The collection begins with a useful overview of 'Fictions of Apocalypse: Taxonomy and Meaning'. In this essay, Brian Russell Graham firstly addresses the question of categories of apocalypse in literature, media and culture. Though the notion of 'apocalypse' points to a total end of 'things as they are,' what we find in representation, he argues, is *degrees* of demise. These categories, however, are not simply coldly, formalist groupings of different types of culture texts. Graham argues that the fact that our culture is characterised by representations of degrees of 'world's end' is deeply suggestive of the actual meaning of these texts. He concludes with a series of reflections upon the meaning of these stories which steers a course away from conservative and pessimistic conclusion about the genre.

The next essay is the first among several in this collection which takes up the theme of 'the end' within a national perspective. In 'Genes, Germans and Genocide: The End of Celtic England?', Robert W. Rix reflects on the Latin *terminus* in relation to the popular understanding that the Celto-British population was effectively eradicated from what is now England. References to 'the end of Celtic Britain' are often found in historical and critical literature, indicating that the Celto-Britons were replaced by Germanic invaders from the continent in the course of the fifth and sixth centuries. The paper examines how this 'endist' notion of total eradication repeats what was in fact the very premise for defining an Anglo-Saxon ethnic identity in the Middle Ages. In a critical context, the paper is a contribution to the re-assessment of the *terminus* myth that has dominated popular conceptions of Anglo-Saxon England. Through a re-examination of several key texts, it is suggested that incorporation and assimilation of Celtic elements may be better models for understanding the foundation of England than genocide.

Frances Carey's paper *'Terminus*: "No vestige of a beginning – no prospect of an end"' picks up on the idea of the divine steering of history that is also discussed in Rix's essay. She begins with the geologist James Hutton in *Theory of the Earth*, a paper he first read to the Royal Society of Edinburgh in 1785. This was one of the landmarks in the Enlightenment's questioning of concepts of time, of purpose and of salvation that had underpinned Western thought. 'God is dead' was Nietzsche's proposition almost a century after Hutton. But Carey shows that God, or at least the imaginative force of the biblical narrative, would cast a long shadow which neither the Enlightenment nor the scientific revolution of the nineteenth century was able to dispel. The essay argues that the 'enchanted' and the 'disenchanted', from the eighteenth century to the present, have continued to reflect the influence of the teleology and imagery of the Bible in ways that both construct and deconstruct meaning.

Camelia Elias's contribution 'The Wheeling End: Tarot as Eschatological Text' offers a mystical parallel to the investigation of scientific paradigms in Carey's article. Ever since the emergence of Tarot as a tool for divination (sometime around 1450), the cards have been associated with modes of self-perception and alternative worldviews derailing the sense of what we call reality. Through the visual imagery of Tarot cards, one travels between states of consciousness in order to look for answers to a problem. In her paper, Elias looks at how the transformative change embedded in Tarot can depict an eschatological validation of the self and the world. In other words, the more one dies and the more the world dies (often represented as a death of cultural beliefs), the more a magical poetic realm manifests itself. Elias suggests that a Tarot pack of cards, due to its several takes on 'endings', aids the creative potential to make visible an invisible world in a process that is neither merely cognitive nor merely psychological, but essentially poetic. The essay is also a close-reading of Robert Browning's 'Porphyria's Lover', which is an examination of abnormal psychology. Elias proposes that the mapping of Tarot cards onto the events in the poem teases out new themes and aspects of the poem. This combines practice and theory in a new and thought-provoking constellation.

The following two essay focus on the U.S. They investigate how national enchantment and disenchantment is engendered in the process of mapping past and future of America as 'new' nation. Joe Goddard's 'Apocalypse and Anniversary: America's Bicentennial' trains its focus on the planning and execution of the American Bicentennial. Planning began in 1966 and cumulated in the 4 July 1976 celebrations. Domestic conflict, spurred on by the war in Vietnam, Watergate, social, sexual, and generational revolutions, systemic estrangement, and a collapse in national self-belief combined to alter the aims and goals of the bicentennial celebrations. A consensus which emphasized American progress broke, to be replaced with scrambles for unity in the (supposedly) less-troubled past. Thus, the bicentennial marked the end of a self-confident era and the birth of a more self-conscious one which leapt backwards by resting upon ideas of a more innocent age. Using government documents, news-media, magazines, and popular culture, this essay suggests that the bicentennial celebrations helped fashion a new heritage consensus.

Bent Sørensen's 'Bob Dylan Sings the Apocalypse' presents a close reading of selected Dylan lyrics that avail themselves of the trope of the apocalypse. This reveals that Dylan's valorisation of the end of the world as we know it alters with his growing old – from an occasionally positive spin on cataclysmic change in the 1960s ('The Times They Are A-Changin'), via cautionary tales (such as 'A Hard Rain's A-Gonna Fall'), to a cynical outlook in 'the last day's last hour of the last happy year' (a line from 'Cross the Green Mountain' from 2003). This development Sørensen reads as emblematic of Dylan's disillusionment with the 1960s youth culture and his whole generation, but also as a more general existential world-weariness on his part.

Like the previous couple of essays, the next two contributions examine issues of nationalism, consciousness and 'ends', but this time in a British context. Jørgen Riber Christensen's '"It was a time for saying goodbye": Humphrey Jennings's *The Silent Village* and *A Diary for Timothy*' employs the two WWII propaganda films to characterize Jennings's style as a documentary film maker. The article also discusses his ideology, and it concludes that it was this complex ideology that determined the style and aesthetics of his films with their use of montage, anticipatory soundtracks and the medium-range shot. The stylistic analysis is used as a tool in the overall aim of the article, which is to examine any dystopian – or terminal – and utopian aspects of Jennings's production. *The Silent Village* is regarded as a counterfactual history and apocalyptical dystopia, and *A Diary for Timothy* as a utopia with its hints at the creation of a welfare state based on class consensus in the post-war period after the apocalypse of the war against Nazi barbarism.

Jens Kirk's paper 'The End and Ends of Walking with Special Reference to Will Self's Psychogeography' shows how, at a point in the history of the West where walking is no longer a necessity, walking must always be staged as an activity with a point, or end, or reason. More particularly, the essay shows how British writer Will Self's texts on walking are minutely preoccupied with the *reasons* for walking and go to great length to make their purposes and ends explicit on the one hand, and, on the other, repeatedly stage walking's *termination* in defeat and failure. An important end for walking remains, nevertheless. Will Self's texts strike up a vital relationship between walking and writing. While his discourse relies on walking for meaningful content, unnecessary and pointless walking relies on his discourse for meaning and significance. Writing produces the activity of walking as significant, relevant and the site of privileged experience. Walking in turn supplies the stuff of writing and discourse, even if that involves its failure to deliver on the promises it was instilled with in the first place. This seems to be the ultimate point or end of walking for Will Self.

The following two articles confront the problem of 'the end' with reference to issues of late modern societies and postmodernism. The first of these discussions is Ben Dorfman's *'Terminus*, Politics and the End of History: Some Thought Questions about Human Rights, History, the State of Global Culture and Political Ends'. This paper addresses *terminus* via politicized notions of history, using Francis Fukuyama's 'end of history' thesis as its springboard. The point is to suggest that, whereas Fukuyama captured a particular mind-set and historical moment in suggesting liberalism as 'the end' of history – a *terminus* of competing ideologies – it may in fact be *human rights* which *de facto* play that role in contemporary culture. This is due to the connection of liberalism and rights – 'rights society' being the goal of liberal culture. However, it also concerns a contemporary cultural relationship with human rights. This concerns rights as artefacts of political culture, certainly, but also popular and consumer culture as well.

On a more concrete level of cultural anxiety, the utopian dream of the nuclear family and the home as a fortress of stability is taken up for revision in 'Suburban Apocalypse: The Haunted House of Capitalism'. In this paper, Steen Christiansen argues for a re-evaluation of the haunted house story as one which sees the current economic crisis as an apocalyptic moment, destroying the picture-perfect dreams of the American family. A number of recent horror fictions have returned to the trope of the haunted house to reveal the anxieties over becoming house-poor. Films such as *Paranormal Activity* insist on the disruption of the hyperhouse/McMansion as a doomed endeavour, one replete with economic disaster. This apocalyptic moment can then only be sublimated into the breakdown of the family, much as it happened in the 1970s. The household economy becomes an image of society's household economy.

The essay that concludes this volume looks into the future, even the far future. Given the volley of natural and ecological disasters, terrorism, deadly viruses, wars, and economic instability, it is no surprise that game creators have projected post-apocalypse scenarios that can be turned into entertainment, at the same time as demanding reflection. Alessandro Canossa and Gordon Calleja's 'The End: Aesthetic and Ludic Topoi in Digital Entertainment' examines the trope of 'the end' both as a recurrent narrative theme and as a fundamental functional gameplay dynamic in computer games ramped up for market profit. Building on theory established in Game Studies, computer games are defined as multi-layered systems of signs, relying both on symbolic representations and affordances that necessitate players making important choices. Within this framework, the theme of 'the End' is examined in three recent games: *Deus Ex 3*, *Mass Effect 3* and *Fallout 3*, which all evidence how aesthetic and ludic elements are embedded within one another.

A collection of essays on *terminus* is to make a beginning. By looking at how ideas of culmination, conclusion, closure, finale and termination from the perspective of a number of various genres, cultural formations and historical contexts, we hope to initiate an invigorating discussion of the how endings *mean* in social and cultural contexts.

Robert W. Rix and Brian Russell Graham

FICTIONS OF APOCALYPSE: TAXONOMY AND MEANING

Brian Russell Graham

As Curtis argues in her *Postapocalyptic Fiction and the Social Contract*, studies of the post-apocalyptic fiction focus on three different issues. Wagar and Mannix stress the genre's 'didactic focus'; Berger and Rosen turn to its 'theoretical association with the postmodern'; and Moylan is concerned with the genre as a 'subtype of the utopian/dystopian genre'.[1] One consideration which is missing from scholarship dealing with this genre is a taxonomy of types of post-apocalyptic fiction: Curtis calls it an 'under-theorized genre'.[2] In this article I provide just such a taxonomy, based on the notion that the different degrees of apocalypse which we come across in this genre point to different types of story. But these considerations are only my starting point. For my argument is that a proper taxonomy of the genre is thoroughly suggestive of the larger meaning of the genre as a whole. The genre might be viewed as a decidedly pessimistic one, morbidly concerned with a terrifying end of times. However, my own taxonomy suggests that the

---

[1] Claire P. Curtis, *Postapocalyptic Fiction and the Social Contract: "we'll not go home again"* (Lanham: Lexington Books, 2010), 12. James Berger, *After the End: Representations of the Post-Apocalypse* (Minneapolis, MN: University of Minnesota Press, 1999); Patrick Mannix, *The Rhetoric of Anti-Nuclear Fiction* (Lewisburg, PA: Bucknell UP, 1992); Tim Moylen, *Scraps of the Untainted Sky* (Boulder, CO: Westview Press, 2000); Elizabeth Rosen, *Apocalyptic Transformation* (Lanham, MD: Lexington Books, 2008); W. Warren Wagar, *Terminal Vision: The Literature of Last Things* (Bloomington, IN: Indiana UP, 1992).

[2] Curtis, *Postapocalyptic Fiction*, 12.

genre urges us to consider positive social goals. Indeed, it compels us to return to religious or spiritual traditions for visions of redemption and restoration which are at the opposite pole of experience from the infernos of post-apocalyptic fiction. Additionally, my discussion is also ground-breaking in terms of its representing the first discussion of the genre to incorporate the works of Nietzsche.

Fictions of the apocalypse are characterized by scenes of devastation, but we might characterize the kind of devastation we come across in particular ways. We might say, to get started, that often a fiction of the apocalypse is a fiction in which the human, animal, and vegetable worlds have been destroyed. Of course remnants of these worlds remain, especially of mankind, but what we see in these works of fiction is that levels of reality have been very nearly destroyed, and the story takes place in the aftermath of the devastation. Figure 1 illustrates the point.

Apocalyptic fiction	Examples
The demise of mankind, the animal kingdom, and the vegetable world.	*The Road* by Cormac McCarthy *The Death of Grass* by John Christopher *The Drought* by J. G. Ballard

Figure 1.

My examples of this kind of degree of apocalypse range from *The Road* by Cormac McCarthy, through *The Death of Grass* (1956) by Samuel Youd, published under the pseudonym John Christopher, to *The Drought* by J. G. Ballard. These texts are representative of the kinds of apocalypses that we come across most commonly in fiction, where these three levels of ordinary existence – human, animal, and vegetable – have been extinguished or very nearly extinguished.

It must be conceded that some fictions of the apocalypse are about Creation – or at least new life in the world. After all, often the destruction done to human beings and animals is wrought by new life forms.

We might think of invasion from Mars (*The War of the Worlds*), a new vampiric race (*I Am Legend*), and exotic new plant life (*Hothouse*). In such narratives, as I say, the emphasis is on not just destruction but new life forms or agency. However, I would argue that here too what is interesting is not the arrival of the new but the passing of the old. These fictions may represent examples of the literature of the fabulous and tell us of new worlds emerging, but even here they primarily represent a nightmare vision in which the categories of reality that we know start to disappear.

I think we can expand the picture somewhat because, although the notion of fictions of apocalypse suggests that what we find are stories in which destruction is more or less total, what we actually find in them are degrees of devastation.

Ever-Greater Decreations	Examples
The demise of mankind	*After London* by Richard Jefferies
The demise of mankind and the animal kingdom.	*The Last Man* by Mary Shelley *I Am Legend* by Richard Matheson
The demise of mankind, the animal kingdom, and the vegetable world.	*The Road* by Cormac McCarthy *The Death of Grass* by John Christopher *The Drought* by J. G. Ballard

Figure 2.

We can see from this table that, in addition to the categories I started out by discussing, there are at least two further categories, these being ones in which the 'end of the world' scenario is less consuming. If we turn to Richard Jeffries's *After London* (1885), in this novel the destruction affects only human life; animal life and plant life are left intact, and those life forms come to characterize life in England, where the story takes place, that world returning to a largely human-free pastoral idyll. Only mankind is affected by this particular end of the world scenario, and perhaps we can create a category for this kind of story. We can create an intermediate category here, too, because there are also stories in which animal life along with human life is destroyed but plant life survives, untouched by the changes. My examples here – the one very different from the other – are *The Last Man* by Mary Shelley and *I Am Legend* by Richard Matheson.

I think we can go even further, because it is also possible to consider the 'apocalypses' which lie on the other side of the central category I started out with. Beyond the stories dealing with the demise of the human, animal, and vegetable categories lie stories dealing with the demise of human, animal, vegetable, and the mineral worlds. Clearly, one kind of story in this category would be the deluge-type story, the point being that in such a narrative human, animal, vegetable life, *and* the mineral world are lost: the mineral world – the cities and even the deserts – is also overwhelmed. Examples include, on different levels of seriousness, Ballard's *The Drowned World* and Kevin Costner's *Waterworld*; other examples would include Kevin Baxter's *Flood* from 2008 and even certain memorable scenes in the blockbuster *The Day After Tomorrow*.

And it is possible, I would argue, to go one step beyond even this, because there are fictions in which all five categories are destroyed: mankind, the animal world, vegetable life, the mineral world, and even the watery world. Those are the fictions in which planet Earth is destroyed. Lars Von Trier's recent film *Melancholia* springs readily to mind, but there are other examples. In his short story 'Finis', Pollack tells the story of the end of the world. A second sun appears in the solar system, and, after a series of cataclysmic events, it proves too much for our planet, which burns up at the end of the short story. Of course fictions in this category need not involve the appearance of a rogue sun or planet. If the previous category involves the rise of water, this level probably involves the rise of fire, and any story in which fire threatens levels of reality belongs here.

Here is the complete table, then, laying out what we should think of as the ever greater 'end of the world'-scenarios of this fiction.

Ever-Greater Decreations	Examples
The demise of mankind	*After London* by Richard Jefferies
The demise of mankind and the animal kingdom.	*The Last Man* by Mary Shelley, *I Am Legend* by Richard Matheson
The demise of mankind, the animal kingdom, and the vegetable world.	*The Road* by Cormac McCarthy *The Death of Grass* by John Christopher *The Drought* by J. G. Ballard
The demise of mankind, the animal kingdom, the vegetable world, and mineral life.	*The Drowned World* by J. G. Ballard *Waterworld* (movie)
The demise of mankind, the animal kingdom, the vegetable world, mineral life, and the watery world	'Finis' by Frank L. Pollack

Figure 3.

Of course what we are looking at is a process whereby apocalypse progressively absorbs the categories of the Great Chain of Being. It is to the idea of the Great Chain of Being that we owe the structure of animal, vegetable, mineral, and so on. This factor suggests to me one further taxonomic point: perhaps we should also consider those texts which deal with the death of God as part of this literature. After all, the level above the human world on the Great Chain is the divine world, and in the nineteenth century the development of atheism was metaphorically spoken of as the 'death of God', or even, and very significantly in this context, the killing of God. In *The Gay Science* or *The Joyful Wisdom*, it is this language that Nietzsche famously uses. In the most famous passage, a madman addresses a crowd, accusing the people of deicide, and his rhetoric, we note, is decidedly apocalyptic in tone:

The insane man jumped into their midst and transfixed them with his glances. 'Where is God gone?' he called out. 'I mean to tell you! We have killed him, you and I! We are all his murderers! But how have we done it? How were we able to drink up the sea? Who gave us the sponge to wipe away the whole horizon? What did we do when we loosened this earth from its sun? Whither does it now move? Whither do we move? Away from all suns? Do we not dash on unceasingly? Backwards, sideways, forwards, in all directions? Is there still an above and below? Do we not stray, as through infinite nothingness? Does not empty space breathe upon us? Has it not become colder? Does not night come on continually, darker and darker? Shall we not have to light lanterns in the morning? Do we not hear the noise of the grave-diggers who are burying God? Do we not smell the divine putrefaction? – for even Gods putrefy! God is dead! God remains dead! And we have killed him!'[3]

The missing element in my table is the divine world, and this kind of discourse fits neatly into my structure.

Ever-Greater Decreations	Examples
The demise of God	*The Joyful Wisdom* by Friedrich Nietzsche
The demise of God and mankind	*After London* by Richard Jefferies
The demise of God, mankind and the animal kingdom.	*The Last Man* by Mary Shelley *I Am Legend* by Richard Matheson
The demise of God, mankind, the animal kingdom, and the vegetable world.	*The Road* by Cormac McCarthy *The Death of Grass* by John Christopher *The Drought* by J. G. Ballard

---

3 Friedrich Nietzsche, *The Joyful Wisdom*, trans. Thomas Common, ed. Oscar Levy (New York: Macmillan, 1944), 167–168.

The demise of God, mankind, the animal kingdom, the vegetable world and mineral life	*The Drowned World* by J. G. Ballard *Waterworld* (movie)
The demise of God, mankind, the animal kingdom, the vegetable world, mineral life, and the watery world	'Finis' by Frank L. Pollack

Figure 4.

If I were to critique my own schema, I might say that what we find in this area of fiction is perhaps not such a 'neat' progression of ever-greater 'world's end' situations. It is easy to point to stories in which the human, animal, vegetable, and watery worlds are dispatched, but the mineral world survives, albeit in the worst possible form. In 'Till A' the Seas Gang Dry' by Barlow and Lovecraft, climate change affects the sea levels, resulting in the disappearance of the oceans, the retreat of human life to the Earth's poles, and the eventual extinction of mankind.

That said, I would argue that such a taxonomy of this type of literary fiction is very valuable, in great part because it is suggestive of the larger meaning of the genre in question. The remainder of this article deals with what this taxonomy suggests about precisely that.

On the face of it, it looks as though these stories are expressive of scepticism about change. In these narratives, the tendency is in the direction of demise. It is as if all 'change' results in demise. At least the Great Chain of Being kept the world turning. Are we, then, supposed to feel nostalgia for the Great Chain of Being and its enduring character?

I would argue that we are not. I'd like to put a positive spin on this kind of fiction. If we look at the worlds of fictions of the apocalypse, what strikes us is the fact that these are worlds characterized by unstable hierarchy and an on-going fight for supremacy. The world was characterized by hierarchy and struggle before the apocalyptic event, and it is still characterized by hierarchy and struggle afterwards. Of course the struggle for pre-eminence in the human world is of paramount importance in this fiction. Many of these stories were written during the Cold War, and a nuclear Armageddon which engulfs most of these categories of reality is obviously central to the socio-historical background to the genre. But this is frequently a mythical genre, and so it constantly expands away from the ordinary human-inspired Armageddon. These worlds are Hobbesian worlds in which the Hobbesian behaviour controls not just human life but also other life types. It is unremarkable for animal life to manifest a fight for survival, but in Brian Aldiss's *Hothouse*, the remaining human-like beings are peripheral to the real fight for supremacy, which goes on between new plants in a far-off planetary vegetable world. In this fiction, we would not be surprised to come across stories dealing with warring mineral-world powers either: any end of the world narrative dealing with machines engaging in a fight for domination illustrates the point.

Another noticeable trend – which is very suggestive for my own conclusions about this genre – is the fact that in these hierarchical and 'fighting' worlds what we often find is that a level of reality has usurped the one or ones above it on the Great Chain of Being. To start off with the categories I first outlined, we can see that in some stories, animal life gains the upper hand; in others, plant life comes to dominate. When we cross the line between the living and the non-living, we come across the same trend. In other stories, machines or computers, representatives of the mineral world, achieve hegemony; the sea, which overwhelms all life in numerous movies, can also be cast as an 'enemy', and so too can the fire which consumes everything in texts such as 'Finis'. Another table suggests itself:

The Rise of Other Categories of Being	Examples
The demise of God and **the rise of men** – specifically Nietzsche's Übermensch	*Thus Spake Zarathustra* by Friedrich Nietzsche
The demise of God and mankind, and **the rise of animals**	*Planet of the Apes* (original novel by Pierre Boulle)

The demise of God, mankind, and the animal kingdom, and **the rise of plants.**	*Hothouse* by Brian Aldiss
The demise of God, mankind, the animal kingdom, and the vegetable world, and **the rise of the mineral world**	Stories in which machines or computers take over.
The demise of God, mankind, the animal kingdom, the vegetable world, and mineral life, and **the rise of the watery world**	*Flood* by Stephen Baxter
The demise of God, mankind, the animal kingdom, the vegetable world, mineral life, and the watery world, **and the rise of fire**.	'Finis' by Frank L. Pollack

Figure 5.

Perhaps the fact that these worlds are characterized by hierarchy and struggle points to how we might consider the kind of positive vision the literature points back to. To moderns, the Great Chain of Being is an image of hierarchy to rival anything in fictions of the apocalypse. Perhaps, then, it invites us to consider what a world that is not hierarchical would look like. We have, however, lost our ideas about what an 'existence' which is free of hierarchy would look like. Marxism tells us of the classless society. Feminism tells us of the demise of the hierarchy in which women are the second sex. Post-colonialism tells us of an end to empire and the subjugation of peoples who are deemed inferior to civilized white men. Environmentalism tells us of the desirability of undoing the hierarchy in which mankind dominates nature. Environmentalism also tells us about habitable cities, which are also sustainable. These achievements may be suggestive of a world free of hierarchy, but it is going to be a much bigger 'free-of-hierarchy' world than that which these stories compel us to imagine. This is, after all, a literature which takes in all these different levels of existence. All of these factors may be characteristics of levels of experience where hierarchy is in the process of being abolished, but it is also possible to go beyond these levels, and I would argue that, in relation to this fiction, we must do exactly that. If I'm right about the death of God being an integral part of this, then what this fiction invites us to consider is even the abolition of the hierarchy of God and Man. If what this fiction demands of us is that we consider what a world that is not hierarchical would look like, the world in question should be as close to the most perfect world of desire as the worlds of fictions of the apocalypse are to the absolute ends of fear. Our ideal, after all, must be every bit as desirable as our infernos are fearful.

No doubt the notion of a world free of hierarchy at the limit of desire has numerous resonances in different religious, spiritual, and even occult traditions. I myself am aware of what this world looks like in the literary theory of critic Northrop Frye, a critic who, like William Blake, believed the Old and New Testaments to be the great code of art. What does a world without hierarchy and struggle look like? In his literary criticism, Frye provides us with an idea. In the first place, Frye argues that literature as a whole insists on the desirability of each category of being – divine, human, animal, vegetable, mineral – uniting in 'one body' on each level of reality. On the level of human society, this means that human society becomes the body of one man. When speaking of liberalism, Frye opposes this 'body' to society as 'mob'. 'A mob always has a leader, but a people is a larger human body in which there are no leaders or followers, but only individuals acting as functions of the group'.[4] Here human society breaks free of the Hobbesian level and achieves unity. But Frye tells us that the world of desire, the 'apocalyptic world' in Frye's vocabulary, is one in which each level of reality is united in one body. In another passage, about human unity, Frye starts out by speaking about the 'body of one man' symbol, but then proceeds to other levels of reality:

---

4 Northrop Frye, *Northrop Frye on Modern Culture*, ed. Jan Gorak (Toronto: University of Toronto Press, 2003), 257.

> In a completely human society man would not lose his individuality, but he would lose his separate and isolated ego, what Blake calls his Selfhood. The prophetic vision of freedom and equality thus cannot stop at the Generation level of a Utopia, which means an orderly molecular aggregate of individuals existing in some future time. Such a vision does not capture, though it may adumbrate, the real form of society, which can only be a larger human body. This means literally the body of one man, though not of a separate man. … The real form of human society is the body of one man; the flock of sheep is the body of one lamb; the garden is the body of one tree, the so-called tree of life. The city is the body of one building or temple, a house of many mansions, and the building itself is the body of one stone, a glowing and fiery precious stone, the unfallen stone of alchemy which assimilates everything else to itself, Blake's grain of sand which contains the world.[5]

The vision Frye is laying out is one in which, having achieved unity, humankind does not blow itself up in mutual destruction; it is also the world at the opposite pole from the world in which nature is 'red in tooth and claw'. It is at the opposite end of experience from worlds constructed by the imagination in which bizarre exotic plant life forms play out a weird fight for supremacy. It is also the opposite of the vision in which squabbling gods slug it out with one another to such an extent that, were they mortal, it would be their end.

Of course fictions of the apocalypse also portray conflict and the fight for supremacy between levels. The genre, then, also asks us to consider what the resolution of these tensions might look like. The world of desire is also a world in which the hierarchy between levels of reality has been abolished. Frye states:

---

5 Northrop Frye, *Northrop Frye on Milton and Blake*, ed. Angela Esterhammer (Toronto: University of Toronto Press, 2005), 197.

> In the human world there is no chain of being: all aspects of existence are equal as well as identical. The one man is also the one lamb, and the body and blood of the animal form are the bread and wine which are the human forms of the vegetable world. The tree of life is the upright vertebrate form of man; the living stone, the glowing transparent furnace, is the furnace of heart and lungs and bowels in the animal body. The river of life is the blood that circulates within that body. Eden, which according to Blake was a city as well as a garden, had a fourfold river, but no sea, for the river remained inside paradise, which was the body of one man ... The more developed society is, the more clearly man realizes that a society of gods would have to be, like the society of man, the body of one God. Eventually he realizes that the intelligible forms of man and of whatever is above man on the chain of being must be identical.[6]

Such is the positive vision which post-apocalyptic fiction compels us to consider. It is a vision far beyond the best that contemporary utopianism produces. Post-apocalyptic fiction suggests we will be haunted by the fictions of collapsing hierarchies until we achieve the world of equality set forth, in Frye's view, in the works of Blake.

---

6 Frye, *Northrop Frye on Milton and Blake*, 197–8.

GENES, GERMANS AND GENOCIDE: THE END OF CELTIC ENGLAND?

Robert W. Rix

When the Romans left Britain (c. 410) it created a power vacuum which enabled what is known as the 'Anglo-Saxon invasion'. This attack from the continent affected the indigenous Celto-British population in significant ways. The view formulated by nineteenth-century writers was one which we would associate today with the term 'ethnic cleansing'. To reflect concretely on the title of this collection of articles, the Latin *terminus* means 'boundary' or 'limit'. This is pertinent to the popular understanding that the Celto-British population was effectively eradicated – either driven away or substantially wiped out – from within the boundary stones of what is now England. Headlines and chapter titles referring to 'the end of Celtic Britain' have often been used to introduce the idea – more or less explicitly – that the Celto-Britons were totally replaced by Anglo-Saxons from the continent in the course of the fifth and sixth centuries.

This 'endist' notion was the premise for defining an Anglo-Saxon ethnic identity. England was seen as quintessentially Anglo-Saxon, its genetic heritage unequivocally Germanic. In turn, this theory became a catalyst for the ideology known as 'Teutonism', by which the merits and greatness of the Anglo-Saxon race were argued on the basis of their absolute distinction from the Celts.[1]

---

1 The most vitriolic formulations of this ideology are found in John Pinkerton's two works *Dissertation on the Origins and Progress of the Scythians or Goths* (1787) and the *Enquiry into the History of Scotland Preceding the Reign of Malcolm III* (1789), and in Robert Knox's *The Races of Men* (1850).

Due to the conspicuous cessation of Celtic culture and language within the borders of England, the 'endist' view has persisted also in non-ideological scholarship. At least until the mid-twentieth century, the idea of *terminus* was the dominant view. Perspectives may have been qualified in recent scholarship on the Anglo-Saxon invasion, but the 'endist' understanding remains an underlying conceptual framework in popular writing.[2] This essay is a contribution to the re-assessment of the *terminus* myth of Celtic Britain.

The notion of expulsion and genocide originates with clerical historians of the Middle Ages, who described the end of Celtic Britain with a pronounced sense of finality. Writing at a time when Germanic hordes were ravaging Britain, the cleric Gildas described in *De excidio Britonum* (The Ruin of Britain) how all major British towns were laid low, foundations stones of buildings tossed to the ground and those who could not flee became bodies scattered in the streets.[3] Gildas therefore found it apt to quote the prophet Isaiah on the Day of Judgment: 'Howl!, the day of the Lord is near ...', adding a number of other biblical prophecies with apocalyptic content.[4] Later, Anglo-Saxon scribes would also frame the invasion in decidedly 'endist' terms. They describe the significant victories over the Britons and how they were driven away as their forefathers took over their kingdoms. It is the purpose of this article to look at some of the central texts that have been used as primary sources for 'the end' of the Celto-Britons. This essay will examine how the statements of extinction, on both sides, can be read partly as rhetorical and ideological representations, serving propagandistic functions. In addition to this, I will examine the indications of Celto-British continuation, assimilation and integration that these texts also offer.

---

[2] See Markku Filppula, Juhani Klemol, and Heli Paulasto, *English and Celtic in Contact* (London: Routledge, 2008), 12–18.

[3] For Latin text and English translation, see *Gildas: The Ruin of Britain, and Other Works*, c. 24.3, ed. and trans. Michael Winterbottom (London: Phillimore & Co. Ltd., 1978), p. 98.

[4] Ibid., citation taken from c. 44.1 (p. 41).

GENETICS AND ETHNICITY

Medieval texts are insufficient to establish any useful idea of the numbers involved in the Anglo-Saxon colonisation, but, recently, help from the science of population genetics has been made available. We may begin with the finding that this has yielded to establish a framework from which a text-based interpretation may proceed. Based on the mathematical frequencies of genetic characteristics, collected from the present gene pool within a particular geographical area, genetic studies provides us with a 'text' that can inform us about past migrations. Tellingly, geneticists use the term *palimpsest* (originally indicating a manuscript that has been written and erased repeatedly) to describe the various overlays of DNA data in a historical perspective.[5] But, as is the case with other texts of which we lack a full understanding of the historical context, a controversy has developed among geneticists over the interpretation of the results which the studies have produced.

A BBC documentary from 2002 included a DNA study led by Mark Thomas. The results were interpreted to show a clear difference between the genetic make-up in Wales and England. This was seen to confirm the 'endist' view that England was created on the basis of ethnic cleansing.[6] Another 2002 study of DNA material, led by Michael Weale with the participation of Mark Thomas, hypothesised that an Anglo-Saxon invasion had replaced between 50 and 100 per cent of the indigenous Celto-British population in England.[7] However, a follow-up study, conducted by Christian Capelli and colleagues, presented a more

---

5 See further Christopher Howe, Adrian Barbrook, Linne Mooney, and Peter Robinson's discusson of the analogues between medieval manuscript dissemination and genetic stemmatology in 'Parallells between Stemmatology and Phylogenetics' in *Studies in Stemmatology II*, ed. Pieter Van Reene (Amsterdam: John Benjamin, 2004), 3–12.

6 BBC series *Blood of the Vikings* (London, 2002), cited in Michael E. Jones, 'Text, Artifact, and Genome: The Disputed Nature of the Anglo-Saxon Migration into Britain', in *Romans, Barbarians, and the Transformation of the Roman World*, eds. Ralph W. Mathisen and Danuta Shanzer (Aldersgate: Ashgate, 2011), 331–42, at 336.

7 Michael E. Weale, Deborah A. Weiss, Rolf F. Jager, Neil Bradman, and Mark G. Thomas, 'Y Chromosome Evidence for Anglo-Saxon Mass Migration', *Molecular Biology and Evolution* 19, no. 7 (2002): 1008–21.

complex picture. Here, evidence was interpreted to indicate that central and eastern England experienced a significant level of intrusion from the continent, while southern and western parts maintained a higher degree of indigenous elements.[8] In 2006, Mark Thomas and others theorised that 'ethnic cleansing' may not be the only reason for the predominance of Germanic genes in some parts of England. It could also be the sign of a small Anglo-Saxon elite that operated an apartheid-like system. Because of the social advantages this introduced, the spread of 'Anglo-Saxon' Y-chromosomes won out in the long term.[9]

The most recent studies have provided a rather different picture. A study led by Bryan Sykes, funded by the European Union and conducted by the Institute of Molecular Medicine at Oxford, matched DNA from 6,000 modern inhabitants of Britain. The study concluded that no more than between 5 per cent in the east and 10 per cent in the north of England were of Saxon, Danish or Norman descent. The genetic similarity between these groups makes it hard to trace the exact origin of genes. But, the northern samples were within the borders of the old Danelaw, which could indicate that this was a result of later Scandinavian settlements during the Viking Age (ninth and eleventh centuries).[10] In any case, the relatively low figure of non-indigenous characteristics makes impossible the 'endist' scenario, by which there was a near total ethnic replacement. The cessation of Celtic language and culture within the borders of England should therefore be seen as the result of the transition to a new Germanic system, rather than genocide on a large scale.

This new interpretation was corroborated by Stephen Oppenheimer, whose findings suggested that the majority of people with north-continental genetic markers actually derived from on-going mi-

---

8 Christian Capelli et al., 'A Y Chromosome Census of the British Isles', *Current Biology* 13, no. 11 (2003): 979–84.

9 Mark G. Thomas, Michael P. H. Stumpf, and Heinrich Härke, 'Evidence for an Apartheid-Like Social Structure in Early Anglo-Saxon England', *Proceedings of the Royal Society B: Biological Sciences* 273, no. 1601 (2006): 2651–7.

10 Bryan Sykes, *Blood of the Isles: Exploring the Genetic Roots of Our Tribal History* (London: Corgi, 2007), 273–82.

grations in the North Sea region as far back as the Palaeolithic Age, or 'old stone age' (commencing in Britain over half a million years ago).[11] Based on a synthesis of genetics, archaeology and linguistics, Oppenheimer argues that the Germanic immigration, beginning in the fifth century, only contributed minimally to the current genetic pool. In other words, the 'Germanic' genes were already a characteristic of the indigenous Celtic population. These findings were substantiated in a 2008 study by John Pattison. Like Oppenheimer, Pattison sees a long-term influx of Germanic genes, pointing to the examples of the Belgae, a presumably Germanic people that had settled in southern Britain, and the Germanic soldiers who formed part of the Roman occupation force.[12]

These latest assessments indicate that the Britons were primarily 'Celtic' in culture and language, not in terms of genetic characteristics. Thus, historical genetics advocates that we see the erstwhile Britons as becoming integrated in the new Anglo-Saxon power structure. Guesstimates of the influx of continental newcomers vary significantly, but some proponents of the integration theory set the immigration ratio as low as 1:50.[13] For Britons of the lower orders, the change of one lord for another may not have been of much significance in terms of living standards. But, over time, knowledge of the new dominant culture and language became a requirement.

If we turn to Anglo-Saxon texts, there are indications that some Britons were incorporated into the new Anglo-Saxon social structure. The noun *wealh* (plur. *Wealas*) stands for 'foreigner', to which the modern term 'Welsh' is etymologically connected. But, it also doubled as

---

11 Stephen Oppenheimer, *The Origins of the British: A Genetic Detective Story* (New York: Carroll & Graf, 2006), 105.

12 John E. Pattison, 'Is It Necessary to Assume an Apartheid-like Social Structure in Early Anglo-Saxon England?', *Proceedings of the Royal Society: Biological Sciences* 275, no. 1676 (2008): 2423–9.

13 Lloyd Robert Laing and Jennifer Laing, *Celtic Britain and Ireland, AD 200-800: The Myth of the Dark Ages* (Dublin: Irish Academic Press, 1990), 84.

a name for 'slave', thus implying low status as well as ethnic origin.[14] Britons are definitely referred to in the West Saxon King Ine's Dooms (*domas*) from the late seventh or early eighth century. In these laws, *Englisc* is a term marking a distinction from *Wilisc*, which refers to British subjects.[15] Ine sets the *wergild* (blood-money) for violating a man of *Wilisc* descent (regardless of his status, slave or free) to roughly half and always lower than that of a man of *Englisc* provenance.

Ine's laws do not express any racist sentiments, but the law code does incorporate a system of segregation. However, when read in context, there is reason to doubt that the distinction made in this law-code was absolute. To a large extent, the *Wilisc* subjects may have been living in the west of the kingdom (territories in Devon and southern Somerset), where the West Saxons were expanding their territory. *Wilisc* could potentially indicate the lower legal status of those who did not speak the language of the Saxon governing class or were yet to conform to their cultural norms. The laws could therefore have been intended to encourage these Britons to accept the rule of the new political elite. The segregation laws could thus be seen as analogous to the laws the Moorish Caliphate in medieval Spain introduced to force allegiance. These laws levied a tax (the *jizya*) on Jews and Christians, but not on Muslims.[16] The analogy is not perfect, since the Moorish tax was a more heavy-handed instrument (non-Muslims refusing to pay were faced with a choice of conversion or death) than it seems to have been the case in Wessex. But the laws discriminating against *Wilisc* subjects may

---

14 *An Anglo-Saxon Dictionary Online*, ed. Joseph Bosworth, s.v. 'wealh', accessed October 1, 2012, http://bosworth.ff.cuni.cz/034770.

15 See *Das Gesetzbuch der Könige Aelfred-Ine*, 'Ine', §§ 23.3, 24.2, 32, 33, 46, 54, 70, and 74, in *Die Gesetze der Angelsachsen*, ed. and trans. Felix Lieberman, vol. 1 (Halle: Max Niemeyer, 1903). The Dooms of King Ine survive only in connection with the laws issued by King Alfred in the late ninth century. There is nothing to indicate, however, that laws contained in the earlier document were changed in transmission. For a discussion, see T. M. Charles Edwards, 'The Making of Nations in Britain and Ireland in the Early Middle Ages', in *Lordship and Learning: Studies in Memory of Trevor Aston*, ed. Ralph Evans (Woodbridge: Boydell Press, 2004), 11–38.

16 This suggestion is made by Bryan Ward-Perkins in 'Why did the Anglo-Saxons not Become More British?', *The English Historical Review* 115.462 (2000): 513–33, at 524.

have been introduced to secure faster integration and allegiance, which was crucial at a time when wars with neighbouring Celtic and Germanic kingdoms were still the order of the day. In Anglo-Saxon England, there was probably a degree of British acculturation to Germanic society and norms; at least there is no mentioning of *Wilisc*, or a correspondent term, in the Wessex laws of King Alfred in the late ninth century.[17]

To sum up, the slave/foreigner identity may not have been biologically fixed and immutable. Social mobility may have been possible if a Celto-British person was free and adapted to a Germanic system of faith and rule. There was no final curtain for the Celtic population, as imagined by earlier historians. What is clear, however, is that new Anglo-Saxon elites took over, imposing their language and culture on the indigenous population, but producing no significant change in the genetic makeup. The suggestion is then that the 'end' to Celtic England was due to the effect of the larger population becoming acculturated to the new order.

THE RUIN OF BRITAIN

In the wake of contemporary critical interest in holocaust and genocide studies, violence in medieval texts has been taken up for renewed scrutiny.[18] That a concept of genocide was in the minds of early medieval writers needs no special pleading. Medieval scribes often saw the fortunes and failures of a people as the result of divine intervention in human affairs. This was a notion inexorably tied up with ideas of wars and invasions: God punished a people for its sins by allowing their defeat and rewarded it with victories in war. In this interpretive paradigm, the misfortunes of Christian societies, especially when it came to being raided by pagan tribes, were seen as punishment for falling away

---

17 *Das Gesetzbuch der Könige Aelfred-Ine*, in *Gesetze*, 46–87.

18 See, for example, James E. Fraser, 'Early Medieval Europe: The Case of Britain and Ireland', in *The Oxford Handbook of Genocide Studies*, eds. Donald Bloxham and A. Dirk Moses (Oxford: Oxford UP, 2010), 259–79; Len Scales, 'Bread, Cheese and Genocide: Imagining the Destruction of Peoples in Medieval Western Europe', *History* 92.307 (2007): 284–300; W. D. Rubinstein, *Genocide: A History* (Harlow: Longman, 2004), 11–44; David Nirenberg, *Communities of Violence: Persecution of Minorities in the Middle Ages* (Princeton, NJ: Princeton UP, 1996).

from God. Such biblically inflected history found notable expression in the Iberian theologian Orosius's *Historiarum adversum paganos libri septem* (early 5th century), an important book that was translated into Old English in the late ninth century. In later formulations of this idea, we frequently find an overlay of typological interpretation, whereby God's castigation of the Hebrews is seen as reenacted in the present. We should, of course, be wary of the historical accuracy when the main purpose of a text is to present events as shadows of biblical narratives.

One text in which historical observation is submerged under a typologising inclination is the primary source for the Anglo-Saxon invasion: Gildas's *De excidio Britanniae* (The Ruin of Britain). Our knowledge of Gildas is scant, but he probably wrote his account sometime in the late fifth or early sixth century.[19] What we do know about him is that he was ordained in the Romano-British Church.[20] The events he describes are virtually pre-historical, since Gildas' work is the only extant source from Britain falling within the first century of the invasion.

Gildas's basic narrative of the events is simple. The British overlord had invited Germanic mercenaries to fight against the troublesome Picts and the Scotti in the north, but the mercenaries decided to revolt and turn against their employer. In chapters 23 and 24, Gildas tells us that his countrymen were murdered in great numbers by the pagans; others were blighted by famine or made slaves. Some fled beyond the seas, while others hid in the mountains and forests. He further describes how his compatriots lay slaughtered in the streets, covered in congealed blood, only with the prospect of ending up in the bellies of beasts and birds. The gory images are observations that undoubtedly

---

19 Full text manuscripts survive from the tenth century or later. For Latin original and English translation, see *Gildas: The Ruin of Britain, and Other Works*, ed. and trans. Michael Winterbottom (London: Phillimore, 1978). All future references are to this edition. The dating of the work is disputed. Gildas informs us in chapter 26 that he was born in the year of the siege of 'Mons Badonicus', forty-three years and one month before the time he wrote *De excidio*. However, there is no consensus on the date of this siege; see Patrick Sims-Williams, 'Gildas and the Anglo-Saxons', *Cambridge Medieval Celtic Studies* 8 (1983): 1–30, at 3–5.

20 Nick Higham, 'Imperium in Early Britain: Rhetoric and Reality in the Writings of Gildas and Bede', *Anglo-Saxon Studies in Archaeology and History* 10 (1999): 31–6, at 32.

have a basis in truth. But we need to look more closely at the motivation and structure of the text, before we accept such accounts of the carnage as the general rule for all of Britain.

As a Romanized Celto-Briton, Gildas's abhorrence at the pagan incursions into British territory cannot be mistaken. He provides an impassioned account, not least because of the on-going devastation of his 'fatherland' (*patria*) and the enslavement of fellow Britons. He is writing with a sense of urgency, since the total destruction of the British is at hand, if they do not reform their ways.

Gildas amplifies the catastrophe at hand to highlight the threat of an imminent end to sub-Roman Britain. He interprets the pagan invasion as punishment for the British leaders' bad stewardship: their sinful ways have compelled divine retribution. Barbarian violence is seen through scriptural example: it is a divine punishment for his countrymen's iniquities against God. Since Gildas believes the Britons are the chosen people, the threat of punishment is conceived within the framework of biblical typology. Thus, in chapter 23, he parallels the decision to invite the Germanic warriors into Britain as mercenaries to the biblical Pharaoh receiving unwise counsel (cf. Isaiah 19:11). The accusation of misguided decisions centres upon the overlord of British kingdoms, whom Gildas calls *superbus tyrannus*.[21] In turn, chapter 24 interprets the devastation wrought by the pagan invaders as a shadow of the biblical story of God raising up the abject race of Assyrians to punish Judea (cf. Isaiah 28).

In deference to God and the punishment he has meted out, Gildas's attitude is one of welcoming the intervention, while showing disgust at the tools employed to mete out the punishment. The invaders are 'wolves', 'death', 'lions', 'dogs', 'barbarians', 'cruel plunderers', 'devils', and 'ferocious Saxons (name not to be spoken), hated by man and God' (*ut ferocissimi illi nefandi nominis Saxones, deo hominibusque in-*

---

21 The British ruler is not named in the oldest MS Cotton Vitellius A VI. In early manuscripts of Bede's *Historia ecclesiastica*, the ruler is named *Vertigernus*, or *Vurtigern*.

visi) (ch. 24)[22] This is the sort of ethnic distancing that is typical of the rhetoric in medieval persecutory societies.[23] But, in this case, it is the rhetoric of the persecuted who look with abjection at the persecutors. The disgust is founded on traditional Christian propaganda against pagan 'others'. But, in Gildas's case, the overblown emphasis on the abhorrent nature of the invaders also helps to highlight the gravity of the sins that God's chosen people have committed.

Gildas is writing with a sense of urgency, since total destruction is at hand. Whether a total annihilation of Britons will take effect depends on their willingness to reform. Gildas himself refers to his work as an 'epistle' (ch. 1), for which readers are asked to draw a comparison with St John writing to the wayward churches in the book of Revelation. As in this final book of the New Testament, Gildas's letter is also intended as a warning against further sinning and a call for reform. Britons both win and lose battles against the invaders, in order for God to test his 'latter-day Israel' (*praesentem Israelem*) and to see if they love him or not (ch. 26). That there is a hope for survival is also borne out in the account of a prophecy with which Gildas was familiar. He writes that the invaders descended upon the Britons

> ... in three *cyulis*, as it is expressed in their language, but in ours, in longships of war with their sails wafted by the wind and with omens and prophecies, in ships of war under full sail, with omens and divinations. In these it was foretold, there being a prophecy firmly relied upon among them, that they should occupy the country to which the bows of their ships were turned, for three hundred years; for one hundred and fifty – that is for half the time – they should make frequent devastations. (ch. 23)

---

22 For a full list, see N. J. Higham, *The English Conquest: Gildas and Britain in the Fifth Century* (Manchester: Manchester UP, 1994), 53.

23 Eric D. Weitz, *A Century of Genocide: Utopias of Race and Nation* (Princeton, NJ: Princeton UP, 2003), 19–20.

Referring to a foreign term here could be in order to allude to Isaiah's account of the Assyrian invasion of Judea, in which it is said that God sent his punishment through 'another tongue' (28:11). That is to say, the Israelites, who would not listen to the voice of God, were humiliated by being forced to hear Assyrian spoken in their streets. The parallel to the foreign Germanic tongue spoken in Britain is clear. But if this is so, the analogy is that of occupation rather than all-out carnage and violent expulsion from land areas.

It should be noted that the genuineness of the passage has been called into question. Most recently, Alex Woolf has renewed the theory that the passage is an interpolation.[24] He suggests that the passage is developed from an interlinear gloss in an early manuscript copy, which was subsequently copied into all other extant manuscript versions. Indeed, words or whole sections could often be added to a manuscript between the lines or in the adjacent margin for explanation. If this was what happened in the case of the Gildas's manuscript, the passage has been incorporated into the text in a way that makes it appear as if it were the author's own words. However, this would make it a highly unusual occurrence in medieval marginalia, which cannot have many parallels. Woolf makes the argument that someone introduced the prophecy of 150 years' devastation in order that the invasion could be assigned to the year 447, which would then make the pagan hold on Britain end in 597, the year in which Augustine's mission arrived in England. Admittedly, this would provide a motive for an interpolation by a scribe associated with the Anglo-Roman Church. But the lack of transparency in calculating these dates speaks against the theory. Most critics have found no compelling evidence to argue in favour of an interpolation in the manuscript.[25]

---

24 Alex Woolf, 'An Interpolation in the Text of Gildas's *De excidio Britanniae*', *Peritia* 16 (2002): 161–7.

25 For other objections to the interpolation theory, see Barbara Yorke, 'Anglo-Saxon Origin Legends', in *Myth, Rulership, Church and Charters: Essays in Honour of Nicholas Brooks*, eds. Julia Barrow and Andrew Wareham (Aldershot: Ashgate, 2007), 15–31, at 20–1.

Practices of omens and divinations are well attested in Germanic religion.[26] And it is most likely that Gildas's information of a prophecy among the invaders shows his knowledge of Germanic tradition. The belief of possessing a right to the land by divine decree would presumably have been developed already in the late fifth century, at a time when the first Germanic settlements had been established, although the exact meaning of the years is not clear.

The claim that the new Germanic rulers were destined to rule in Britain was translated into Christian terms by later Anglo-Saxon writers, who came to look back at the invasion as divine Providence. It is to this, we will now turn.

BEDE'S ECCLESIASTICAL HISTORY

The fact that the Anglo-Saxons came to see themselves as God's chosen people is an understanding that informs the Old English biblical poems Genesis A, Exodus, Daniel, and Judith, it has been argued.[27] The idea of the English as divinely elect is certainly evident in the writings of Alcuin, the prolific writer and monk.[28] Alcuin was directly inspired by another Northumbrian monk, known as the Venerable Bede. In *Historia ecclesiastica gentis Anglorum* (Ecclesiastical History of the English People), completed in 731, Bede read Gildas's account intensively.[29] Since it was the major written source on the invasion, Bede follows Gildas's narrative closely in the early chapters.

Like Gildas, Bede also believed in a providential or teleological unfolding of history. He therefore concurs with Gildas's view of the Germanic invaders as the tools of divine punishment for British sins.

---

26 The first-century Roman historian Tacitus, for example, wrote that the Germanic people practised divinations to the widest possible extent; see Tacitus, *Germania*, 1.10; in *Agricola, Germany, and Dialogue on Orators*, ed. and trans. Herbert W. Benario (Reprint, Indianapolis, IN: Hackett, 2006), 68.

27 See Andrew P. Scheil, *The Footsteps of Israel: Understanding Jews in Anglo-Saxon England* (Ann Arbor, MI: University of Michigan Press, 2004).

28 For a study of this interpretation, see Scheil, *Footsteps of Israel*.

29 All references to this work will be to the Latin and English texts in *Bede's Ecclesiastical History of the English People*, eds. and trans. Bertrand Colgrave and R. A. B. Mynors (Oxford: Clarendon, 1979), cited by book and chapter numbers.

But whereas Gildas saw the Britons as the New Israel, Bede sees the 'English' (a collective ethnic notion he was instrumental in establishing) as the chosen people.³⁰ Bede presents the invasion as God ordering a definitive end to British rule: the 'just judge [*iusto Iudice*] ordained that the fire of their brutal conquerors should ravage all the neighbouring cities and countryside from the eastern to the western sea, and burn on, with no one to hinder it, until it covered almost the whole face of the doomed island' (1.15). The key word here is 'just', alluding to the idea that destruction can function as a necessary tool to further the will of God on earth.³¹ At several junctures in Bede's text, it is clear that British rule must come to an end in order to make way for the English, God's chosen people.

We must understand this in the context of medieval Christianity, for which peace may have been preached as an ideal, but it was not overwhelmingly pacifist in the way Christianity later came to be. The modern historian Len Scales describes a commonplace ideology in medieval Christian historiography: the 'destruction of certain peoples was inseparable from the making of others, an essential motor of historical change, underpinned by biblical narratives of divine election and condemnation'.³² Often the root-and-branch termination of a people is recounted without flinching, since it was seen as the fulfilment of God's plan on earth, the necessary and inevitable punishment of a wicked people. Medieval national history writing was based on such premises of divine rights to land.

---

30 A central passage is the legend of the future Pope Gregory, who sees two Anglian boys in Rome and (through a liberal play with near homonyms) understands that they are 'angels' (*angli/angeli*). See my 'Northumbrian Angels in Rome: Religion and Politics in the Anecdote of St Gregory', *Journal of Medieval History*, 38, no. 1 (2012): 1–21.

31 For a discussion of the concept of the war of righteousness in Anglo-Saxon texts, see Ben Snook, 'Just War in Anglo-Saxon England: Transmission and Reception', in *War and Peace: Critical Issues in European Societies and Literature 800-1800*, eds. Albrecht Classen and Nadia Margolis (Berlin/Boston, MA: Walter de Gruyter, 2011), 99–120.

32 Scales, 'Bread, Cheese and Genocide', 284.

An example of this can be found in Book I of *Historia ecclesiastica*, which concludes with an account of King Æthelfrith (died c. 616) from Bede's own native Northumbria. We learn that Æthelfrith 'ravaged' (*uastauit*) the Britons more extensively than any other English ruler. For this achievement, Bede aligns him with the biblical King Saul (only with the caveat that Æthelfrith was ignorant of the true religion). The comparison with Saul is certainly overdone. For example, the Bible tells us that Saul punished the Amalekites by making war upon them, leaving none alive, beginning with the women and the infants (Samuel 7:1). This was probably not the case in Northumbria. But, Bede holds that Æthelfrith 'exterminated or conquered the natives' (*exterminatis uel subiugatis indigenis*).

Do we here have an avowal of ethnic cleansing to some degree? Colgrave and Mynors's English translation offers 'exterminate' in this sentence, but the reference could well be to the Latin verb *exterminare* (to drive something beyond (*ex*) the boundaries (*termini*) of something else).[33] If we consult concordances of classical texts, it appears that the verb is relatively rare and most often occurs (beyond Cicero) in ecclesiastical Latin, where the term mostly denotes the sense 'banish'.[34] The context here, we must remember, is the establishment of a Northumbria, whose border (*terminus*) Æthelfrith helped to define.

Bede uses the verb *exterminare* on several occasions in the *Historia ecclesiastica* (1.16, 1.22, 1.34, 3.34, and 4.16). It is used at junctures when some form of violence is undoubtedly involved, but in none of the examples is all-out genocide the best interpretation of this term. The question is whether 'the natives' is an all-encompassing term or only refers to the elite and their upper military ranks. When the verb is used in the account of the West Saxon conquest of the Isle of Wight in the 680s (4.16), we are told that king Cadwælla 'endeavoured to wipe out all

---

33 For the problem of interpreting this verb, see James E. Fraser, 'Early Medieval Europe: The Case of Britain and Ireland', in *The Oxford Handbook of Genocide Studies*, eds. D. Bloxham and A. D. Moses (Oxford: Oxford UP, 2010), 259–79.

34 Examples are found in the Vulgate Bible and in Bede's ecclesiastical hero Gregory the Great. For Gregory's use, see Ann Julia Kinnirey, *The Late Latin Vocabulary of the Dialogues of St. Gregory the Great*, vol. 4 (Washington: Catholic University of America, 1935), 42.

the natives by merciless slaughter and to replace them with inhabitants from his own kingdom' (*ac stragica caede omnes indigenas exterminare, ac suae prouinciae homines pro his substituere contendit*). It is not reasonable to conclude that Bede intends this statement to mean an all-out eradication of the population of Wight (an Anglo-Saxon kingdom at this time) with an ensuing total re-colonisation from Wessex. Throughout, Bede focuses his history on dynastic and elite culture. Thus, 'all the natives' probably refers to figures of rank, not the *vulgus*. That is to say, it was a question of elites killing and replacing each other.

To illustrate how ethnic identity was tied to status, we may take the story Bede tells only a few chapters later in connection with the war between the kingdoms of Northumbria and Mercia. Imma, a Northumbrian nobleman and warrior, was captured by the Mercians after a battle at the Trent in 679. When questioned by the Mercians, Imma found it wise not to disclose that he was a warrior (miles) of the Northumbrian King Ælfwine's army, and pretended to be 'a peasant and a poor man [*rusticus*]'. The purpose of this was to avoid death, as the war was a feud between elites. That Imma would feign low status shows us that to count as a full member of the Northumbrians, one needed to be a freeman of a certain status (4.22). To the extent that eliminating 'a people' refers primarily to elites, it may also affect the way in which we interpret the descriptions of the violence against the Britons.

For Bede, the destruction or banishment of the Britons is never a desired goal in itself. Instead he emphasizes the English in their role as missionaries to the other peoples of Britain. In Bede's history, it is the peaceful conversion of the Celtic churches to Roman orthodoxy through the agency of the English, which provides the most triumphant climaxes.[35] In fact, Bede begins his book with a statement of ethnic co-existence which fits the typological framework he has established. He observes that there are five languages in Britain 'just as the divine law is written in five books' (i.e. the Pentaeuch, the first five books of

---

35 For a selection of the more important passages dealing with reconversion to the Roman model of beliefs and practices, see *Historia ecclesiastica* 3.25–29, 4.2 and 18, 5.15 and 22. For discussion, see H. E. J. Cowdrey, 'Bede and the English People', *Journal of Religious History* 11, no. 4 (1981): 501–23, at 511–3.

the Old Testament). These Bede enumerates as *English, British, Scotti, Pictish*, and *Latin* (1.1). The last on the list is the shared language of the church. The simile that Bede draws indicates that his own ecclesiastical history (perhaps not by coincidence also in five books) is about the establishment of a unified set of religious laws and observances like that described for Israel in the Pentateuch. Nonetheless, a happy analogous ending, which would be that the whole island lives in accordance with the doctrines of the Roman Church, is frustrated. Bede expresses his discontent: 'to this very day it is the habit of the Britons to despise the faith and religion of the English [i.e. the canon of the Roman Church] and not to co-operate with them in anything any more than with the heathen' (5.20). Throughout Bede's work, the Britons are represented as rebellious for their unfaithfulness, both to the English people and to God.[36] Thus, a perfect, typological conclusion to his history cannot be reached.

THE ANGLO-SAXON CHRONICLE

We will now make a few observations on the 'end of Celtic Britain' in relation to the *Anglo-Saxon Chronicle*. This is a text found in seven different manuscripts. The common stock for these manuscripts has been identified as a no longer extant text receiving its finishing touches c. 892. The *Chronicle* was not directly related to the writing activities of King Alfred's court, but it is generally acknowledged that it contains a fair degree of West Saxon propaganda.[37]

The early entries in the *Chronicle* provide an account of the invasion, listing some of the spectacular victories over the Britons that led to the establishment of Anglo-Saxon kingdoms. An idea of the Anglo-Saxons, as a people favoured by God, putting an end to British rule, is never made as explicit as it is in the writings of Bede. Nor is there

---

36 Throughout *Historia ecclesiastica*, Bede writes acrimoniously about the Britons and their church practices, as enumerated in W. Trent Foley and Nicholas J. Higham, 'Bede on the Britons', *Early Medieval Europe* 17, no. 2 (2009): 154–85.

37 The text cited below is the oldest surviving version, the Winchester Manuscript (also known as The Parker Chronicle or MS A). The edition used is *The Anglo-Saxon Chronicle, A Collaborative Edition*, vol. 3, MS A, ed. Janet Bately (Cambridge: D.S. Brewer, 1986).

anything resembling the combination of ethnic hostility and millennial hopes that are found to characterise many premodern texts seeking to justify crusades or violence against another people.[38] The underlying script in the *Chronicle* is rather that the great victories were provided due to the heroic efforts of the English forefathers. It is the heroism of the ancestors that is praised without any vested interest in pointing out the religious wickedness of the Britons.

In relation to our central question of what kind of 'end' was wrought upon the Britons in England, some of the accounts of the victories clearly show us that it was not a root-and-branch elimination of the indigenous population. We may take Kent, the first Germanic kingdom established in Britain, as an example. The *Chronicle* has an entry under the year 449 which tells us that the British overlord invited the Germanic warriors Hengest and Horsa to fight for him as mercenaries. However, these warriors turned against him and became invaders. In the entry for the year 455, we are told that Hengest and Horsa battled with the Britons at *Agelesþrep* (Aylesford?). Nothing specific is said about the scale of this battle, only that Hengest and his son Æsc afterwards reigned in Kent. It is unlikely that the population of the kingdom would have suddenly been replaced by large numbers of immigrants from the continent. Rather the existing inhabitants would simply have found themselves living in a British kingdom one day and in an Anglo-Saxon kingdom the next through the change of dynastic regime. To those of the lower orders, this may not have meant much of a difference.

In the entry for the year 457, the chroniclers inform us that Hengest and Æsc fought at *Crecganford* (Crayford?) and there slew four thousand men, so that the Britons forsook Kent for London 'with great fear' (þa *Brettas þa forleton Centlond 7 mid micle ege flugon to Lundenbyrg*). The fact that a large army could be raised so soon after Kent was taken by Anglo-Saxon warriors indicates that the events of 455 cannot have been a battle on a large scale. And how are we to understand the flight

---

38 See Abbas Aramat, 'Introduction: Apocalyptic Anxieties and Millennial Hopes in the Salvation Religions of the Middle East', in *Imagining the End: Visions of Apocalypse from the Ancient Middle East*, eds. Abbas Aramat and Magnus Bernhardsson (London: I. B. Tauris, 2002), 1–23.

of 'Britons'? This is unlikely to have been a mass exodus of all Kentish Britons to the then small town of London. Rather, it would make more sense to conclude that this refers to a number of wealthy families who were seeking refuge in a nearby fortification under British control.

For comparison, we may turn to the legendary material about Kent in the Celto-British text *Historia Brittonum* (compiled c. 830; surviving in eleventh- and twelfth-century manuscripts). Here, we find a slightly different 'spin' on the takeover of Kent. In chapter 37, we learn that Hengest marries his daughter to Vortigern, the overlord of Britain, and as a bride price received the kingdom of Kent. The erstwhile king of Kent, Guoyrancgonus, apparently had no choice but to yield to Vortigern's wishes on this occasion. The ensuing battles that are also mentioned in this text must therefore be interpreted as revolts against this negotiated takeover.[39]

Returning to the description in the *Anglo-Saxon Chronicle* of the takeover of Kent in 455, the phrase used about Hengest and his son Æsc is that they *feng to rice*, which means 'took the kingdom'[40] This is ambiguous. In the present case, it occurs after the mentioning of a battle victory, but, when used elsewhere, the phrase can simply refer to one king replacing another in the royal Anglo-Saxon lines.[41] The chroniclers' predilection for formulaic phrasing is an obstacle for assessing what may have taken place in each individual case.

It further complicates matters that the chroniclers (or their sources) favoured a symbolic approach to the invasion. For the year 449, we learn that the number of ships that arrived on the British coast was three; in 477, the number again is three; in 497, five ships arrive; in 501, two ships appear; and in 514, there are three again. The subsequent movement of auxiliary soldiers to fight in the battles described in the *Chronicle*, as well as the subsequent influx of non-military settlers, are

---

39 For text and English translation, see *British History; and the Welsh Annals*, ed. and trans. John Morris (London: Phillimore, 1980).

40 The OE *rice* is cognate of Scandinavian *rike/rige* and German *Reich*.

41 The phrase is also used about peaceful ecclesiastical succession, such as Pope Stephanus replacing Pope Leo (for the year 814), or Ælfric replacing Sigeric to the bishopric (*arcebisceoprice*) of Wiltshire in 994.

not mentioned. We are left wondering to what extent the accounts of the invasion are symbolic and follow the rules of foundation legends, where it is often a small band of warriors that migrate to establish a new people. This was a *topos* known elsewhere in early Anglo-Saxon legend.[42] The sparse numbers recorded in the entries for the fifth and sixth centuries stand in glaring contrast to the 250 Danish ships that attacked in 893. If some historians believe this number to be exaggerated, at least the account is an attempt at giving an impression of a capable invasion force.

The *Chronicle* operates with the notions of Germanic invaders slaying the Britons (for example, under the year 491, *ofslogen*), as well as putting a people to flight (for example, under the year 514, *geflymdan*). We must not forget that the chroniclers, like Bede, are writing the history of kings and elites, expressing little or no interest in the common people. Hence, their nomenclature must also be read as reflecting this rather exclusivist approach. The killings and banishments of indigenous inhabitants may therefore have been limited to the elite classes. There are certainly entries in the *Chronicle* which suggest that, in some cases, the 'end' of the Britons was indeed a well-organised elimination of dynastic rulers. In the entry for the year 501, for example, we are told that 'Port and his two sons Bieda and Mægla came to Britain with two ships'. The Germanic invaders landed at Portsmouth, where they 'killed a young British man of very high rank'.[43] The stress placed on a singular killing seems to indicate that a strategic elimination of key persons in the existing power structure was often an effective means to attain power.

In the earliest A-text of the *Chronicle*, the Saxon brothers Cynric and Cerdic are said to have invaded the Isle of Wight in the year 530, on which occasion they *ofslogan fea men* (slew a few men). Interestingly, some discrepancy can be found between the various manuscript

---

42 See chapter one in my forthcoming *The North in the Anglo-Saxon Imagination*.

43 My base text is the Winchester Manuscript (also known as the Parker Chronicle, or MS A of *The Anglo-Saxon Chronicle*): Cambridge, Corpus Christi College MS 173, ff. 1ᵛ–32ʳ. This is the oldest surviving MS of the *Chronicle*. For comparisons between manuscripts, see the XML editions at http://asc.jebbo.co.uk/.

recensions on this specific point. For, where the later B- and C-texts maintain this reading of 'few', all other manuscripts change this word to *feala* (many).⁴⁴ At some point, a scribe either made a slip, or, more likely, invented a significant victory as proof that the takeover was divinely ordained. Certainly, legends of victory and mass immigration are known to have formed part of the ideology of political legitimacy.⁴⁵ This clearly shows us the problem of reading texts that exist in several recensions: each individual manuscript may present a moment of faithful transmission of a precursor text, a faulty attempt at reproduction, or a rewriting for later political purposes.

Another such rewriting may be seen in relation to the West Saxon chroniclers' treatment of their own royal history. Despite promoting an unveering Germanic ideology, there are possible hints at the continuation of British influence to be found. At least, it is peculiar that the names of the earliest West Saxon kings – Cerdic, Cynric, Cædwalla and Ceawlin – are clearly names of Celtic origin. These kings are prehistoric in the sense that we have no historical documents, law codes or any non-legendary texts to corroborate the historicity of their reigns. However, the inclusion of Celtic names in the West Saxon royal line does not concord with the legend presented in the *Chronicle* that Cerdic and Cynric arrived in Hampshire in 495 from the continent.

It has been suggested that the inclusion of Celtic names in dynastic legend may represent an attempt at Anglo-Saxon spin directed at their British subjects. This could have been advantageous when seeking the allegiance and loyalty of the indigenous population.⁴⁶ However, another interpretation is possible. If we were to assume that Cerdic and his son Cynric were historical rulers, it is possible that they arose from a British dynasty which became collaborators and acted as sub-kings,

---

44 The tenth-century ealdorman Æthelweard used an early version of the *Anglo-Saxon Chronicle* for his Latin account of English history. In his work, the number is indicated as *paucos Brittanos* (small number of Britons).

45 See Helena Hamerow, 'Earliest Anglo-Saxon Kingdoms', in *The New Cambridge Medieval History*, ed. P. Fouracre, vol. 1 (Cambridge: Cambridge UP, 2005), 263–88, esp. 269.

46 For this suggestion, see Yorke, 'Anglo-Saxon Origin Legends', 23.

adopting the language and culture of the Anglo-Saxon overlords. The *Anglo-Saxon Chronicle* may therefore be an attempt at obscuring their real identity by rerouting their origin via an overseas journey. This would be done in order to avoid the stigma of low-status 'Britishness' that developed as an ideology in the new Anglo-Saxon England. The West Saxon genealogy is clearly muddled and has probably come down to us in the form of a redaction of several sources. It has already been shown that the early names in the lineage are based upon a root pedigree borrowed from the line of Bernician kings, whose ancestry is recorded in the so-called Anglian collection of royal ancestors.[47]

The possible re-identification of British kings to fit later political ideology finds a parallel in the documented remaking of the British shrine of the local St Sixtus. When Augustine arrived from Rome, he turned this into a religious site for the similarly named (but Roman) Pope Saint Sixtus II – in this way keeping the name but changing the identity to fit the new Romano-Christian order.[48] However, what is most remarkable in connection with the use of Celtic names in the West-Saxon royal lineage is that it seemingly caused no problems for the Anglo-Saxon chroniclers. This may indicate that the division between Germanic and British blood, even at dynastic levels, may not have been absolute, as supporters of the 'endist' argument have otherwise supposed.

CONCLUSION

Above, I have put forward arguments which contradict the received perception that England was completely purged of Britons through mass expulsion and genocide. The latest genetic studies do not support the idea of large-scale change, nor do the legendary and historical records of the Anglo-Saxon invasion present evidence of a mass replacement of the Celtic population.

---

[47] Kenneth Sisam, 'Anglo-Saxon Royal Genealogies', *Proceedings of the British Academy* 39 (1953): 287–348, at 302–4.

[48] For the case of this shrine, see Peter Hunter Blair, *An Introduction to Anglo-Saxon England*, 3rd ed. (Cambridge: Cambridge UP, 2003), 24.

In some cases, Germanic rulers took over already established Romano-British power structures and dominated Celtic populations. It is possible that Roman, or indeed pre-Roman boundaries, were maintained in these cases. As we know, this was a model also followed elsewhere after the collapse of the Western Roman Empire.[49] However, such a model is not plausible as a general principle for all of England. Pre-invasion political geography was surely disrupted in many cases and the *Terminus* stones of early Germanic kingdoms were likely erected as the result of political competition and warfare, where survival operated according to a Darwinistic model.[50] In terms of Germanic violence on British populations, what happened in different kingdoms may have varied, and some conquests may have been more ferocious than others.[51] After all, the Anglo-Saxon invasion was not a concerted effort engineered from a central source, and no general strategy was followed. But, from the evidence discussed above, it seems most reasonable to conclude that it was Celtic culture and language that was eradicated within Anglo-Saxon England. The Anglo-Saxon invasion did not spell 'the end' for the Celto-British population at large.

---

49 Barbara Yorke, *The Conversion of Britain: Religion, Politics and Society in Britain c. 600-800* (Harlow: Pearson Longman, 2006), 44.

50 For a discussion of kingdom formation, see Helena Hamerow, 'The Earliest Anglo-Saxon Kingdoms', in *Cambridge Medieval History*, ed. Paul Fouracre (Cambridge: Cambridge UP, 2005), 263–88; at 280–7.

51 See John Hines, *Voices in the Past: English Literature and Archaeology* (Cambridge: Boydell & Brewer, 2004), 39.

TERMINUS: 'NO VESTIGE OF A BEGINNING – NO PROSPECT OF AN END'

Frances Carey

Endings presuppose beginnings; both are symbolic as well as actual markers that anchor our lives within a narrative structure which gives individual and collective meaning – an ineluctable momentum towards an ultimate goal. To dispense with such obvious framing devices and the connecting trajectory of purpose remains surprisingly disorientating even for a largely secular audience after more than a century of experimentation with narrative structure in every form of artistic expression, from serial musical composition without clearly signposted beginnings and endings to fiction such as J. L. Borges' *The Book of Sand* in which the recipient of the eponymous work is terrified because of the enormity of something that is infinite: 'neither sand nor this book has a beginning or end'.[1]

But far more challenging was the conclusion made by James Hutton (1726–1797), Scottish physician, chemical manufacturer, agriculturalist and geologist, in his *Theory of the Earth*, the paper he first read to the Royal Society of Edinburgh in 1785. The paper was published in 1788 then incorporated in 1795 into two volumes of the same title which ended with: 'The result, therefore, of our present enquiry is that we find no vestige of a beginning – no prospect of an end'.[2] Often quoted since – on the third track of the *No Control* album released by

---

[1] J. L. Borges, *The Book of Sand* (London: Penguin, 1998), 91.
[2] James Hutton, *Theory of the Earth with Proofs and Illustrations; In Four Parts*, vol. 2 (Edinburgh: Creech, 1795), 567.

the American punk rock group *Bad Religion* in 1989, for example – it has come to stand as a watershed in the understanding of 'deep time', the challenge to biblical authority for the creation of the world, and to a directional view of history. The 'beginning' was most famously calculated by Archbishop Ussher of Armagh, the Anglican Primate of Ireland in the mid-seventeenth century, as having taken place on the night preceding 23 October, 4004 BC. The Flood, which he placed in 2349–2348 BC, was central to this history of the earth, marking a cataclysmic rupture between an antediluvian age and the world thereafter that was inhabited by the survivors from Noah's ark and their descendants.

Hutton espoused a Plutonist theory for the creation of the earth – that of a hot centre driving the creation of new rock which was then deposited in the sea, the heat causing sediment to consolidate and rise to make new lands. These were in turn eroded, submerged, then subjected to further deposition and uplift. The opposing Neptunist argument was that all rocks had been precipitated out of a single enormous flood. Slow incremental change rather than sudden catastrophe, or uniformitarianism as it became known, was what Hutton deduced from his observation of landscape features such as 'Hutton's uncomformity' at Jedburgh in Scotland, one of the illustrations to the 1795 publication. An uncomformity is a fossil surface of erosion, a gap in time separating two episodes in the formation of rocks. The science of stratigraphy did not begin with Hutton whose major precursor was the Danish pioneer in anatomy and geology Nicolas Steno or Niels Stensen (1638–1686), a Lutheran convert to Catholicism in 1667, who became a priest some eight years later. In his *Dissertationis Prodromus* of 1669, he is credited with defining the laws of superposition, original horizontality and lateral continuity, and with the theory that the fossil record was a chronology of creatures living in different eras, with the oldest on the bottom and the most recent on top. Steno's ideas were key to Hutton's and to those of one of Charles Darwin's principal mentors, Charles Lyell (1797–1875), whose *Principles of Geology* (1830–1833) Darwin read on the voyage of the *Beagle* to South America in 1832–1836. As one French popular science writer, Louis Figuier (1819–1894), wrote in *The World before the Deluge* of 1865: '… from the study of fossils, science has not only reanimated the animals; it has reconstructed the theatre of their existence'.[3]

Interest in geological formation captured the attention of mid-nineteenth century artists such as Peter Christian Skovgaard (1817–1875) and his views of Møns Klint at Liselund, a famous Danish beauty spot, where the cliffs created as a result of pressure from glaciers pushing the terrain upwards, are comprised of the shells from microscopic creatures living on the seabed more than 70 million years ago. In Britain, one of Henry Fox Talbot's early photographs of c.1844 was of geologists, poised with their hammers to prize fossils from the limestone rock face behind them in Chudleigh, Devon, which dates from about 416–345 million years ago, the subject of an important paper given to the Royal Geological Society in 1840. The impact of geological interest was especially notable among those who came under the influence of John Ruskin whose fourth volume of *Modern Painters* appeared in 1856, devoting much space to mountain ranges and rock formation. Inspired by this John Brett (1831–1902) spent the summer of that year at Rosenlaui in Switzerland, leading to the *Glacier of Rosenlaui* (Tate Britain, London), one of the masterpieces of Pre-Raphaelite landscape painting.

The most famous of these 'geological' pictures was William Dyce's *Pegwell Bay, Kent – A Recollection of October 5th, 1858–60* (Tate Britain, London), exhibited at the Royal Academy in 1860. Dyce grew up in Aberdeen in Scotland in an atmosphere of scientific inquiry, first studying medicine then theology before he became a professional painter. The subject captures an autumn holiday on the Kent Coast with members of the artist's family gathering shells in the foreground; the geological strata on the chalk cliffs, formed during the Cretaceous period (c.145–65 million years ago), are clearly visible and the white tail of a comet streaks across the sky. This was Donati's comet named for the Italian astronomer who first observed it on the 2 June 1858. 5 October 1858, was the date when the comet (the first to be photographed) was predicted by the *Illustrated London News* to be at its most brilliant in the sky: 'It is

---

3 Louis Figuier, *The World before the Deluge*, (London: Chapman and Hall, 1865), 336.

sixty-two million miles from us ... It would seem that this comet will return in 2,100 years' time, but with comets of this period ... calculators cannot be certain to a few centuries.[4] However, the artist's inclusion of the date within his title was for symbolic as much as for astronomical reasons; he was concerned with capturing an image of a specific and very personal moment in time, which became the vehicle for juxtaposing human, geological and astronomical timescales, moving from the particular to the universal.[5]

The discovery of 'deep time' as evidenced by the fossil record was more troubling even than Newtonian physics and what had been revealed about the planetary system, because it concerned the terrestrial world and was in every sense closer to home. Man's position was relegated to one of utter chronological insignificance. Yet, the superior position of man in the larger scheme of things had been the primary justification for 'intelligent design', one of the concepts with which empirical science endeavoured to reconcile sacred and profane history. The philosopher and theologian William Paley (1743–1805) attempted to do just this in his *Natural Theology; or, Evidences of the Existence and Attributes of the Deity* (1802), read by Charles Darwin, among many others. Paley's famous analogy was between a watch and the universe, claiming that from the complexity of the latter, we have no option but to deduce the guiding purpose of an 'intelligent' creator. (This was the argument, among others, that Richard Dawkins sought to demolish in *The Blind Watchmaker* of 1986.) Nor could Hutton dispense with the notion of an *a priori* cause which conferred meaning on the universe and its operations. He began his *Theory of the Earth* by setting out the proposition that:

> When we trace the parts of which this [the terrestrial system] is composed, and when we view the general connection of those several parts, the whole presents a machine of a pe-

---

4 Quoted in Marcia Pointon, *William Dyce 1806–1864* (Oxford: Clarendon Press, 1979), 172. On this painting, see also Tim Barringer, Jason Rosenfeld and Alison Smith, *Pre-Raphaelites: Victorian Art and Design* (London: Tate, 2012), 110.

5 Pointon, *William Dyce*, 171.

culiar construction by which it is adapted to a certain end. We perceive a fabric, erected in wisdom, to obtain a purpose worthy of the power that is apparent in the production of it. ... We shall thus also be led to acknowledge an order, not unworthy of Divine wisdom, in a subject which, in another view, has appeared as the work of chance, or as absolute disorder and confusion.[6]

Hutton concluded some 1,181 pages later with:

This end, the subject of our understanding, is then to be considered as an object of design; and in this design, we may perceive, either wisdom, so far as the ends and means are properly adapted, or benevolence, so far as that system is contrived for the benefit of beings who are capable of suffering pain and pleasure. But, in this physical dissertation, we are limited to consider the manner in which things present have been made to come to pass, and not to inquire concerning the moral end for which those things may have been calculated.[7]

Hutton, along with others challenged the literal interpretation of the Bible and presented a history of the earth that was cyclical and indeterminate. Yet he accepted mankind's ultimate responsibility to a divine Creator and the importance of constructing a narrative that would explain the physical world past and future, as well as present: 'Man is not satisfied, like the brute, in seeing things which are, he seeks to know how things have been, and what they are to be'.[8] This, *par excellence*, was what the biblical accounts from Genesis to Revelation had provided, whether understood literally or metaphorically and imaginatively. Time's arrow was the primary metaphor of biblical history seen as an irreversible sequence of unrepeatable events. It was an image of time

---

6 Hutton, *Theory of the Earth*, vol. 1, 3.

7 Ibid., vol. 2, 566.

8 Ibid.

that was also one of salvation traditionally opposed to the Aristotelian notion of a changeless or cycling eternity, though the two concepts were never mutually exclusive, as Stephen Jay Gould pointed out in the Jerusalem lectures that he published in 1987 as *Time's Arrow. Time's Cycle: Myth and Metaphor in the Discovery of Geological Time*.[9]

Hutton's equivocation between 'natural' and revealed religion sat within a distinguished scientific tradition. Francis Bacon had counselled that the Book of Scripture and the Book of Nature should be read differently, but eminent mathematicians such as Joseph Mede in the first half of the seventeenth century and Isaac Newton in the early eighteenth century, devoted considerable effort to investigating the meaning of the figures in Revelation and their true application to history. Newton's work in this connection on the book of Daniel, the Old Testament forebear of Revelation, and on Revelation itself, was posthumously published in 1734. Among the related manuscript material, now in the National Library of Israel in Jerusalem, is his conclusion that the world will not end before 2060:

> It may end later, but I see no reason for its ending sooner. This I mention not to assert when the time of the end shall be, but to put a stop to the rash conjectures of fanciful men who are frequently predicting the time of the end, and by doing so bring the sacred prophecies into discredit as often as their predictions fail.[10]

The 'disenchantment' or secularization of the world has been seen as lying at the heart of Enlightenment thought, though the Enlightenment concept of progress created a teleological narrative of its own, which

---

9 Stephen Jay Gould, *Time's Arrow. Time's Cycle: Myth and Metaphor in the Discovery of Geological Time* (Cambridge MA: Harvard UP, 1987). For more recent discussion of the European context of 'geotheories' in the eighteenth and early nineteenth centuries, see Martin J.S. Rudwick, *Bursting the Limits of Time* (Chicago: University of Chicago Press, 2005) and *Worlds Before Adam* (Chicago: University of Chicago Press, 2008).

10 Isaac Newton, 'Newton's Views on Prophecy, Revelation and the End of Times', Yahuda Ms. 3, www.newtonproject.sussex.ac.uk/.

presupposed 'Time's arrow' heading towards an ultimate goal of human perfectibility. It was Immanuel Kant (1724–1804) who explored most fully, and certainly most influentially in terms of modern philosophical inquiry, the status and role of the concept of God. Against the view that God was the fundamental explanatory principle and the ultimate causal ground, Kant argued that the concept of God properly functions only as a 'regulative' principle in the ordering of the world. But he also considered there was a justification to affirming a supreme cause of nature because objects of moral faith are necessary to bring about the highest good for all, which was the 'end' in sight. His philosophy of history, as developed from the *Critique of Pure Reason* in 1781 onwards, hinged on questions such as 'What can I know?', 'What ought I to do?' and 'For what may I hope?' He explored the early chapters of Genesis in *The Conjectural Beginning of Human History* (1786). In 1791, he offered a reflection on the book of Job and then in *The End of All Things* (1794) he applied himself to the book of Revelation, to explore the moral significance of the doctrine of the Last Judgement:

> It is a common expression, especially when speaking piously, for a dying man to say that he is *passing from time into eternity*. In fact this expression would mean nothing if by "eternity" one were to understand the infinite passage of time; for then surely man would never emerge from time, but would always only pass from one moment to another... Why do men expect an end of the world *after all*? And why, if this is granted to them, do they expect an end that is terrible (to the greatest part of the human race)? ... The basis for the *first* expectation seems to lie in this, that reason tells them that the duration of the world has a worth only insofar as the ultimate ends of the existence of rational beings can be met within it; but if these should not be attainable, creation itself would appear to those who believe in an end of the world to be as purposeless as a play that has no upshot whatsoever and no rational design.[11]

---

11 Immanuel Kant, *Perpetual Peace, and Other Essays on Politics, History and Morals*, trans. Ted Humphrey (Indianapolis: Hackett, 1983), 93 and 96.

By the mid-nineteenth century, the 'scepticism of the clerisy', to borrow Frank Kermode's term,[12] had chipped away at many of the fundamental tenets of orthodox Christian belief. Ruskin complained to Henry Acland in 1851 of the imagined clink of the geologists' hammers at the end of every cadence of the Bible verses, but by 1858 he had lost his religious faith, as would the painter John Brett, who had been a fervent Congregationalist, a couple of years later. The weakening of conventional, doctrinally sound religious faith did not mean the disappearance of the eschatological terms of reference. The necessity for these was rooted in reason according to Kant, whereas for others, among them the notable twentieth-century literary critic Northrop Frye, it was rooted in imagination and 'a vision of accomplished cultural destiny'.[13] The Old Testament's legacy of prophecy as history, with its fulfilment in the book of Revelation, had a pervasive influence even for the 'unconverted'. It permeated the conscious and the unconscious mind in ways to be explored through Jung's theory of archetypes during and after the First World War. Kant himself was from a German Pietist background. Nietzsche (1844–1900), son of a Lutheran pastor and initially a student of theology, proclaimed the death of God but wrapped himself in clothes of apocalyptic rhetoric; D. H. Lawrence (1885–1930) was to identify Revelation as the most 'Nietzschean' of the books in the Bible, in his own work on the Apocalypse (1931). Max Weber (1864–1920), the founder of modern sociology and author of the phrase 'the disenchantment of the world', was the son of a devout Calvinist, while Ruskin came from a background so evangelical that he knew 'most of the Apocalypse, every syllable by heart'.[14] In 1843 Ruskin ended the first volume of *Modern Painters* with a vision of the artist J. M. W. Turner that was to be paralleled by the imagery of the latter's painting *The Angel Standing in the Sun*, a direct quotation from the book of Revelation, exhibited at the Royal Academy in 1846:

---

12 'Clerisy' refers here to a learned elite. Kermode's first use of the term is in Frank Kermode, *The Sense of An Ending. Studies in the Theory of Fiction* (Oxford: Oxford UP, 1967), 24.

13 Steven Goldsmith, *Unbuilding Jerusalem* (Ithaca: Cornell UP, 1993), 11.

14 John Ruskin, *Praeterita*, vol. 1 (London: George Allen, 1905), 3.

> He stands upon an eminence, from which he looks back over the universe of God, and forward over the generations of man. Let every work of his hand be a history of the one and a lesson to the other. Let each exertion of his mighty mind be both hymn and prophecy, – adoration to the Deity, – revelation to mankind.[15]

Notwithstanding the rejection of his mother's evangelism at the end of the 1850s, Ruskin often had recourse to apocalyptic imagery to express his increasing sense of alienation and doom about the contemporary world. Of the Franco-Prussian War of 1870, he wrote under the heading of 'Storm Cloud of the Nineteenth Century':

> Blanched Sun, – blighted grass, – If in conclusion, you ask me for any conceivable cause or meaning of these things – I can tell you none, according to your modern beliefs; but I can tell you what meaning it would have borne to the men of old time ...[16]

The role of the Bible as the defining mythological framework for western culture was the central theme of Northrop Frye's career, from *Fearful Symmetry*, his landmark study of William Blake in 1947, to *The Great Code: The Bible and Literature* of 1982.

Ways of seeing are crucially important to the enduring power of eschatological imagery, the very concrete nature of the book of Revelation differing markedly from the abstract formulations of much of the New Testament, the Gospel of St John and Epistles of Paul in particular. For Blake and for Frye, the imagination rather than the senses was the true door of perception.

'Seeing' is susceptible to many interpretations, with the capacity of the beholder – intellectual and spiritual – being of paramount importance.

---

15 John Ruskin, *Modern Painters*, vol. 1 (London: Smith, Elder & Co.,1851), 422.
16 John Ruskin, *Storm Cloud of the Nineteenth Century* (Orpington: Allen, 1884), 61–2.

St Augustine at the very end of the *City of God* returned to the conundrum of how we will encounter God in the world to come, when St Paul defines Faith as the evidence of things not seen, while promising that we 'shall no longer see through a glass darkly, then we shall see face to face'. The solution lies in seeing 'with the heart' and seeing in the spirit. William Blake's watercolour *Vision of the Last Judgement* (1808) was characterised in his *Descriptive Sketches* as an example of 'seeing with the heart and in the spirit', even though it was realised within a well-established iconographic tradition. In fact, it referenced Michelangelo and much else besides. It was a commissioned work done for the Countess of Egremont to hang in the Picture Gallery at Petworth House, which Blake fully described in a letter to his friend the painter Ozias Humphry (a letter which came up for sale in 2011). Outlining the left hand side of the painting, Blake related how this was 'appropriated to the Resurrection & Fall of the Wicked.'

> The Book of Death is opend on Clouds by two Angles: many groupes of Figures are falling from before the Throne & from the Sea of Fire which flows before the steps of the Throne ... many Figures Chaind & bound together fall thro' the air, & some are scourged by Spirits with flames of fire into the Abyss of Hell which opens to receive them beneath, on the left hand of the Harlots seat; where others are howling & descending into the flames & in the act of dragging each other into Hell & of contending in fighting with each other on the brink of Perdition ... Such is the Design which you my Dear Sir have been the cause of my producing and such: but for you might have slept to the Last Judgement. (January 18, 1808).[17]

Teleological purpose has framed any number of secular narratives, not least those concerning the progress of civilization and the arts. Between 1817 and 1845, James Stephanoff (1788–1874) exhibited at the Society of

---

17 Geoffrey Keynes, ed., *The Letters of William Blake with Related Documents* (Oxford: Clarendon Press, 1980), nos.108–9, 132–3.

Painters in Water-Colours (later the Royal Watercolour Society) a series of six large, highly finished compositions based on works in the British Museum's collection. The following caption accompanied the culminating piece, *An Assemblage of Works of Art, from the Earliest Period to the Time of Phydias* which was indeed 'a vision of accomplished cultural destiny':

> At the base of the picture are specimens of Hindu and Javanese sculpture, and on either side are the colossal figures and bas-reliefs from Copan and Palenque; those above them are from Persepolis and Babylon, followed by the Egyptian, Etruscan, and early Greek remains, and surmounted by the pediment from Aegina; bas-reliefs and fragments from Xanthus and Phygalia; the Theseus, Ceres and Latona, the Fates, and other figures from the Parthenon; and terminating in a portion of the equestran bas-reliefs of the Panathenaic procession in the Temple of Minerva.[18]

Such indeed was the Western paradigm from which museum displays have yet to be wholly emancipated.

The advent of cinema opened up new possibilities of teleological rhetoric and the manipulation of time, combining both time's arrow and time's cycle. Originally conceived as a screenplay, Blaise Cendrars's *La fin du monde, filmée par l'Ange N.-D.* (1919) was published as a book illustrated by Fernand Léger when funding for the film fell through. It was a satire in which God, depicted as an American businessman, promotes an apocalyptic war on earth for profit and for the amusement of the god Mars. There are many layers of irony to the narrative which maintains the fiction of being a film that can be rewound to create the world anew – only this time God is bankrupt. Christian Marclay's *The Clock* (2010), a twenty-four hour montage of film and television clips that are about time, played in real time but on a loop, subverts in an-

---

18 James Stephanoff, *An Assemblage of Works of Art, from the Earliest Period to the Time of Phydias* (1845), watercolour over graphite, http://www.britishmuseum.org/explore/highlights.

other way the concept that time is a series of irreversible, unrepeatable events. Part of its fascination is that we suspend awareness of the true passage of time, yet experience a mounting anticipation of a grand finale in which the significance of all that has passed will be revealed – but the denouement never comes.

Thus endings even more than beginnings have remained supremely important in terms of how we create meaning for ourselves. Our deaths are foretold and that focuses the mind even for those who believe in reincarnation. The maxim that 'life is just one damn thing after another' is peculiarly unsatisfactory, somewhat at variance with the dramatic end to the life of the author of the remark, Elbert Hubbard (1856–1915), an American writer and libertarian socialist who together with his wife, died on the *Lusitania* when it sank off the coast of Ireland in 1915. Without the moral purpose that 'the sense of an ending' imparts, as Kant said, creation itself would appear to be as 'purposeless as a play that has no upshot whatsoever and no rational design'. Something of this philosophical premise is captured in the film *Groundhog Day* of 1993 where the key to breaking the cycle of endless and meaningless repetition is for the weatherman to find a moral purpose. 'The search for meaning in a preposterous universe'[19] continues unabated, though contrary to James Hutton's conclusion recent research in the realm of atomic science is of the view that there may very well be 'the prospect of an end'.

---

19 Sean Carroll, *From Eternity to Here: The Quest for the Ultimate Theory of Time* (New York: Dutton, 2010), 373.

THE WHEELING END:
TAROT AS ESCHATOLOGICAL TEXT

Camelia Elias

Ever since their emergence as a tool for divination, sometime around 1450, tarot cards have been associated with modes of self-perception, alternative world-views that derail our sense of what we call reality, and shamanistic practices. Through the visual imagery of tarot cards, one travels between states of consciousness in order to find answers to some problem. Depending on the aim, the way in which a querent's consciousness alters depends on the quest. If the quest is one of self-discovery, then a useful definition of the function of tarot is to suggest that it uncovers blind spots. However, unlike in shamanism, where the quest is undergone in a state of trance induced by drumming or some other ecstatic manifestation, it is possible to 'enter' the tarot cards with a fully conscious mind, and yet experience the often very direct message from the cards as magical. In this sense tarot can be said to perform what others, such as filmmaker and author Alejandro Jodorowski, have called a form of psychomagic.[1] In this paper I am interested in looking at how transformative change seems all the more powerful when associated with the specific cards in tarot that depict an eschatological validation of the self and the world. In other words, the more one dies and the more the world dies – often represented as a world of cultural beliefs – the more a magical realm of poetry manifests itself. My claim is that a Tarot pack of cards, due to its several takes on endings, is partici-

---

[1] See, for example, Alejandro Jodorowsky, *Psychomagic: The Transformative Power of Shamanic Psychotherapy* (Rochester, Vermont: Inner Traditions, 2010).

patory in anyone's creative potential to make visible an invisible world in a process that is not merely cognitive, nor merely psychological, but poetic and therefore, par excellence, 'out of this world'.

In many cultures, the idea of an end is expressed as a continuum. This continuum can manifest in a nominal act followed by conjunction. We can say the following: death/and. In this relation the point of finality, death, comes with a tag in the form of a supplement, or a trace, a plus. In this sense, we understand the end as a transitional point, and although we may think of death plus the beyond as emphasizing either a material state or a spiritual or metaphysical state, the beyond is here not that which exceeds death as an end but the thing itself. In many cultures, the beyond is nothing other than the thing itself, an interstitial state, a state between worlds, a gate. With this thought in mind, we can say that divinatory tools such as tarot provide the user with the potential to experience 'being in' the phenomena. Being in the phenomena is the same as saying that one participates in a magical act, the act that joins the world of *logos* with the world of *mythos*. And whereas the world of rationality can be said to be sustained by what we can observe as a fact of reality, the world of the irrational is sustained by the way in which we participate in the creation of alternative reality. In a magical setting, what we can observe about a flying bird can shift to an act of participation. By considering flying itself, rather than what a bird does while moving through the air, we can participate in the act of flying, and thus achieve an experience of flying. Likewise, if in the physical world we may consider the wind making the leaves of a tree move, then, in a magical setting, we may just as well consider that it is not the wind that is moving but our own mind. In a magical setting, what we aim at is to experience a shift in our consciousness away from rational precepts.

How to account for the understanding of magic has been a difficult task in the world of science, and many anthropologists and philosophers of science have tried to advance arguments about magic which either make magic appear more rational than it is or more mystical than it is. In her ground-breaking book, *The Anthropology of Magic,* Susan Greenwood points to the important debate between anthropologist Edward Evans-Pritchard and philosopher Lucien Levy-Bruhl that took place in 1934. As Greenwood remarks, Levy-Bruhl's ideas, which acknowledge the existence of an altered state of consciousness as a primary mode of living among 'primitive' men, had a major impact on the work of Evans-Pritchard. In turn, Evans-Pritchard sets out to show that what Levy-Bruhl calls a pre-logical order and life-style is in fact more logical within its magical context – Levy-Bruhl refers here to tribal rituals. Greenwood brings out the implications of this debate and poses a significant question: Why is it still necessary for science to claim that the world of magical thinking is very rational and consistent with its own internal regulations instead of allowing for the magical world to be just that, magical, and thus comparable to corresponding dimensions rather than what we call the world of physical reality or the age of enlightenment.[2]

The point to grasp here is that due to the scientists' commitment to the world of observable fact, an important message about magic has been missed, namely that magic does not need science to explain it, nor does it need belief to enforce its existence. In other words, the world of *mythos* is best understood as a world whose very condition for existence is a web of connections. Within this world, we make associations and we work towards understanding via analogical thinking. Time here is also of another dimension. In contrast, what we call our physical reality is ruled by logic, gravitational time, and linearity. In contrast to this, magical analogy connects us to an alternative mode of reality which exceeds the observable fact, since logic binds us to limiting measures. This means that in magical analogy the act of thinking transfers to feeling, which further entails that if a sense of reality is grasped then it is so only by means of uncertainty. In other words, if a sense of precision emerges in the magical world, comparable to what we may find in our physical reality as an appreciation in nature of geometrical patterns and perfect numbers, we can only be sure about this precision as it manifests itself precisely within the framework of analogical rather than logical time.

It is my contention in this article that through visual material such as dreams, near-death experience, and out-of-the-body experience, we

---

[2] Susan Greenwood, *The Anthropology of Magic* (Oxford: Berg Publishers, 2010), 10–27.

can arrive at a state of altered consciousness that opens towards what we may term *magical eschatology*. One way of understanding what magical eschatology may mean is to think of the shamanic experience, in which a shaman, after passing through a tunnel into an altered state of consciousness, may begin his/her journey with its own 'end'. Here, I sympathise with Greenwood's account of how on a shamanic journey to the underworld she experienced her own death by having morphed into bones. But she was not quite dead, or quite finished, as she was able to look at herself as a pile of bones, which later were eaten by a black cow. The cow then transformed into a white owl, and she felt emerging as a shape-shifted shaman flying like a master.[3] Such experiences, which are not uncommon for shamans, show how the experience of death in an altered state of consciousness is a circuitous end. Events are put into motion, the dice are cast into the wheel, and what may come comes. The act of magic here is subsumed not by the perception of the event of finality but by that of coming. This coming is in fact entirely consistent with traditional eschatological thinking in which the end is perceived precisely as a supplement: to death we normally add a gate. Death relocates us.

In his book, *Getting Back into Place,* Edward S. Casey, states the following:

> What is important ... is *the course and direction of the journey itself,* its tenor and import, whatever its precise path may be. To demand literalism of the path, whether in word or in image is to convert the plasticity of places into the rigidity of sites .... What matters on a journey is not movement as such but the form of motion. At the limit, one can travel without moving.[4]

Although Casey makes this remark within the context of the importance of place in our lives, I want to see how this translates into a con-

---

3 Susan Greenwood, *The Anthropology of Magic* (Oxford: Berg Publishers, 2010), 7.
4 Edward S. Casey, *Getting Back into Place* (Bloomington, Ind.: Indiana University Press, 2009), 306.

text of working with oracular images, namely the tarot cards, which direct us to specific places, such as classic pieces of poetry. The tarot's most reproduced images are those of the 22 cards called the major arcana cards. If laid in a pattern of progression from 1 to 22, it is clear that what we are dealing with is a soul's journey, or as others like to point out, a fool's journey, the *Fool* card being the only card without a place in the pack due to its numberless status. The *Fool* is card zero in the pack, functioning also as a wild card, disturbing and destabilising all relations it comes into contact with. If one takes the 22 cards and lays them in a sequence of seven cards distributed over three rows, it is clear that what emerges in the first row is the idea that man comes into this world to learn how to interact socially. The second row emphasises inner psychological drama when man learns about himself. The third row shows man in relation to forces that exceed his control. Here man realises that he must give back something of what he has learned and perform some action in the world that demonstrates how balance can be achieved in a lifetime and how to respect all that is living, nature and the universe included.

For those who have some familiarity with a tarot pack, the fact that the *Death* card appears in the middle of the major arcana cards (*Death* being number 13) does not come as a surprise. For what *Death* is doing there, in the middle of the journey, is not to say something about movement, or about moving ahead into the great beyond, but to say something about the form of movement. This form invites us to reconsider the idea that only in death may we come to possess an otherwise fleeting movement. Here, we may appropriately take the example of Robert Browning's poem 'Porphyria's Lover', in which a powerless and distressed young man decides to empower himself by robbing his beloved of her life only so that he can possess her, stop time, and silence the voice of god, which insists on remaining uncondemning – at least according to the speaker in the poem. The last lines in the text are a great testimony to the consequences of the man's act of self-denial, although here emblematic of the rational mind. What is fascinating in this poem is the fact that while self-denial goes hand-in-hand with a persuasive argument, it comes from a place of fantasy. The speaker reasons with fate and himself, holding Porphyria's dead body in his arms, and justifying his murder by convincing himself that sending Porphyria's soul to meet its maker is not only the right thing to do, but also serves to redeem his love, lifting it from scorn to a place of power and gain. In an uncanny image, Porphyria's dead body becomes a medium for the speaker's dead spirit. What is gained in this conjoining is a discursive moment that becomes magical:

> And thus we sit together now,
> And all night long we have not stirr'd,
> And yet God has not said a word![5]

As Porphyria says nothing, we never get to hear anything about her own experience of her purported love for the speaker in the poem. Browning seems to suggest that the reason why the lover is fascinated with Porphyria is because she is of an 'other' world, a goddess, or even a benevolent spirit. But this magical world is too much to handle for a man interested in concrete action, a man who ends up saying, 'Marry me now or die'. That fact that Porphyria only wants to keep him as her lover makes him shift his focus from his own inability to persuade her to take him as her husband to assigning agency to the futility of love. While love itself cannot be blamed, futile love can. Or else, as a goddess Porphyria cannot be blamed, but her supposed vanity can. The speaker thus creates a space between worlds where love free of either guilt or commitment can occur. This is the place that Browning, here and elsewhere, often suggests is in fact 'a spirit of place'.[6] As such, just as it can be invoked as a blessing deity, it can also be banished as evil. Here, however, what is happening is that we see a shift in the speaker's consciousness to a form of dark shamanism: Porphyria will be saved from her vanity and the lover will claim power over his impotence to rule over a goddess. Justice is done, or so the speaker thinks.

---

[5] Robert Browning, 'Porphyria's Lover' (1836). Available at www.onlineliterature.com.

[6] Charles Hobdey, *A Golden Ring: English Poets in Florence from 1373 to the Present Day* (London: Peter Owen Publishers, 1998), 13–15.

The poem illustrates perfectly the failure of trying to map a logical world unto an analogical one. We get a glimpse into the universe of this dramatic monologue and see how the speaker's desire to participate in Porphyria's world by means of logic and reason at the expense of stripping her of her magical power over him is bound to go wrong. Browning's poem, while indicating a sense of an ending, also shows what happens when death in the middle of it, as it were, is denied the form of movement, is denied its supplement.

What I find interesting in this example that bridges over to my discussion of magical eschatology in tarot is the fact that Browning allows his protagonist to speak in the language of the oracular, the language that both predicts an event and also instigates to action. This language is also the language of reverie, which situates itself above judgment. As such, it is the language of the thing itself, a spiritual phenomenon that renders death as a marriage of heaven and hell. However, the fact that an end may be experienced without judgment, without a day of atonement, is not an idea easily entertained by Christianity, and the fact that there may exist a redeeming underworld that offers reconciliation is a disturbing thought in Western culture, where we are weaned on images taken from Dante and Milton. Here, Browning senses another dimension. This is the dimension of a poetic space that Gaston Bachelard associates with a form of movement conducive to natural reveries. Bachelard writes:

> Whosoever goes to the bottom of reverie rediscovers natural reverie, a reverie of the original cosmos and the original dreamer. The world is no longer mute. Poetic reverie revives the world of original words. All the beings begin to speak by the names they bear... In the cosmic reverie, nothing is inert, neither the world nor the dreamer; everything lives with a secret life, so everything speaks sincerely. The poet listens and repeats. The voice of the poet is the voice of the world.[7]

---

7 Gaston Bachelard, *The Poetics of Reverie: Childhood, Language, and the Cosmos* (Boston, MA: Beacon Press, 1971), 188.

What Bachelard does here is to formulate the very physical reality of what can be termed a shamanic word-and-image experience. If the image redeems the word from getting stuck in a rationalist discourse, the word lends the image a name.

In tarot, after the Death card, which also bears the name of *L'Arcane Sans Nom*, the Nameless Arcane, we encounter the card called *Temperance*. The woman of chalices, the alchemist, prepares a magical potion that can save the traveller from getting stuck in the underworld, the world of dark forces, of possessiveness, of pride, artificial distinctions and inauthentic living. Incidentally, according to Mary Greer's *Who are You in the Tarot*, a book about associating tarot cards with dates of birth, Browning embodies the *Devil* card, seeking to explore evil through art, while constantly being preoccupied with his fortune, or the fate that deals one's lot in life in a reverse order: 'as if true pride / Were not also humble'.[8] Here we have an instantiation of the supplement in the form of humility which adds to the pride that is always already complete in itself. If one looks at the *Wheel of Fortune* card, one notices that the movement of the creatures caught in the eternal turning of the wheel is counter-clockwise, as if suggesting that if the cyclical pattern were to end – someone can take the handle of the wheel and change the course of events – then this change would not end with a final liberation but in a movement that tests man's courage to revise his life and transform it through introspection. Often the first step into introspection is done through the realisation of our own nothingness. Introspection thus allows for the situation of being most humble when we are also most proud.

Tarot images create poetic language, and we can easily see how their wisdom maps onto the poet's desire to be the voice of the world. The tarot card *Strength*, card 11, following the *Wheel of Fortune* and turning it forcefully, suggests that mastery over the art of speech must also come as a result of the poet's ability to eat his own words so that he can make space for listening, for suspending between worlds where vision includes seeing both physical and spiritual entities. Browning's lover talks too much, betraying the world of magic of which he wants to be

---

8 Mary K. Greer, *Who are You in the Tarot* (San Francisco, CA: Weiser Books, 2011), 131.

part. The *Hanged Man*, the one who always has a different perspective on everything, is allowed to break the pattern of living but only to an extent. As *Death comes to the Maiden*, rather than the man himself, the work of self-recovery fails where he is concerned. Perhaps God would like to clear his throat, as we have it suggested in the *Tower* card, and thus let his wrath shatter the illusion of solid constructions. But in the case of Porphyria's lover, it is clear that such an option is denied God. The *Star*, following the *Tower*, has been reduced to rosy cheeks. This means that the potential work of guidance, healing, and hope gets lost behind the *Moon*, leaving the lover disillusioned. 'God is not saying anything. I want God to say something', one can almost imagine hearing the desperate words of the lover that are not articulated properly. In the realm of the *Moon* card, it is never disclosed clearly what the agenda is, who does what to whom and why. While the *Sun* can also shine on the madman, he fails to see where it rises. His coordinates are screwed up. Still fumbling in the dark, the lover also fails to hear the sound of the trumpet. 'All rise to Judgment', the *Judgment* card says, and one can notice that here, unlike in other sacred texts, everyone is forgiven. Everyone rises to a higher consciousness, and the work of knowing oneself finds completion in the universe.

The *World* card indicates that the end is here as another wheel. Perhaps magical eschatology can be thought of in terms of an elliptical movement. One gets there by taking the long road up, feeling the path narrowing by getting closer to the parallel line, and coming down as if through a tunnel. A magical end is not an endless point going in a circle, but an end plus something else. A magical end is an end that resists finality, it is an end that shows that the on-going nature of experience is the real end. 'What goes up comes down', we are reminded by all discourses on wheels, at least since Boethius and others, which means that all attempts to produce closure are in fact a mere footnote to the continuation of life and death, an etcetera to rational understanding. The physical world of *as is* cannot be without the magical remainder, the cetera of the *otherwise*. The end understood as a full-stop to everything, as an apocalyptic moment, has less of the roundness of this cycle. After the apocalypse we don't ask the question: 'What does it all mean?', but, 'What is happening? How do we regroup?' Consequently, any investigation into the symbolic aspect of the 'after' is bound to be more of a pragmatic, rather than epistemological project. In this context, when meaning dies with the old world, participation in the new can occur. As a first, this participation would be the experience of the thing itself. In this sense, the end of the world is very much symbolically understood through direct communication. As new images form new impressions, they can also be seen to act as redemptive tools. We understand what the images tell us. Whereas the apocalypse itself is not a vision quest, the end is, if esoterically understood, a beginning beyond the symbol.

The transformational power of the tarot cards, whether read for divination purposes, or whether employed to map out alternative modes of reading literary texts, resides in their potential to bring out what is most magical about understanding life cycles through words and images taken together. Tarot cards speak in the language of participation. They teach us to view endings at a collective level, the level that goes beyond culture. At a collective level, there is no division; there are no false distributions and distinctions. At an archetypal collective level, no difference between living things exits. In other words, while there is something unsubstitutable about the singularity of death – it happens only once to all of us – it is still subject to contextualisation.

This notion has been explored successfully by critic and fiction writer Italo Calvino, particularly in his work *The Castle of Crossed Destinies* (1969), in which tarot readings are taken to a higher ground. My own understanding of what happens in *Porphyria's Lover* follows his method. What this higher ground suggests is the idea that between word and image, or meaning and message, much can happen. The experience of tarot is all about what we make of transition, and then determine what 'the end' does for us.

A tarot pack is a pack of playing cards, cards that work by virtue of carrying individual numbers. In analogy to reading a piece of literature, we think of transitions when reading cards. By that token, what happens between 2 and 3 is not the same as what happens between 8 and 9. And yet there is a sense of things being repeated, which we experience as either going from contraction to expansion, or from expansion to contraction. This is a lesson that some of the best-known tarologists and philosopher poets such as Enrique Enriquez teach.⁹

By bringing divination closer to the academic world of humanistic sciences, we learn that literature also teaches its lessons by degree, or by numbers, which means that we learn to distinguish between protagonists who constantly go through 'intense' feelings and our own response to situations that do not elicit such an experience. *Porphyria's Lover* is very much an example of one such protagonist who, while calling for sympathy, also calls for a 'cold' reading. My main point with bringing the tarot into reading a poem about death is to emphasise the idea that, particularly in *Porphyria's Lover,* what I think Browning does is draw our attention to a simple yet forgotten awareness, namely the awareness about the fact that there is a difference between what is essential and what is inessential in a poem at the chance level. Here one could point to the often controversial scholarship on Robert Browning and the ideas about crafting poetry under the sign of thinking of poetry as a tool for divination.¹⁰ At least, we know for a fact that Browning used bibliomancy to inquire about the fate of his love for his beloved, Elizabeth Barrett Browning. In one of his letters he recounts randomly choosing a book and deriving a message from a paragraph picked at random. While being disappointed in having a book of grammar fall into his lap, as it were, the book *Cerutti's Italian Grammar* fell from the shelf. Upon randomly opening it, he thought better of it. His eyes caught the following sentence: 'if we love in the other world as we do in this, I shall love thee to eternity'.¹¹ Thus, even a translation book, when used for divination purposes, can prove very useful indeed.

This example gives us a clear idea about the immediacy of a message and its practical applicability in interpretation. I find it particularly rewarding to interpret works of literature through the lens of divi-

---

9 Enrique Enriquez, *Tarology* (London: EyeCorner Press, 2011).

10 See, for instance, Mary E. Gibson, *Critical Essays on Robert Browning* (London: MacMillan Publishing Company, 1992) and Harold Bloom and Adrienne Munich, *Robert Browning: A Collection of Critical Essays*, 20th Century Views (New Jersey: Prentice Hall, 1980).

11 Robert Browning, *The Letters of Robert Browning and Elizabeth Barrett*, vol. 1 (Harper and Brothers, 1899), 470.

nation insofar as divination has a final ring to it – that and the fact that we essentialise all the time. That we should be allowed to distinguish between what is essential and what is not essential is something that Calvino insisted on in his lessons about experiencing the immediacy of a message in a literal, rather than a symbolic form. We should not respond in the same way to the literal strangling of Porphyria as we do when we see her strangled metaphorically in the sense of her being a victim of her time and age. While the events evoked in such lines may be similar, they are not congruent.

In our thinking about how to cross the literal bridge into the cultural setting that informs the writing of literature we invariably think about how transitions always leave a trace. In this sense, whatever we may make of renewal – 'and God never said a word, and therefore I can get on with my life' – becomes an act of 'bringing together', of agreement. The old stuff cannot be got rid of, only reworked, or reincorporated. Consequently, as any transition carries with it contamination, a spilling over, a remainder, or residue, it creates a supplement that is bound to haunt all exits.

In any great storytelling – which tarot is a tool for – we can think of what the philosopher and a follower of Calvino, Jacques Derrida, said in his book *The Gift of Death* (1995):

> Everyone must assume his own death, that is to say the one thing in the world that no one else can either give or take: therein resides freedom and responsibility... Even if one gives me death to the extent that it means killing me, that death will still have been mine and as long as it is irreducibly mine I will not have received it from anyone else. Thus dying can never be taken, borrowed, transferred, delivered, promised, or transmitted. And just as it can't be given to me, so it can't be taken away from me.[12]

---

12 Jacques Derrida, *The Gift of Death,* trans. David Willis (Chicago, IL: University of Chicago Press, 1995), 44.

Shamanically speaking, we may have to fulfil different functions – act as psychopomps, give advice, or heal the disconnected ones – but what underlies our existence is a deep-seated respect for everything. In the culture of living and thinking collectively outside of a magical realm hierarchies are imposed. These create a kind of obligation to fulfil inauthentic positions, such as the one Porphyria's lover inhabits. In that poem, it is clear that what the man cannot tolerate is dealing with a woman who has a mind of her own. Her life is not taken because her lover desires it, but because he feels that he owes it to the entire patriarchal culture to show who is in control. Thus 'reason' taken without a measure of magic leads to a loss of respect. Tarot cards remind us that the question is not about who is to be master, but about what can end forms of oppression, allowing the wheel to turn against the tyranny of rationalism, positivism, and literalism.

APOCALYPSE AND ANNIVERSARY: AMERICA'S BICENTENNIAL

Joe Goddard

The decade-long bicentennial planning process and the execution of the festivities cumulating in 1976 gave many Americans pause for thought. For some, two hundred years after its inception, the nation was in a possibly apocalyptic decline. For others, the festivities afforded a post-apocalyptic opportunity to arrest decline and begin again, by ending the destabilization of the 1960s and early 1970s. But what should that new start entail? Should the bicentennial offer a return to an appreciation of traditional America, to values which had served the nation well, or should it offer a pluralistic remaking of the nation which built on the social and cultural transformations of the previous ten or so years? Ideas of decline suggested that the celebrations should be focused on a diminishing canvass, as local and community affairs. Conversely, ideas of a new start suggested redemption, both for conservative visions of tradition and more liberal or radical visions of transformation.

On July 4, 1976, journalist Walter Cronkite called US bicentennial celebrations the 'greatest, most colossal birthday party in 200 years'. Others saw the festivities in less complementary light. Supposed as a tribute to progress when planning began in 1966, the official celebrations became preoccupied with backward-looking and comfort-seeking re-enactments of past triumphs. Planning the bicentennial celebrations presented huge opportunities for policymakers to mold the public mood. To exemplify: In 1966, President Lyndon B. Johnson argued that the

Declaration of Independence had lit the fire of revolution and still inspired people. Since 1776, despotic and tyrannical forces had declined worldwide, as men were 'inspired by the ideals' expressed in the Declaration.[1]

This essay argues that negotiating the increasingly troubled bicentennial era (roughly 1966-1980) forced policymakers and officials into the past in search of a common platform for the celebrations. This celebration of the past struck a chord with many Americans. Delving into the past helped advance a durable 'heritage' consensus, taken up in popular mindsets and manifested itself in a number of ways. This heritage consensus looked to the earlier twentieth century and beyond for inspiration. One example is in terms of living patterns and lifestyles best exemplified by the Americana and 'country living' booms established from the early 1970s, which extend towards the present and remain evident in popular and middlebrow culture.

Some work has been done in the field of Bicentennial Studies. Historian Christopher Capozzola has charted the overall bicentennial planning process, John Bodnar has considered the role of public memory in American commemorations, and David Lowenthal has discussed heritage and public memory, but the relationship between America's sixties 'apocalypse' with the bicentennial and an emerging heritage consensus has not yet been fully developed.[2] This essay aims to help explain the heritage consensus seen in relief against the troubles of the bicentennial era. It begins by looking at the context of bicentennial planning, moves on to discuss how professional historians viewed the celebrations, and then reflects over the role of stories in common more generally. From there it considers the role of the bicentennial in popular culture (TV), before examining the development of imagery and text of anti-urban

---

[1] Lyndon B. Johnson, cited in Alvin Shuster, 'President Signs the Bicentennial Bill', *New York Times*, July 9, 1966.

[2] See Christopher Capozzola's account of the planning process: 'It Makes You Want to Believe', in Beth L. Bailey and Dave Farber, eds., *America in the Seventies* (Lawrence, KS: University of Kansas Press, 2004), 29–49; John Bodnar, *Remaking America: Public Memory, Commemoration, and Patriotism in the Twentieth Century* (Princeton, NJ: Princeton UP, 1992); and David Lowenthal, *The Heritage Crusade and the Spoils of History* (Cambridge: Cambridge UP, 1997).

rusticism in the bicentennial era by surveying imagery in *Good Housekeeping*, *Country Living*, *Mother Earth*, *Town and Country*, and *Americana* magazines from the sixties to the nineties, the period in which the cultural influence of the bicentennial celebrations extended. These magazines built or serviced huge readerships and earned very substantial advertising revenues. Michael Kammen's ideas on the selectiveness of heritage, David Lowenthal's thoughts on the construction of heritage, and marketing scholars' insights into the world of creating new meanings in marketing help guide the essay.[3]

Contested notions of heritage are embedded in this essay. Two major elements of heritage are used here, a popular/practical one used for political purposes and to build consensus, and the more contemplative use of heritage by historians. The first, practical one stems from *Heritage '76* which remarked (retrospectively) that 'Through *Heritage '76* we sought to remember our form of government, our founding fathers, our forgotten people, the places and things of our past, the events of our past and, more importantly, our freedoms'.[4] This statement widened the earlier intent (1970) to 'recall our heritage and to place it in its historical perspective'.[5] Put differently, popular and practical heritage was encouraged from the top down in the bicentennial planning.

The second element of heritage concerns the exploration of much more amorphous and troubled notions of heritage residing in public memory which historians must untangle. These notions see heritage as essentially constructions which are seldom identifiable within more critical discussions of history, despite holding influence over ordinary people and being understood as history by the general public. This essay aims to establish that heritage was present in a generalized way in

---

3 Michael Kammen, *In the Past Lane: Historical Perspectives on American Culture* (Oxford: Oxford UP, 1997); and Marcy Darnovsky, 'The New Traditionalism: Repackaging Ms. Consumer', *Social Text*, no. 29 (1991): 87–88.

4 American Revolution Bicentennial Administration (ARBA), introduction to *The Bicentennial of the United States – A Final Report to the People: Prepared and Submitted to the Congress of the United States by the American Revolution Bicentennial Administration* (Washington, DC: U.S. Government Printing Office, 1977).

5 American Revolution Bicentennial Commission (ARBC), *America's 200th Anniversary* (Washington, DC: U.S. Government Printing Office, 1970), 6.

people's minds. In this, I am following Michael Kammen and David Lowenthal, who argue that popular views of heritage and history often overlap and conflict.

As the bicentennial planning unfolded, the event's planners delved into the past to reaffirm that they could overcome contemporary challenges to the nation. Bringing people together in troubled times proved complicated, in the volatile space between official, national, public, and local memory.[6] Constructing the bicentennial allowed reinterpretations of the past, and arguably aided the emergence of more open and noisier consensus on what it meant to be American. The American Revolution Bicentennial Administration's (ARBA) 1977 final report remarked plaintively that the bicentennial took place during some of the nation's bitterest times, and that Americans 'cried out' to be drawn together again.[7] ARBA's chief, John Warner, argued the celebrations proved 'America was alive and well' again. America had, in Warner's view, risen from terminal decline.[8] ARBA and its forerunner the American Revolution Bicentennial Commission (ARBC) were the foremost federal agencies planning the nation's anniversary. Both organizations included politicians, administrators, and included citizens and cultural luminaries within their membership and advisory boards.[9]

Potent change scoured the nation in the years leading up to 1976.[10] Tales of national progress, war victories and the benevolence of governmental power-stories celebrating the feats of modern America were challenged at home and abroad. Desegregation, gender equality, the deepening war in Vietnam, moral challenges, and the unfolding of new

---

6 Bodnar, *Remaking America*, 20.

7 ARBA, *Bicentennial*, 4.

8 ARBA, *Bicentennial*, 267

9 Altogether, numbers varied between approximately twenty and fifty, including advisory members. ARBC members grew in numbers and diversity in response to grassroots pressure, leading to the counter-charge that decision making became difficult. In the revamp of ARBC to ARBA in 1974, decision making was 'facilitated' by a reduction in membership and an accretion of power around ARBA Administrator John Warner.

10 Tom Mathews, 'The Bicentennial Summer', *Newsweek*, July 14, 1975, 28.

social mores led some people to see American society as shattered, its 'basic institutions and traditions of the United States have been distorted or besmirched'[11] on the one side, or reformed and liberated by other people. Religious thought fluxed between fundamental revivalism, and an intensely individualistic experientialism.[12] That same year, the First ARBC Report (1970) reflected over the nation's divisions:

> We desire peace, yet find ourselves at war. We believe in justice and equality, yet there are wrongs and injustices in the land. We proclaim reverence for our God-given environment, yet tolerate its pollution. We believe in the brotherhood of man, yet there is violence in the streets, prejudice of the mind, distress and discord on the campuses.[13]

Many people felt the country had strayed from its course, and was no longer the beacon of hope and freedom. President Nixon, in office for much of the planning period, fought for positivity for the celebrations in his September 1970 address to Congress. Nixon argued that the bicentennial granted an 'occasion for looking ahead', and he clearly wanted to re-focus the bicentennial events on the future.[14] Critics feared that the ARBC governmental machine would make centralized cultural policy and that Nixon would soak the celebrations with top-down jingoism and partisanship: inappropriate given the ongoing hot war in Vietnam and domestic cultural battles.[15]

Debate focused on what the national bicentennial celebrations

---

11 Eric F. Goldman, 'Topics: The Real Revolution-Or Doodle Dandy?', *New York Times*, September 27, 1969.

12 For the first, see Hal Lindsey's *The Late, Great Planet Earth* (Grand Rapids, MI: Zondervan Publishing House, 1970); for the second, see Richard Bach's *Jonathan Livingstone Seagull* (New York, NY: Macmillan, 1970).

13 ARBC, *America's 200th Anniversary*, 3.

14 ARBC, appendix to *Official Documents of the American Revolution Bicentennial Commission* (Washington, DC: U.S. Government Printing Office, 1972).

15 See Peter Carroll, *It Seemed Like Nothing Happened: America in the 1970s* (New Brunswick, NJ: Rutgers UP, 2000), 184. See also Kammen, *In the Past Lane*, 95, and Herbert Mitgang, 'The Spirit of '73', *New York Times*, November 20, 1973.

should involve. Should private enterprise fund the festivities, to epitomize the American spirit and economic system and a 'get rich' mentality, as business interests and supporters of the 'Freedom Train' argued? The steam-powered Freedom Train steel-wheeled across the country carrying 500 Americana objects – material and immaterial relics which typified the nation, sponsored by some of the nation's biggest corporations.[16] Or should they celebrate the American people, their diversity, and a new 'independence from big business' in a grass-roots and bottom-up celebration – as some on the left, including the influential People's Bicentennial Commission (PBC) suggested, and resist the Nixon administration's attempt to frame and 'steal' the people's event?[17]

How should minorities – including African Americans, Chicanos, and Native Americans – be recognized and represented? One advocate of minority participation argued: 'What kind of celebration do you have if you leave out the Indian American, the Asian American, the Spanish American, and the black American?'[18] And would such groups even want to take part?[19] What would the bicentennial mean for them; was it something they could celebrate?

Understandably, some African Americans were cool towards bicentennial talk precisely because they took the nation's foundational ideas seriously and couldn't see them reflected in their specific history and experience.[20] Native Americans turned notions of progress upside-down by pointing to their tragedy: the loss of land, the subjugation and marginalization of their societies and culture. Could they *really* be expected to 'celebrate 200 years of being shot, killed, and reservated?'[21]

---

16 Eileen Keerdoja, 'Bye-Bye Bicentennial', *Newsweek*, April 18, 1977, 18.

17 See People's Bicentennial Commission, *America's Birthday: A Planning and Activities Guide for Citizens' Participation in the Bicentennial Years* (New York, NY: Simon and Schuster, 1974). John Hess, 'A Day of Picnics, Pomp, Pageantry, and Protest', *New York Times*, July 5, 1976.

18 Vincent De Forrest, cited in Mathews, 'The Bicentennial Summer', 28.

19 See Christopher Capozzola, in Bailey and Farber, *America in the 1970s*, 30.

20 Byron Tushing, Director of Boston Museum of African History, quoted in Anthony Lukas, 'Who Owns 1776?', *New York Times*, May 18, 1975.

21 Bunny Woods, Yakima social worker, in Tom Mathews, 'The Bicentennial Summer', 28.

Americans split over whether national or local celebrations should feature most prominently in the festivities – especially as scandals afflicted the core of the nation, and especially given traditions of localism.

Professional historians reflected on the significance of the bicentennial for seventies' America. Historians grappled with the ideas of the nation's fundamental ideas and documents and held them up against the present, asking what their importance was. Presidential addresses in the *Journal of American History* and the *American Historical Review* devoted column space to discussions of the Bicentennial.[22] Frank Freidel's address and Richard Morris' response underlined the significance of this landmark event for the historical profession.[23] Freidel wrote that people held little knowledge of the past and that the history profession was in crisis, in an age in which historical memory and interpretation was singularly in a state of construction and historians were more needed than ever before. For Freidel, the bicentennial emphasized the need for 'enlarged and ... more useful role for this nation's historians'. In tumultuous times, historians could help the citizenry interrogate, recover, and establish memory.[24]

Richard Morris pressed more directly didactic goals by diving back into the revolutionary era and showing the diversity of thought at that time. The revolutionary era had been one of churning, contradictory change – similar to the late 1960s and 1970s, and certainly not much like the coherent unity proposed by top-down bicentennial celebrations. Morris spotlighted the absurdity of unitary and jingoistic conceptions of the past projected in the present and instead supported Freidel's call for historians to decode such fallacies. The bicentennial era was no historical aberration in its spectrum of opinions but echoed with jumble and conflict, much like the early years of the Republic.

---

22 Frank Freidel, 'American Historians: A Bicentennial Appraisal', *Journal of American History*, 63, no. 1 (1976); and Richard Morris, 'We, the People of the United States: The Bicentennial of a People's Revolution', *American Historical Review*, 82, no. 1 (1977).

23 C. Vann Woodward, 'The Aging of America', and Arthur Schlesinger, 'America: Experiment or Destiny?', *American Historical Review*, 82, no. 3 (1977).

24 Freidel, 'American Historians', 19.

The 1970s offered opportunities for people, and presented the growing conception of the people – an *inclusive* people – as sovereign. A 'people's revolution' led to social change two hundred years previously: The rededication of its spirit in the bicentennial bore the potential to transform the nation.[25]

Contributing to the discussion, Vann Woodward pointed at the uneasy tension between an American self-image as a young nation and its status as one of the world's oldest. Americans had trouble maintaining the myth of a virtuous nation in a wicked world, 'save by preserving the fantasy of youthful innocence'.[26] Celebrants chose the symbols of youth when commemorating the nation's birthday: marching in revolutionary-era uniforms, traipsing in period costumes, exhibiting historic firearms, carts, and tools. These symbols molded the kind of ahistorical fixed constellations that Morris had warned of, leaving Americans in denial between a chronological status as a mature society, and a self-conception of early adulthood. Arthur Schlesinger, Jr. suggested that the national psyche wavered between foundational ideas of self-doubt, redemption, salvation, and providence, inherited from Calvinism. These ideas connected with the idea of America as experiment, destiny, a promulgator of righteousness, and of grand design, but also of the terrible consequences of failure where righteousness was lost. Messianism afflicted American policy makers, ultimately bearing them back to a pre-apocalyptical era, into the realm of the constructed history which vexed Morris.[27]

ADMINISTERING THE BICENTENNIAL

The bicentennial 'framers' hoped that agreement over the past could bind the frayed threads of identity: not the America as it was (in Morris's eyes), but America as it should be. Heritage could console a nation which had lost faith in one of the nation's foundational concepts – progress.[28] Nevertheless, it proved difficult to reach consensus over

---

25 Morris, 'We, the People of the United States', 1.
26 Van Woodward, 'The Aging of America', 589.
27 Arthur Schlesinger, 'America: Experiment or Destiny?', 505–22.
28 See Lowenthal, *The Heritage Crusade*, xiii.

the intensely politicized present, to then gaze into the past.[29] On July 4, 1966, the formal mechanics and organization of the federal bicentennial celebrations empowering the ARBC with authorship of the overall program emerged from a joint congressional resolution. The precise time span of the commemorations remained open till Nixon decreed that the celebrations would cumulate in July 1976, as his second administration would be ending, linking him to Jefferson, Washington, and the creation of the nation.[30] Nixon's administrations covered much of the substantive planning of the event.

ARBC established three main themes for the celebration: *Heritage '76*, *Open House '76*, and *Horizons '76*. *Heritage '76* would concentrate on history, *Open House '76*, which became *Festival '76*, centered on people, while *Horizons '76* would emphasize technology and progress. The weightiest was always *Heritage '76*, and it gained more emphasis over time. *Heritage '76* was charged with concentrating the 'substance of our collective memory' and examining the nation's values and achievements: clearly dovetailing with the reimagining of the nation in the present through deliberate selection and interpretation of the past.[31] Ill-formulated *Open House '76* celebrated hospitality and movement before mutating into *Festival '76*, and ditching some its overt tourism components for arts and crafts. Progress-minded *Horizons '76* focused the commemoration by peering into the future, but it also concentrated on local improvement schemes.[32] Despite *Heritage '76's* increasing influence, critics still considered the ARBC plans unlikely to excite the nation as they were too timid, too bureaucratic, too unfocussed, and too unimaginative.[33]

In 1971-2, critics charged ARBC with partisan behavior, secrecy, boosterism, commercial, political and nationalistic exploitation, an ide-

---

29 The Civil War centenary events provided a rough experiential matrix for national celebrations. See Bodnar, *Remaking America*.

30 Eugene Meyer, 'The Big Birthday Bungle', *Washington Post*, July 2, 1972.

31 ARBC, *Official Documents*, 5

32 ARBC, *Official Documents*, 9.

33 Editorial, 'Letting Our Heritage Down', *Washington Post*, August 1, 1972

ologically-narrow focus, and that it reflected the ideas and values of the dominant mainstream, which fitted well with Nixon's manipulation of the bicentennial finale.[34] Among the most strident and influential voices was the People's Bicentennial Commission, which attacked the celebrations from the left while sympathizing with America's revolutionary foundation. ARBC responded with a reorganization which accepted greater diversity, firstly by broadening and increasing the commission's membership to include African Americans, Native American, youth groups, other minority groups, and women, and secondly by holding more open hearings on the nature of the celebrations.[35] Still, and perhaps unsurprisingly, top ARBC organizational positions remained exclusively in older, white, and male hands.[36]

The original ARBC planning sketches focused on top-down national celebrations in Philadelphia and on State Bicentennial parks plans.[37] Both ideas foundered over cost – the parks alone would have cost over one billion dollars, and the idea of favoring one city with national celebrations drew criticism.[38] More and diverse commission representation complicated the organizational work, leading to calls for a core-decision group and a simplified structure. Diversity and decisiveness seemed at odds, mirroring the atmosphere in the country at large.

In 1974, in a victory for critics of ARBC's now-convoluted decision making, ARBC was replaced by the American Revolution Bicentennial Administration (ARBA). Ex-Secretary of the Navy John Warner – appointed by President Nixon and confirmed by Congress – provided

---

34 Editorial, 'Boosting the Bicentennial', *Washington Post*, August 17, 1972; Editorial, 'More on the Bicentennial Commission', *The Washington Post*, August 22, 1972.

35 ARBC, *Official Documents*, 1; ARBA, *Bicentennial*, 200; and Editorial, 'More on the Bicentennial Commission', *Washington Post*, August 21, 1972.

36 Eugene Meyer, 'Bicentennial Director Quits: Management Was Criticized', *Washington Post*, August 2, 1972.

37 See Ada Louise Huxtable, 'Bicentennial Panel Urges Network of Parks', *New York Times*, February 23, 1972.

38 Editorial, 'Marching Towards '76', *Washington Post*, February 9, 1973.

ARBA with strong leadership.[39] Warner vowed to stick to Nixon's unitary views of bicentennial ideas, and suggested the celebrations should 'forge a new national commitment – a new spirit for '76', and revitalize 'the ideals for which the Revolution was fought' as he saw them.[40] Still, ARBA's role was quickly defined in limited terms, to 'stimulate, encourage, and coordinate' rather than plan nationally.[41] Local events, it was hoped, would aggregate to a national celebration. ARBC retained ARBC's three central themes and its congressional funding.

ARBA favored private funding more than ARBC, and sanctioned the 1976 Freedom Train. The Freedom Train's five million dollar bill was split between PepsiCo, General Motors, Prudential Insurance, Kraft Foods, and ARCO, and its staff claimed that theirs was a truly 'national event'.[42] The Train's wagons contained a veritable feast of Americana relics (from moon rock, to Judy Garland's *Wizard of Oz* dress), and were dedicated to the American 'go-getter' spirit to buttress the argument that 'freedom, individual initiative, and the free-enterprise system allowed our nation to grow and prosper for 200 years'.[43] The pursuit of happiness as a measurement of progress was one prescription for a resurrected nation, based on one conception of America's common story. Other private organizations pitched in with ventures to celebrate the nation's birthday and make a profit, such as Walt Disney. For $5.25 admission, customers could marvel over a Walt Disney Productions' spectacle which gave people 'the feeling that they had actually celebrated the birthday of the nation'. Hot air balloons, floats, 4,000 flags, and Mickey Mouse, Goofy and Donald Duck as the Spirit of '76 (a well-known ren-

---

39 Byline, '1976 Commission Scored in Report', *New York Times*, December 30, 1972; Byline, 'President Proposes A New Unit to Plan/U.S. Bicentennial', *New York Times*, February 2, 1973; Byline, 'New Plan Urged for Bicentennial', *New York Times*, April 25, 1973; Paul Friedlander, 'Bicentennial Reports: Bits and Pieces', *New York Times*, November 4, 1973.

40 ARBA, *USA '76: The First Two Hundred Years*, (Washington, DC: U.S. Government Printing Office, 1975), 1.

41 ARBA, *Bicentennial*, 248.

42 Keerdoja, 'Bye-Bye Bicentennial'.

43 Edward Yalowitz, ed., *All Aboard America* (Crossroads, VA: The American Freedom Train Foundation, Inc., 1976).

dering of Yankee Doodle from 1876) were included in Disney's event. This ARBA-supported venture took two years to plan and cost eight million dollars to develop. Disney hoped that twenty-five million people would see this show, showering $125 million dollars in revenues on the corporation. John Warner approved: Disney was 'trying to do some real Americana'.[44] Disney's event, preserved as a six-minute *You Tube*, film begins thus: 'In the Spirit of '76, Walt Disney Productions proudly presents "America on Parade – a Salute to America's 200th Birthday", two centuries filled with challenges, achievements, and world contributions', and ends (without irony) thus: 'God Bless America. May liberty's flaming torch and out great symbols of freedom shine like beacons and inspire all mankind to live together in peace and harmony'.

Behind the commercialism, the Disney film touches on important episodes in American history. However, it omits the Civil War – and represents the flattening of knowledge that worried Morris, as well as promoting simple and uncritical statements of peace and harmony which contradicted America's Vietnam-era experience. Not surprisingly, private initiatives like Disney's attracted heavy criticism from grass roots organizations. Critics howled against the commoditization of revolutionary spirit and the unacceptable merger of the private and the governmental: ARBA co-hosted the Disney celebration event announcement at the State Department. PBC, meanwhile, proposed reinvigorating the 1776 revolutionary spirit and its radical tradition to inspire social change, to promote real equality, protect the environment, check the military, and deepen democracy. Clearly, PBC's ideas were very different from the smug tones emanating from the Freedom Train and Disney.[45] In fact, some critics cast the ARBC leadership as anti-revolutionary Tories rather than authentic American patriots.[46] Critics caus-

---

44 Tom Mathews, 'Three Cheers for the Red, White and $$', *Newsweek*, June 9, 1975, 48; James T. Wooten, 'Disney will Join the Bicentennial', *New York Times*, February 19, 1974.

45 In Mitgang, 'The Spirit of '73'.

46 In Meyer, 'The Big Birthday Bungle'. See 'Report of the Subcommittee to Investigate the Administration of the Internal Security Act and other Internal Security Laws of the Committee of the Judiciary of the United States Senate, Second Session, March 1976', *The Attempt to Steal the Bicentennial: The People's Bicentennial Commission*.

tically claimed that the administration and business were 'planning to sell us a program of plastic Liberty bells, red, white, and blue cars, and a Manichaean "love it or leave it" political program'.[47]

Lambasted for enlisting free market forces to help arrange the celebrations, Warner retorted that the pursuit of happiness – economic freedom – endured as a core American value and had enthralled generations of immigrants. In Warner's words, 'For every person who migrated to the US for religious or political freedom, there were ten who came for the purpose of participating in the free enterprise system and to get into the economic mainstream'. Warner connected American values with getting ahead. Critics, on the other hand, named religious freedom and civic perfectionism as motivating immigration to the United States.[48] This clash precisely illustrates the contested notions of what a common American heritage was construed as meaning in the bicentennial period as both views were defensible.

Concentrating a two-decade revolutionary process into a July 4, 1976 holiday weekend was problematical – even if essential for an extravaganza of compacted memory and clearly condensed opportunities for unity and division. One-weekend events obscured complexity, crushed understanding, and stifled dissent. Yet, there were precursors in the commemoration of other revolutionary era events.

The reenactment of the 1773 Tea Party in Boston on December 16, 1973 demonstrated the thick brew of opposing currents bubbling out of the debate over the bicentennial celebrations, themselves pouring out of America's fractured self-image. Crowds witnessing the re-enactment got and gave more than a replay of Tea Party tax strife, as the event turned into a 'happening' which showed how tussled the nature of the bicentennial celebrations was, and how the bicentennial's contemporary interpretation could not be controlled. 'Official' Tea Party re-enactors echoed the revolutionary protests of two centuries earlier by chanting 'Down with King George'. Crowds at the festivities retorted with 'Down with King Richard' – President Nixon, then under investigation

---

47 People's Bicentennial Commission, *America's Birthday*, 9.

48 Cited in Marylin Bender, 'Will the Bicentennial See the Death of Free Enterprise?', *New York Times*, January 4, 1976.

for Watergate wrongdoing with the approval of a meager quarter of voters. Nixon's actions were highly instrumental in the collapse in support for America's political institutions. During Nixon's period in office trust in government fell from over 60 % to around 35 %.[49]

Some protesters, then, linked the anti-establishment protests of the early 1970s with the anti-British protests two hundred years earlier. Power and privilege, the cozy corporate sponsorship of the public Tea Party event and the growing power of oil corporations motivated protesters to dump empty oil barrels instead of tea. One libertarian anti-tax group protested peacefully by sailing a yacht festooned with the banner 'taxation is theft'.[50] This protest linked the tax revolt of the 1770s with the onerous tax rates of the 1970s (and forward to the Tea Party Movement). The revolutionary past and rebellious present bubbled together in the re-enactment, the crowd's retort, the barrel dumping, and the yacht protest. Heritage and history refused to be confined in official narratives. Other events and reenactments were similarly contested. In 1975, *The Harvard Crimson* compared 'embattled Concord farmers who fired the shot heard around the world', and the 'embattled farmers of Indochina – who ... fight the world's strongest power'.[51] *The Harvard Crimson* joined dots that Disney's sermon of 'peace and harmony' couldn't see.

Turning back from events to themes, the central focus for the bicentennial events became 'heritage' which was expressed through *Heritage '76*. Michael Kammen maintained that heritage, rather than consisting of physical things or relics, is amorphous, relational, and obscures as much as it explains. Given the imperative to help bring Americans together, heritage was laden with positive meaning in the celebrations. Kammen described the 'heritage syndrome' as the selective 'impulse to remember all that is attractive or flattering and to ignore the rest' – matching the remit of the bicentennial planners to unify peo-

---

49 Pew Reseach Center for the People and the Press, *Distrust, Discontent, Anger and Partisan Rancor: The People and Their Government*, April 18, 2012, accessed Aug. 7, 2013, http://www.people-press.org/2010/04/18/distrust-discontent-anger-and-partisan-rancor/

50 ARBA, *Bicentennial*, 106.

51 Cited in Lukas, 'Who Owns 1776?'

ple quite precisely, and following Morris's critique. The propagation of understanding inherent in bicentennial heritage bore risks, including the 'commercialization, vulgarization, oversimplification, and tendentiously selective memory' which risked a 'warping and whitewashing' of a 'fenced-off past'.[52] Kammen's heritage critiques chimed well with citizens' critiques of the official celebrations. In correction Kammen recommended locating the whole of history in heritage – to open up 'heritage' – to liberate the term from pastel uniformity; however, this option would have clashed with the political and cultural aims of politicians and officials alike during the bicentennial.

David Lowenthal, meanwhile, worried more over the danger that heritage poses for sober reflection of history. The purpose of heritage, many people felt, was to aggregate sentiment upwards, to find commonalities linking people into exceptional communities, and to explain why people are special. Popular ideas of heritage ideas are susceptible to political interference, and to being harnessed for specific unity-creating purposes, as Nixon intended. This can leave people blind to the difference between heritage as a set of beliefs of the past projected into the future, and history as an attempt to understand the past on its own terms. Heritage is the handmaiden of the present. One Congressman commented (around 1995) on the Smithsonian's efforts to communicate American history: 'I don't want 16-year-olds walking out of there [the Smithsonian] thinking badly of the United States'. A Smithsonian Regent put this view more graphically, declaring that 'We've got to get the patriotism back in to the Smithsonian ... to reflect real America and not something that a historian dreamt up'.[53]

Heritage '76 was increasingly intended to mend America's crumbling self-perception and manifested itself in material culture in physical and felt terms. Over 3,600 building heritage restoration projects commenced during the run-up to the bicentennial festivities, including repairs to preservation-worthy log cabins and the restoration of buildings, railroad stations, theaters and other important sites.[54] Natural

---

52 Kammen, *In the Past Lane*, 220–1.
53 Lowenthal, *The Heritage Crusade*, 160–1.
54 ARBA's final five-volume report catalogued local and state projects.

history projects favored included tree-planting and local bicentennial park dedications. These projects projected attention into the past by celebrating relics of American history and, in their re-construction, of the bicentennial process itself as an intended (through the buildings restored) and unintended (through listings) agent of heritage.[55] The National Register of Historic Places saw a 3,000 % increase in buildings listed.[56] In the certification of past relics, people were taught to revere their local heritage through a set of approved ideas and objects across the nation, relics now known, recognized, and locally significant through registration. One way this worked was through the encouragement of the establishment of local historical societies and associations. Such organizations helped maintain the past's legacy and narrate its relevance to the present.[57]

Reenactments in the bicentennial festivities often spoke to popular or public memory of the mind rather than the built environment.[58] Restaging national myth, horse-drawn wagons reversed national expansion by riding from points west to Philadelphia. Thundering across the continent, riders in this event evoked western settlement and the 'hopes and bravery of pioneers'.[59] Massive popular interest accompanied these events: over 60,000 riders rode stages of the journey.[60] Revolutionary battles were re-enacted, including at Lexington and Bunker Hill. These re-enactments reaffirmed – or more accurately constructed – knowledge and pride in the creation of the country, connecting imaginations of the past with alternative understandings of the pres-

---

55 Reconstruction did not always go uncontested, as disagreement often centered on precisely *what time* to restore physical relics to. In a lifetime perhaps stretching centuries, the moment of authenticity was not always obvious. See also ARBA, *Bicentennial*, 34.

56 Rising from 400 in 1969 to 13,000 in 1976. See ARBA, *Bicentennial*, 92 & 122.

57 ARBA, *Bicentennial*, 124, and Philip Jenkins, *The End of the Sixties and the Making of Eighties America* (Oxford: Oxford UP, 2006), 69.

58 Following the precedent of the Civil War centenary celebrations in the early 1960s.

59 ARBA, *Bicentennial*, 119.

60 ARBA, *Bicentennial*, 61.

ent which jumped back and forth over recent division. The creation of history-by-doing had been one bicentennial aim from the outset, by encouraging hodgepodge local organizations to become involved in celebrations which 'would make every American ... eager to participate' in a form of celebratory elective republicanism which married top down and bottom up approaches.[61] Mass support for these small scale celebrations suggested the participatory appeal struck home. Nationally sanctioned, these grassroots activities allowed local freedom and agency.

The bicentennial era also fostered awareness of impending natural catastrophe. In 1776, limitless bounty seemed to provide 'food, clothing and shelter, and energy for a young nation on the move'.[62] Unconstrained, Americans could reap without worries of the future. By the 1960s, however, the cornucopia of natural forests and countryside was endangered on multiple fronts, with oil-pipeline arteries of modernity crossing the last wilderness in Alaska.[63] Since Frederick Jackson Turner in the 1890s, wilderness had been popularly identified as steeping an 'American' quality to the nation.[64] Retaining wilderness required protection and patronage, a realization recognized by ARBA.

ARBA produced a key exhibit which talked to human and natural heritages, *USA '76: The First Two Hundred Years*. This exhibit advanced ARBA's ideas for the representation of the bicentennial and featured landscape painting, folk art, photography, film, and printed matter, and recognized the connection between America's imagined origins and the present in its catalog.[65] ARBA activity included protection measures for the natural treasure trove: tree plantings, watershed retention, city

---

61 ARBC, *America's 200th Anniversary*, 2, and Paul Friedlander, 'Bicentennial Reports: Bits and Pieces', *The New York Times*, November 4, 1973.

62 ARBA, *Bicentennial*, 173, and James Field, 'America: Experiment of Destiny? Comments', *American Historical Review*, 82, no. 3 (1977), 526.

63 See Peter Coates, *The Trans-Alaska Pipeline Controversy: Technology, Conversation and the Frontier* (London: Associated UP, 1991).

64 Frederick Jackson Turner, *The Frontier in American History* (Boston, MA: Henry Holt, 1953).

65 ARBA, *USA '76*, 4.

parks sponsorship, and roads beautification.[66] Instructed to appreciate nature, people became more sensitive to it and the value of landscapes. With rustic origins eulogized, rural populations rose for the first time in a century and Americans recorded increasing keenness to live outside of major cities.[67] Meanwhile the urban crisis provided an equally important factor in this rural population rebound, fueled by mixes of white prejudice, African American assertiveness and plummeting tax revenues: all of which reduced the allure of cities.

While the bicentennial ultimately facilitated a renewal of spirit in the thousands of local celebrations, this rejuvenation came at a cost as hope and apathy swirled together. Hopeful moments in mending America's apocalypse: bringing troops home, the ending of the Watergate nightmare, the resignation of President Nixon, and the installation of Gerald Ford as president in 1974 evaporated for many when Nixon was pardoned shortly thereafter, and domestic politics remained bedeviled by disagreement and falling public confidence as evidenced in opinion polls.

Increasingly distrustful of the federal government, many younger Americans turned inwards in pursuit of meaning and quality-of-life.[68] From 1964 to 1980 trust in government fell by two-thirds. A broad assessment suggested that people's focus had moved from a belief that their success in the present resulted from the correct adherence to tradition, towards a rejection of the present for the past, to a rejection of authority, and then on to a rejection of the collective for individual and local salvation. Generalized antigovernment passion exploded during the 1966-1976 bicentennial decade, opinion polls consistently noted. Was this any surprise, given the assassinations of John F. Kennedy, Bobby Kennedy and Martin Luther King, the demise of Lyndon Johnson

---

66 ARBA, *Bicentennial*, 175–7.

67 Calvin Beale, *The Revival of Population Growth in Non-Metropolitan America* (Washington, DC: Economic Research Service, United States Department of Agriculture, 1975).

68 Levels of trust for local and State governments remained buoyant. See The Pew Research Center for the People and the Press, *How Americans View Government: Deconstructing Distrust*, March 10, 1998, accessed August 13, 2013 http://people-press.org/report/95/.

over Vietnam, the disgrace of Richard Nixon over the Watergate cover up, the discrediting of Vice President Spiro Agnew, and the disappointment of Gerald Ford and then Jimmy Carter in an era of continued decline?[69]

POPULAR CULTURE AND PRINT CULTURE

For many Americans, shelter in the past became increasingly attractive as a search for commonalities in shared and unifying experiences. A celebration of American history and heritage was, of course, always integral to the bicentennial design. Three sub-tracks to this 'heritage' process which emphasized the past deserve a little more attention. The first track saw increased appreciation of rural roots, landscape and farming society, as these 'folk' memories offered qualities circumventing contemporary divisions, a supposed time before disagreement. Solace and unity in the imagined byways of the past surfaced in popular culture, including TV shows. Examples included *The Beverly Hillbillies, Green Acres, The Waltons,* and *Little House on the Prairie,* all of which captured top-twenty television audiences year after year in the sixties and seventies with the spellbinding imagery of uncorrupted lifestyles – before the nation fell from grace. *The Waltons* (1972-1981) and *Little House on the Prairie* (1974-1983) acted as moral foils for bicentennial era strife; they showed how conflicts could be resolved in multigenerational homes, in local schools and in forgiving churches – beyond the blue glare of television in suburban living rooms which illuminated the familial fragments divided by the 'generation gap' between younger and older viewers.

Younger people in particular tuned out by 'returning to the land' – although not all successfully or lastingly. Still, they showed that some people willingly reinvented themselves and sought 'authenticity' and salvation in their rural past rather than in a present judged contaminated beyond restitution. Back-to-the-land stories emerged strongly in

---

69 See Bruce Schulman, *The Seventies: The Great Shift in American Culture, Society, and Politics* (New York: Da Capo Press, 2001), 51. See also Pew Research Center for the People and the Press, *Public Trust in Government: 1958-2010,* January 31, 2013, accessed August 8, 2013, http://people-press.org/trust/.

the booming alternative magazine culture catering to younger readers around 1970; these urban refugees did not express inherently conservative ideas, but oftentimes rejected parts of modern life. Some avowed an unwillingness to participate in the 'plasticity' of the rat race or support the 'military-industrial complex'. Urban renegades sought inspiration in the simple lifestyles propounded by an earlier generation of simple living gurus and many hoped that technological solutions could ultimately be found to modern problems.[70]

From 1970, the alternative magazine *Mother Earth News* advised urban refugees, connected them in a network through several pages of lineage ads, and reached over a million readers. *Mother Earth* targeted people eager to leave pollution, congestion, strife, and artificial lifestyles behind: 'the "hip" young adults. The creative people. The doers ... Heavy emphasis is placed on alternative life styles, ecology, working with nature, and doing more with less'.[71] Taken together, the magazines' articles, advertisers, and public sustained communities who had simply separated themselves from contemporary problems, and who sought inspiration from the nation's rich history of utopian communities. Enthusiastic readers flocked towards the magazines and publications like *Mother Earth News* savvy enough to showcase 'simple living' ideas and examples.

Mainstream people also fled to the perceived simplicity of the suburbs and countryside, Predominantly WASP, this 'white flight' fuelled suburban growth and the 'rural (population) turnaround' recognized by the U.S. Department of Agriculture in 1975.[72] City-edge counties saw markedly increased numbers of smallholdings in the bicentennial era, dubbed 'ranchettes' and 'farmettes', reported in local press, magazines and journals, in the national media, and visible in U.S. Census Bureau

---

70 Scott and Helen Nearing, *Living the Good life: Being a Plain Practical Account of a Twenty Year Project in a Self-subsistent Homestead in Vermont, Together with Remarks on How to Live Sanely and Simply in a Troubled World* (Harborside, ME: Social Science Institute, 1954); and *The Mother Earth News*, January 1970.

71 'Mission Statement', *The Mother Earth News*, May 1970, 5, and "How to Make it Your Way," *The Mother Earth News*, January 1970, 6.

72 The term was coined by Department of Agriculture demographer Calvin Beale, in *Revival of Population Growth.*

statistics. Urban refugees hoped to combine an updated yeoman farmer ideal, their existing salaries, and leave city problems behind.[73]

A third expression of a growing preoccupation with the past around the bicentennial is reflected in the blend of images projected in the magazine world. Rural Americana' celebrated heritage in the form of the objects and ideas of pre-mechanized farming and life, and became a 'national' design style by the mid-seventies. Rural Americana hearkened back to America's youth, and away from contemporary division. Mainstream women's and lifestyle magazines like *Good Housekeeping* and *Town and Country* changed their appearances strikingly – precisely the magazines which could be expected to showcase the development of ideas in popular culture. They rejected the bright, colorful, slick, and linear modernism of the fifties and early sixties in favor of an earth-hued rustic and organic revivalism. Upper crust *Town and Country* wrote of increased collector and investor interest in the decorative arts of the nineteenth-century, suggesting that arts and crafts were becoming central to contemporary understandings of America's past.[74] Documenting the allure of heritage, articles in *Town and Country* wrote of the explosive growth of clubs and organizations, while museums began to pay homage to American arts. *Town and Country* signaled that the enthusiasm for nineteenth-century Americana reconnected readers with feelings of hope and pride which were lost in the 1970s.[75]

The rise of an 'Americana' heritage in the nation's consciousness also surfaced in new magazines which attempted to channel 'country style' living readers and their advertising dollars. One example, *Country Living*, included imagery awash with aesthetic rural Americana furniture: hand-made, rustic items and patchwork quilts. These objects filled the backdrops of shows such as *The Waltons* and *Little House on the Prairie*.[76] Rural Americana also connected with green, as earlier home-

---

73 See Joe Goddard, *Being American on the Edge: Penurbia and the Metropolitan Mind, 1945-2010* (New York: Palgrave, 2012).

74 Monica Meehan, 'A Nineteenth Century Look', *Town and Country*, September 1970.

75 Monica Meehan, 'Living with Americana', *Town and Country*, March 1976, 76.

76 See 'Come Quilt with the Waltons', *Good Housekeeping*, October 1976, 150.

spun lives stood in contrast to the unsustainable use of resources in modern agriculture, industry, and homes. Magazine and moving images teased out deep, dream-like cultural memories. Country magazines' readerships grew into the millions, while advertising takes soured into the hundreds of millions, catapulting these kinds of publications onto lists of America's top 100 magazines in readers and revenue.[77]

Serious interest in folk art gained support from the bicentennial's focus on heritage. Exhibitions of rustic objects and folk art spawned innovative shows and auctions at the Whitney Museum of American Art and Sotheby's Auctioneers in New York.[78] At the Whitney three hundred items exhibited numbered 'paintings and sculptures ... furniture, quilts shop signs, toys, rugs, embroidery', and a number of other material artifacts linking the nation to its past.[79] New York's Metropolitan Museum was encouraged to establish an Americana Museum while the American History Museum in Washington, DC, under the Smithsonian was rededicated to the 'collection, care and study of objects that reflect the experience of the American people'.[80] *Americana* magazine, founded in 1973, witnessed an enthusiastic, growing readership for magazines communicating serious rustic country style for collectors. *Americana*'s editor Michael Durham believed the magazine helped readers appreciate how the past could enrich and be consumed by the present.[81] The publishing industry, prominent auctioneers, and local and national museums built and reflected growing sensibilities favoring the nation's earlier material culture.

---

77 *Country Living* was not alone in the market, and with its nearest direct competitor, *Country Home*, produced nearly $300 million in advertising revenue by 2004. Several other magazine titles were published from the early 1980s, most of which still exist.

78 Jean Lipman and Alice Winchester, *The Flowering of American Folk Art, 1776 1876* (New York: Courage Books, 1974).

79 Hilton Kramer, 'New Perspectives on American Folk Art', *New York Times*, February 1, 1974.

80 For the Americana Museum, see ARBC, *Report to the Congress of the United States* (Washington, DC: U.S. Government Printing Office, 1972), 7.

81 Alan and Barbara Nourie, *American Mass-Market Magazines* (New York, NY: Greenwood Press, 1990), 21–3. *Americana's* readership soon outstripped that of the parent.

Cultural ideas persist even when we can't see them on the surface. These ideas are intangible and ethereal, yet despite this they link people in different places and times together cognitively. Cultural ideas are constantly being reworked and refashioned, narrated and related. The growing obsession with the past at the expense of the present mixed existing ideas such as the frontier, prejudice against the city, environmentalism, and veneration for the small-scale community, reified them in the bicentennial process, and reinterpreted them to fulfill contemporaneous needs to create meaning. Yet rather than solely a spontaneous and simultaneous reaction on the part of Americans, this reinterpretation was also a created phenomenon. Marketing scholars acknowledge the great power that practitioners of these skills have in recognizing and mobilizing contemporary issues, dissembling them symbolically, cracking them into their constituent parts before recombining them 'into compelling new meanings and identities'.[82] The bicentennial era provided a volatile backdrop for such work. The depth of the retreat from the present in terms of ideas and tastes almost certainly outstripped the expectations of the professionals, politicians and administrators involved, and perhaps illustrates how acutely Americans of different origins, politics and beliefs collectively felt the nation was flailing

The bicentennial celebrations' emphasis on heritage articulated an appreciation of older and uncorrupted ideas as the celebrations increasingly became conceived as commemorating past achievements, changing contemporary minds and affecting material fashions. With the demise of progress, modernist design slipped out of fashion. Man-made, factory design materials and colors suffered by comparison with the craftsmanship of the past, exemplified in the rustic and traditional Americana design styles and lifestyles of quilts, bed-throws, wood, stoneware, and homemade breads and jams expressed in magazine features which expressed domesticity, serenity, and unhurriedness. The long bicentennial gestation made an impact, as it allowed for a pride in earlier, authentic, and untainted material culture to unfold. Contemporary observers, experiencing a cultural reorientation, found difficulty

---

82 Darnovsky, 'The New Traditionalism', 87–8.

in separating cause from effect. One columnist maintained appreciation of country-style fed off the post-bicentennial backlash against high-tech styles which encouraged the development of a patriotic, values-embracing country design movement.[83] Yet articles, photo essays and advertisements in *Good Housekeeping*, *Town and Country*, and *Country Living* magazines demonstrated that a rustic, rural, traditional style had already captured the mainstream earlier in the bicentennial era, leaving the question of whether *Heritage '76* was an agent or reagent of cultural change.[84]

CONCLUSION
Bicentennial planning and celebrations were simultaneously the result of changing attitudes and an agent of their change. Ingrained cultural ideas and the apocalypticism of the bicentennial era played in during the preparations, yet the planning itself created a frame for thought which both influenced and empowered people. Planning the bicentennial became part of a backward-looking exercise which aimed at bringing Americans together by celebrating their past despite their present-day divisions. The celebrations came to be conceived more as an appreciation of older and uncorrupted ideas and a festival of past achievements than of present prowess and future progress.

The combination of social, political, generational, and environmental upheavals, the urban crisis, Watergate, Vietnam, and ecology allowed latent cultural preferences and prejudices to surface among Americans. The decade of bicentennial planning and the discussion it brought invigorated deep, yet ill recognized cultural memories, activated by the churning spirit of the late sixties and early seventies. Celebrating the country's rural and frontier 'heritage' past became immensely important during the bicentennial era. Celebrations created

---

83 Jeff Gremillion, 'Country Style: Titles Celebrate the Heartland', *MediaWeek*, April 21, 2003.

84 See 'Old Fashioned Baking: We've Made it Easier', *Good Housekeeping*, February, 1976, 110; 'Do It Yourself Bedrooms with the Decorator Touch', *Good Housekeeping*, July, 1976, 108; 'How to Decorate with Personal Treasures', *Good Housekeeping*, August, 1976, 90; 'Come Quilt with the Waltons', *Good Housekeeping*, October, 1976, 150.

a sense of pride shorn from the corrupted present and extolled views of a youthful, simpler nation which chimed with traditionalists who pitted themselves against permissiveness, as well as with progressives who employed the motif of a younger America against the present. The young and the not-so-young could unite to celebrate a community transcending the disconnection between older and newer conceptions of the nation. An orgy of commemorative preservation and reconstruction projects emerged prior to 1976, with local projects in the forefront. Personal senses of quality of life became important around the bicentennial. Empowered by wealth most other countries could only envy, and embittered to see political power abused and ineffective, many people tuned out of the national and in to the local. Perhaps this was the 'greatest, most colossal birthday party in 200 years', but if so it was one in which a wide variety of guests partied and celebrated in wildly different ways. For some the bicentennial was a wake, while others looked forward to a new beginning.

BOB DYLAN SINGS THE APOCALYPSE

Bent Sørensen

This article discusses the function of tropes of the apocalypse in the songs of 1960s US counterculture icon, Bob Dylan. Dylan draws on older folksong traditions, and often models his work on ballad lyrics from the past. He, however, updates the political and ethical thrust of the lyrics to address issues of relevance to his contemporary audience. The main concern of this article is what makes the apocalyptic discourse particularly pertinent for the 1960s and beyond.

The role of apocalyptic discourse has been increasing within popular culture in the US since the 1960s where the counterculture movement started utilizing the trope of the apocalypse for various purposes, partly connected with a positive wish for complete spiritual change from a Christian, patriarchal hegemony exalting materialism above all else, partly connected with a fear that if such change was not brought about within a generation the world would really come to an end, either in a nuclear holocaust, or in a combination of various ecological disasters. The duality of the phenomenon of the apocalypse as text, that of both prophecy and revelation, is thus neatly reflected in the discourse work being done by the counterculture spokesmen and –women, who alternated between two types of speech act: prophecy as cautionary tale (if we do not act the fire will descend upon us), and revelatory description (this is what will happen as we descend towards the apocalypse).

Philip Beidler[1] has appropriately described the production and consumption processes surrounding such prophetic texts as constructing 'a true people's priesthood, a whole consumer-cult of young believers, mixing their sacred texts high and low into a total myth of consciousness. Here, as well as in science fiction, fantasy, and a host of other styles of semiotic experimentation, they tried to recast the word itself as a kind of wiggy, Day Glo shamanism, the ultimate magic and light show. [T]hey fixed the nation's attention one last time on the idea that words could still be holy and that the newest emanation into the world could still create America as the beacon of History'.[2] This focus on the logocentric belief in the power of the word to bring about changes in perception, as well as action, is emblematic of the counterculture project of the 1960s and not least of its prophets who took upon themselves to describe and warn us of the apocalypse.

Chief among these prophets of the apocalypse were the singer-songwriters of the early to mid-1960s in America. Often also labeled protest singers or folk singers, lyricists such as Phil Ochs, Peter LaFarge and many others continued an earlier leftwing, pro-union, working-class songwriting tradition stretching from Woody Guthrie to Pete Seeger in the preceding decades, and themselves became forerunners for later decades' figures such as Joni Mitchell, Leonard Cohen and Neil Young (all three in reality Canadians who to varying degrees repatriated themselves as Americans), who all wrote apocalyptic and utopian songs in the late 1960s and onwards. Towering over all these figures, however, is that of Bob Dylan, whose importance as spokesperson for a generation of seekers and protesters alike cannot be overstated.

For a few years in the early and mid-'60s Dylan's every word and move was eagerly watched by hundreds of thousands of young fans and followers. Dylan's first three albums, especially his second – *The Freewheelin' Bob Dylan* (1963) – were received as reports from the frontline

---

1 Philip D. Beidler, *Scriptures for a Generation: What We Were Reading in the '60s* (Athens, GA: The University of Georgia Press, 1994).

2 Beidler, Scriptures, 11.

of the battle for change,³ and the figure of Dylan as the lone troubadour with an acoustic guitar bringing back insights and vision in plain, mobilizing speech was revered. Dylan's fourth album, released in the fall of 1964 (*Another Side of Bob Dylan*), signaled a change to come, but still contained protest anthems such as 'Chimes of Freedom' which could be read as either topical comments or apocalyptic warnings. Nonetheless this particular song also constitutes a departure from the plain language of troubadours such as Guthrie and Seeger, and can be regarded as a Symbolist poem whose religious imagery and almost medieval tonality moves Dylan's vision beyond politics and topical commentary towards a greater universality in a message that has been described by music critic Paul Williams as Dylan's 'Sermon on the Mount'.⁴

There are quite obviously too many Dylan songs that contain cautionary tales of the impending end, or visions from beyond the grey everyday life of political protest for this chapter to cover them all. However, a quick tour of selected Dylan lyrics that avail themselves of the trope of the apocalypse reveals that his valorization of the end of the world as we know it alters with his growing older and older, much as his role as a spokesperson finally collapses as he turns to electrical instrumentation of his songs and becomes a part of a musical collective in 1965,⁵ only to return sporadically when he lends his voice to causes over the following four decades.

What Thomas Beebee has dubbed Dylan's 'apocalyptic ballads' (composed of a blend of 'allusive lyric ... musical idiosyncrasy ... and critique of culture through reference to his own position within

---

3 See for instance Nat Hentoff's 'Folk, Folkum and the New Citybilly',*Playboy*, June, 1963, 95–98, 168–170. Later critics and biographers such as Andy Gill (see note 9) and Howard Sounes in *Down The Highway: The Life Of Bob Dylan* (New York, NY: Grove Press, 2001) concur.

4 Quoted in Nigel Williamson, *The Rough Guide to Bob Dylan*, 2nd ed. (London: Rough Guides Ltd., 2006), 219.

5 I refer to the practice of performing with a backing group which commenced with Dylan's notorious 'going electric' at the Newport Folk Festival that year, after which he rarely performed solo anymore. During his Woodstock residence throughout 1967 Dylan was part of a musical collective in the sense that he rehearsed and recorded with his current backing group, The Band, on a daily basis.

it')[6] have developed from an occasionally positive spin on cataclysmic change in the 1960s. Dylan has said of 'The Times They Are A-Changin':

> This was definitely a song with a purpose. It was influenced of course by the Irish and Scottish ballads... 'Come All Ye Bold Highway Men', 'Come All Ye Tender Hearted Maidens'. I wanted to write a big song, with short concise verses that piled up on each other in a hypnotic way. The civil rights movement and the folk music movement were pretty close for a while and allied together at that time.[7]

In this instance, we see a young songwriter lending his voice to an attempt at mobilizing his generation for change, snatching the future back from the brink of disaster.

Earlier records had already featured more staccato-like, fear-filled cautionary tales such as 'A Hard Rain's A-Gonna Fall' – about which Dylan has said: 'Every line in it is actually the start of a whole new song. But when I wrote it, I thought I wouldn't have enough time alive to write all those songs so I put all I could into this one'.[8] This instance shows the songwriter emulating the Biblical Revelations, reporting from beyond the brink of final destruction.

As a much later counterpoint to these two youthful lyrics the chapter ends with a look at a song that presents a world-weary and cynical outlook, imagined to be observed and spoken in 'the last day's last hour of the last happy year'[9] ("Cross the Green Mountain', 2003, originally commissioned for the soundtrack of *Gods and Generals*, a Civil War epic, financed by Ted Turner).

'The Times They Are A-Changin' starts with an image of the impending flood, and calls for the scattered people to awake and realize the predic-

---

6 Thomas O. Beebee, 'Ballad of the Apocalypse: Another Look at Dylan's "Hard Rain" ', *Text and Performance Quarterly* 11 (1991): 18–34, quotation at 18.

7 Quoted from Cameron Crowe's liner notes to the album *Biograph*, 1985.

8 Quoted from the liner notes to *The Freewheelin' Bob Dylan*, 1963.

9 Released on *The Bootleg Series Vol. 8 – Tell Tale Signs: Rare and Unreleased 1989–2006*.

ament they are in: 'Admit that the waters / Around you have grown'. The exhortation of these lines indicates that people are in denial of the reality of the impending apocalypse that will sweep away the world they 'roam', and this is a call of assembly as well as an alarum sounding to waken those who are, metaphorically speaking, going about their business like sleepwalkers. The next three stanzas are particularized calls to three groups who especially need to wake up to realities: first the writers, next the legislators, and finally the parent generation, or the elders of society. Each of these three groups is issued a specific warning, pointing to a well-known weakness of the players of these roles or functions: The writers should not speak too soon, the legislators should not stall the initiatives of the new electorate, and the parents should not patronize their young offspring and preach the old ways as the best. The final stanza turns the warning more towards a threat: 'The line it is drawn / The curse it is cast' – and if one is not careful with the new generation and its program, the old will, sooner rather than later, be left behind in the dustbin of history.

In this song the apocalypse is thus two-fold. There is the one created by the indifference of the system that is currently in place, an indifference that will lead to a swift death by drowning for all, both the keepers of the system and those unaware sleepwalkers who have let themselves be dulled by the system's constant reassurances that all is well. Then there is the much more active, reversed apocalypse that will sweep through the system and 'shake your windows / And rattle your walls' – which is the youth-created counter-flood that the 'battle outside' causes to come and cleanse the old institutions. The apocalypse in this troubadour-like lyric can therefore in some ways be harnessed for good, and ultimately perhaps can even be ameliorated in consequence if only the 'old road' sees the errors of its ways and begins to 'lend a hand' to the new one.

As with all Dylan's apocalyptic lyrics, 'The Times' draws heavily on Biblical language. Writers and critics are hailed as prophets, and the reference to the first flood is unmistakable (just as the listener will instantly hear echoes of God's reassurance that it will be the fire next time). As Andy Gill has pointed out in his Dylan biography *My Back Pages*, the lyrics echo lines from the book of Ecclesiastes which Pete

Seeger adapted to create his anthem 'Turn, Turn, Turn', and the climactic line about the first later being last is a direct scriptural reference to Mark 10:31: 'But many that are first shall be last, and the last first'.[10] 'First' here of course refers less to speed than to status and grandeur, and this meaning would have had obvious resonance with the counterculture's disenfranchised membership.

In 'A Hard Rain' from 1962, Dylan had already introduced a symbolic language that he would later revisit in 'All Along the Watchtower' and 'Desolation Row', which are all set in worlds and spaces beyond the immediate ken of the average American citizen. However, 'A Hard Rain' has a distinct medieval tone to it, which is perhaps not surprising given its obvious intertextual relation to the traditional Anglo-Scottish border ballad 'Lord Randall'[11] from which Dylan borrows the call-response structure that he twists into something that more resembles a set of impotent, almost rhetorical questions asked by the old prophet/king of his youthful messenger whose answers the old man is unable to interpret in any way, means or form. Instead it is the young generation's representative, the returned pilgrim (or prodigal son) who leaves the old man again, having reported in full on the sad state of affairs abroad in the land. He pledges to return to the badlands, not as an observer, but rather as a spokesperson and advocate for change ('And I'll tell it and think it and speak it and breathe it / And reflect it from the mountain so all souls can see it'), having carefully thought and absorbed the horror before formulating well in song his findings. Again there is some hope in this early song that the apocalypse may thus be averted, although the 'blue-eyed son' is not so blue-eyed and naïve that he does not know that he may well 'start sinkin'' in the process of his battle for enlightenment.

In this ballad we of course again observe the Biblical intertextualitics, and nowhere more clearly than in the just quoted position of the young man's: 'I'll stand on the ocean' – as a latter-day Jesus, but also in yet another reference to the flood. Whereas Lord Randall in the

---

10 Andy Gill, *Classic Bob Dylan: My Back Pages* (London: Carlton, 1999), 42–43.

11 See *The English and Scottish Popular Ballads*. Edited by Francis James Child. 5 vols. Mineola, NY: Dover Publications, 2003. Child calls his version of the ballad 'Lord Rendal'. It is number 12 in his collection.

original ballad ends up poisoned by his 'true-love's' pan of fried eels, the young man of Dylan's ballad is a savior attempting to rescue those who themselves have fallen victims of starvation and the poison of pollution: 'Where the people are many and their hands are all empty / Where the pellets of poison are flooding their waters'.

Forty years later, in ''Cross the Green Mountain' an aging Dylan projects his imagination into the mind of a Civil War soldier who is so traumatized by the war that he knows not whether he is dreaming a 'monstrous dream', seeing visions of the future or just being lost in memories 'sad yet sweet'. Something terrible is – again – abroad in the land, but it is unclear whether it has risen from the bottom of the sea in the form of a monster, or has crossed the mountain in pursuit of our narrator, or is simply the return of an Old Testament 'avenging God'. This entity, who may well simply be God come to settle old scores with humanity, is thus for the first time named outright, given, as it were, its Christian name. This late ballad also contains the first images of the apotheosis that is otherwise reserved for Judgment Day: 'I'm lifted away / In an ancient light / That is not of day'. This light is quite possibly the same light that the narrator has seen 'coming forward' signaling the progress of God as 'all must yield' – all perhaps except him who seems to be the one righteous Abraham left in all of this American version of Sodom and Gomorrah.

The landscape of the ballad is American (the chilling reference to the evergreen 'Stars Fell on Alabama' is a give-away, despite the changed connotation of 'stars' in this nightmare vision), and yet one can only describe it as post-apocalyptic, of the future as well as a realistic description of the US of 1865. The surviving humans are raging, altars are burning, there is 'blasphemy on every tongue', and the leader has been 'killed outright ... by his own men'. Calling this particular leader 'our Captain' is an obvious reference to Whitman's salute to the assassinated President Lincoln, 'O Captain! my Captain!' – constituting one of the few specific, albeit implicit, anchorings in the Civil War epoch for the lyrics. The lyrics refer to the 'land of the rich and the free' – a parody of 'the land of the free and the home of the brave' of 'The Star-Spangled Banner' where the word 'brave' has been dislodged and shipped to the last line of the third stanza: 'More brave blood to spill'. The complacency of this land has forever been disrupted, and this time not by the poor and the un-free, although the Civil War had been said to be about liberating just those groups, just as the 1960s revolution-that-never-was claimed that it aimed to do.

There truly seems no escape from this late version of the Dylan-esque apocalypse. Although the calamity has been brought about by virtually the same forces as in the youthful apocalyptic ballads - greed, hatred against one's fellow man, pride, complacency and sloth - this time there is no conquering hero, surviving prophet or bearer of witness, allowed exemption from the harvest of the horseman.

Only the righteous and resigned soldier who 'was loyal / to truth and to right' will be taken up into 'a far better land', where 'virtue lives / and cannot be forgot'. Perhaps this is a self-portrait of Dylan no longer as a young man, but as a weather-beaten, orphaned and brother-less Abraham, ready to go home. Images of such figures can certainly be found in other Dylan lyrics such as 'Knocking on Heaven's Door', and 'Trying to Get to Heaven'. If this is the case, Dylan has traveled a long way, textually speaking, from using the trope of the apocalypse to warn a whole generation of its calling and the perils of not following them, and from cursing a whole (older) generation for complacency and overweening pride – to simply using the palimpsest of the American Civil War and the story of Abraham and Lot to paint a self-portrait of his ageing sensibilities. In such an analysis one could perhaps remark in closing that Dylan has then reversed the '60s slogan that the personal is political into its opposite: the political – and the apocalyptic – is personal.

A brief summation of the above article would suggest that Dylan never leaves the tropes of the apocalypse behind in his body of work, but that the valorization of the apocalypse which in the beginning was seen as a potential cleansing of a morally corrupt world has changed toward a much more pessimistic attitude of world-weariness and resignation. This shift mirrors Dylan's growing disillusionment with his generation and those following it, and coincides with his desire to abdicate as a spokesperson for political change.

'IT WAS A TIME FOR SAYING GOODBYE': HUMPHREY JENNINGS'S *THE SILENT VILLAGE* AND *A DIARY FOR TIMOTHY*

Jørgen Riber Christensen

The British director of documentary films, Humphrey Jennings, is mainly known for his relatively few propaganda films made for the Ministry of Information during the Second World War. Working within this official system with its restrains, but certainly also opportunities, Jennings became an auteur, and he has had almost uninterrupted fame as one of the leading directors in British film history. Jennings's film style, it will be argued in this article, is characterized by a method of continuity presented through narratological rupture and startling juxtapositions. These narrative ruptures are of a positive nature as they are used paradoxically to create a sense of connection between the specific subjects of his films and time, history and tradition, and this will be a leitmotif in the article. This stylistic analysis is, however, only a tool in the overall aim of the article, which is to examine any dystopian – or terminal – and utopian aspects of Jennings's production. Here the focus will be on two films: *The Silent Village* (1943), a counterfactual history and apocalyptical dystopia, and *A Diary for Timothy* (1945) with its possibility of the utopia of the post-war period with hints at the creation of a welfare state. The final, rather complex subject which the article will consider is Humphrey Jennings's ideology.

The research question of the article has its origin in the observation of a surprisingly large amount of references to and use of British cultural heritage in Jennings's films. The research question which the article tackles is what Jennings's ideology was like and if and how this ideology determined the style and aesthetics of his documentary films? To answer this question the article travels three different paths. These three are a detection of dystopian and utopian themes, stylistic analyses of the films, and examination of the ideological context of Jennings and his film production. This latter path goes back in cultural history to Edmund Burke's continuity thinking and it also goes through Pierre Bourdieu's concept of the cultural field, which will be used to explain how Jennings's supposedly left-wing views could be connected to the conservative ideology of Burke. In the conclusion of the article hopefully these three paths converge or connect in an answer that will offer an understanding of the wartime appeal of Jennings's film production.

UTOPIA, DYSTOPIA AND THE POST-APOCALYPTIC WORLD: *TERMINUS*

The Silent Village is about the end of the world, and *A Diary for Timothy* about its rebirth as a better place. The latter of the two films illustrates the dramaturgic challenges of the utopian genre. Basically, the ideal world of a utopia is without conflicts, whereas a narrative cannot be constructed without any. E. M. Forster's short story 'The Machine Stops' (1909) and James Cameron's more recent film *Avatar* (2009) demonstrate this narratological dilemma and typical solutions to it. The initial harmony of the seemingly perfect, technological world of the main character of Forster's short story is broken by his ennui, and similarly the harmony of the perfect, ecological world of *Avatar* is broken by an invasion from a technological world.

The utopia and the dystopia are not far apart. The dystopia can be regarded as a utopia in the form of a warning, and very often a utopia has its origin and theme in the depiction of a future or remote society from which contemporary conflicts have been removed. The warning or dystopian form of a utopia can here be regarded as science fiction with the aim of preventing the future from taking place. Though the utopia genre is often embedded in science fiction it is nevertheless not totally fictional. It is primarily a pre-scientific and artistic project or plan for a future societal formation, and as such it may be translated into a scientific theory, and subsequently into social practice.[12] There is a cycle in which a society runs through a number of steps until it reaches the apocalypse and slips into barbarism, and after a post-apocalyptic period it re-emerges in a purified societal formation. The pre-apocalyptical conflicts and disasters, the apocalypse itself and the barbarism in the post-apocalyptical world are of a dystopian nature, whereas the reborn and purified society is utopian. In European utopias, the new society is often reminiscent of the early-bourgeois historical period in the Age of Enlightenment and its ideals, and in America it is based on early, populist frontier ideals. Because of this cyclical interconnection between dystopias and utopias they are regarded as one genre in this article. The Latin meaning of '*Terminus*', boundary stone, is apt here, as the apocalypse may well signify the end of the road, but there is something new at the far side of the boundary, which is not only the barbarism of a post-apocalyptical existence, but also a utopian rebirth of the world.

THE SILENT VILLAGE

The subject of Jennings's *The First Days* from 1939 is about London preparing for Britain's entry into the Second World War before it had really begun. The film's aim is the mobilization of Britain's home front. In the film millions of sandbags are being filled, and the commentary states that '[t]he thousand classes of London came to work for the common good'. This is the basic theme in Jennings's wartime film production: national unity and consensus between the social classes in the face of the common foe; but the sense of loss is also apparent at the surface of the film. Pets are being killed, the National Gallery is emptied of works of art, and three quarters of a million children are being evacuated. 'It was a time for saying good-bye', as the commentary puts it. In 1943 the full, apocalyptic tragedy of the war is the subject of Jennings's *The Silent Village*. In the following this film will be presented, and the focus of the presentation will be on the narrative style with metonymical representations of the enemy, incremental sound and Jennings's use of the medium close-up camera distance. The aim of focussing on the nar-

---

12 Georg Seesslen, *Kino des Utopischen: Geschichte und Mythologie des Science-Fiction-Films* (Reinbek bei Hamburg: Rowohlt rororo, 1980), 59–60.

ratological and cinematographic elements is to examine the ideological implications that Jennings's use of them may have.

This 36-minutes long film is a recreation in a Welsh coal-mining village, Cwmgiedd, of the Lidice massacre, which took place in Czechoslovakia in 1942. As retaliation for the assassination of Reich Protector Reinhard Heydrich in Prague all men in this mining village were shot by soldiers from the SS and the German army. The women and the children of the village were sent to concentration camps, and after the war only 153 women and less than 20 children returned. In all, around 340 people were murdered. The village itself was burnt and totally destroyed. Nazi propaganda actually publicized the fate of Lidice as a déterrent, and Allied propaganda did likewise to show the nature of Nazi occupation.[13] Jennings went location-hunting in Wales, and he found Cwmgiedd, which was suited for his conception of history, as not only mining but also farming were widespread in the area, just as the Welsh language was spoken there. Jennings described the area's double tradition in a BBC broadcast in May 1943:

> In this picture you see not only the reconstruction of the Lidice story, but also the clash of two types of culture: the ancient, Welsh, liberty-loving culture which has been going on in these valleys way, way back into the days of King Arthur and beyond, still alive in the Welsh language and in the traditions of the valleys; and this new-fangled loudspeaker blaring culture invented by Dr. Goebbels and his satellites. And it is through the clash of these cultures that the mechanism of the film so to speak is presented and not simply as a blood-and-thunder story of some people marching into a village.[14]

The title sequence of the *Silent Village* is ominous. It says, 'The story of the men of Lidice who lit in Fascist darkness a lamp that shall never be put out'. As a contrast the first eight or nine minutes of the film present life in the village as idyllic, and an intertitle says, 'Such is life at Cw-

---

13 Jan Kaplan and K. Nosarzewska, *Praha: The Turbulent Century* (Köln: Könemann, 1997), 239.

14 Kevin Jackson, *Humphrey Jennings* (London: Picador, 2004), 271.

mgiedd in the Western valleys of Wales – and such too was life in Lidice until the coming of Fascism'.

The middle part of the film begins with the arrival of a black car with the sign of the swastika and a ridiculously oversized loudspeaker on its roof shouting 'Achtung! Achtung!' A harsh voice with a German accent tells the people of the village that they have come under the protection of the Greater German Reich. Only the loudspeaker and the car are seen, never the people inside it. In his films Jennings was always careful not to make the enemy explicit. For instance the passive voice of the title itself of the film about the Blitz *Fires Were Started* is indicative of this tendency, and the Germans are hardly mentioned in this film. In *The Silent Village* there is merely a metonymical representation of the barbaric invaders. Only sound is e.g. the loudspeaker voice, radio announcers, military music, and gunfire. No humans are shown, and the visual sources of the sound are the loudspeaker and the radio sets. It is noticeable how the enemy is represented by non-human machinery.

Resistance begins with the miners using the traditional weapon of the class struggle: strikes. The car with its loudspeaker returns, yet Welsh history and tradition are not to be vanquished yet. The Welsh harp is used as underscoring for an establishing shot of a resistance meeting in a castle ruin in the mountains, and the resistance movement gathers force. Jennings uses sound incrementally in *The Silent Village*. First of all the film's title itself initiates the stress on sound, in particular when the title of this film is compared to the title of Jennings's *Listen to Britain* made the year before. In *Listen to Britain* it is precisely sounds of many diverse aspects of life in Britain that are used, not only as a structural device of the film but also as what ties a society as such together. When a village becomes silent this social fabric is destroyed.

The assassination of Heydrich now leads to harder repression, and the radio threatens the people repeatedly to hand over the assassins. Also, everyone must be registered by the authorities. Jennings uses this measure to give an individual portrait of the villagers in a low, medium close up as they are standing in line. We see them and we hear their names, ages, and occupation before they move out of the picture. This use of the medium shot depicting individual characters is typical of Jennings. He does not use the close-up here, as this camera distance would exclude the context of the character. People in Jennings's films are almost always shown – as individuals – in a social context.

In the homes people are stoically waiting for their deaths, as nobody is prepared to give in to the demands of the Germans. The next morning, marching feet cannot quite drown out the voices of the men who are defiantly singing as they are lined up in front of the church to be shot. The children are sent off in vans to a concentration camp; their crying mothers are also marched off. There is a cut-away from the men to the graveyard as the firing squad is heard. The incremental sound has reached its fatal climax. As the camera pans across the burning ruins of the village, a German radio is heard with an announcer and Wagner music. The announcement is translated and printed in Gothic lettering with the burning village as background:

> [A]ll the male adults of the village have been shot, the women have been sent to a concentration camp, the children have been handed over to the appropriate authorities. The buildings of the locality have been levelled to the ground and the name of the community has been obliterated.[15]

However, the film's postlude claims that this is not the end of the story as it says in an intertitle. A shot of the Welsh landscape now leads the audience into another village where a miner speaks up against the German proclamation: 'No comrades. The Nazis are wrong. The name of the community has not been obliterated. The name of the community has been immortalised', and he continues that miners the world over will not become slave labour, they will fight against the Nazis so that the people of Lidice have not died in vain. It is at this point in its postlude that the film leaves the genre of counterfactual history, as it is clearly stated that it was about Lidice and not Cwmgiedd. The miner's voice is illustrated by shots of a working mine pit with its machinery,

---

15 Humphrey Jennings, *The Silent Village* (The Crown Film Unit, 1943).

which can be regarded as the Welsh miners' necessary contribution to the British total war effort.

The liquidation of Cwmgiedd and its men, children and women is the apocalypse as the consequence of the dystopia of a Nazi society. *The Silent Village* is about dystopian barbarism at its worst because although the film is counterfactual historiography of the what-if type, it is only so to a certain extent. When Jennings's film answers the question of what would happen if Britain was defeated in the war, the answer given is based on the cruel fact that the Lidice massacre did actually happen, and so the counterfactual nature of the film is tempered by real events and by horrible facts. Therefore Jennings's use of the apocalyptical dystopia can be the stronger in its effect. The film supports the total war effort. The working classes, particularly miners, and more particularly Welsh miners, are mobilised to take their part in this effort.

Jennings's ideological openness is crucial. The miners in Cwmgiedd use their traditional weapons of the class struggle against the fascist enemy. Their initial response to the repression is to lay down tools, and the class war becomes a weapon against the barbaric Nazis. Class war can in other words be encompassed by the consensus model of the British war effort. In *The Silent Village* it becomes apparent that Jennings's propaganda film production and his ideology cannot be separated. The inclusive nature of Jennings's ideology as it manifests itself in the film is stressed by the fact that also the national or regional conflict between England and Wales is represented in it. The Nazis' suppression of the Welsh language in the film is reminiscent of the way Welsh, national culture and its language are threatened by England or Great Britain, and it is significant that one of the lessons in the village school is about the conquest of Wales – by the English.

The dystopia-utopia genre's cyclical form, with the apocalypse and barbarism being followed by the rebirth of a purified and utopian society, is in itself not developed in *The Silent Village*; but it is in Jennings's total film production, in which *A Diary for Timothy* about the last months of the war and post-war life can be understood as his utopian vision of a new and reborn Britain.

THE NEW WORLD: A DIARY FOR TIMOTHY

The theme of change, modernity, tradition and continuity being interconnected is seen in *A Diary for Timothy* (1945), which is a film about the last year of the war. Happily, the change in this film, on which Jennings began working in the autumn of 1944, is the war approaching its end with victory, and as such one might assume that this film is a purely utopian picture of post-war life in Britain with its rebirth after the near-apocalypse of the war. Yet Jennings uses this film to ask the not uncritical and troubled question of what it was, then, we were fighting for? As we shall see, the answer is ambivalent, but in itself the overall narrative technique of this film offers an implicit answer of a utopian nature. In the following presentation of the film the narrative technique, such as Jennings's special use of montage and the film's soundtrack, will be considered in connection with the ideology inherent in it.

The birth of Timothy Jenkins exactly five years after the war broke out symbolically represents the utopian rebirth of a society. Obviously Timothy Jenkins himself is the future. The commentator addresses him directly, and in this way the film's audience is addressed indirectly. This rhetorical narrative device creates identification between the audience and new-born Timothy, who is also the audience's future after the war. Regarded in this way, Timothy becomes almost a sort of Hitchcockian MacGuffin, i.e. a catalyst to initiate the action of a film,[16] as he is not the main character that develops through the story. The main characters are Alan, a farmer, Goronwy, a Welsh miner, who gets wounded in an industrial accident down the pit, Bill, a train driver, and Peter, a wounded, but recovering pilot. These characters must change, as society and their world are changing. The overall narrative structure of the film is the cross-cutting between these four representatives of the British people and its social classes, and it is when new-born Timothy is added to this cross-cutting that the film constructs its premise about consensus and continuity.

Immediately after the film's prelude with a radio news announcer, the presentation phase establishes the coherence and unity of representatives of the British population. It consists of a montage sequence

---

16 François Truffaut, *Hitchcock* (New York, NY: Simon & Schuster, 1983), 138–139.

with these diverse elements: Timothy, his mother, marching soldiers, three boys walking through ruins, a coal-pit, the countryside, a passing bomber, a train driver, and a hospital ward with wounded patients. However, the commentator ties everything in the presentation phase together when he addresses the new-born baby directly: 'All these people, Tim, were fighting for you, though they didn't exactly know it'.

Michael Redgrave's voice-over is not the only commentary, as Alan, the farmer, now in his own words explains how land was cleared at the start of the war. The soundtrack is changed to a clearly diegetic siren and the drone of a V1 bomb, and this sound's diegetic nature is stressed by a reaction shot of a dog that raises its head and listens. Non-diegetic underscoring music follows, but there is a lack of consistency. Is Redgrave's commentary diegetic or not? His immediate listener is Timothy, who as a baby cannot understand him, so in actual fact it is the film's audience that he addresses, and as such the commentary is a non-diegetic voice-over. The audience is consequently spoken to as a child, and it may feel patronized, especially so as Michael Redgrave's voice-over voice is decidedly posh or upper-class. This inconsistency of the communication model of the film may be an indication also of an ideological inconsistency, or perhaps rather of an ideological openness, which will be discussed later on in this article, but here already it may be pointed out that the content of the commentary, which was written by E. M. Forster, is hard to pinpoint ideologically in its openness. Early in the film, the voice-over explains that Timothy was lucky as he was born in a nursing home near Oxford, 'very comfortable' and not 'in wartime Holland and Poland, or a Liverpool and Glasgow slum'. E. M. Forster's commentary here aligns the misfortunes of war with the misfortunes of class and poverty, and the conflict of the war between nations is continued in a subdued voice by Jennings as a conflict between classes.

The relationship between the film language or aesthetics and the ideology of the film is also in this film, as in *The Silent Village*, found in Jennings's use of camera distances. Characters are nearly always shown in medium-range close-ups, which allows for a clear identification of the character and of his surroundings as well. Jennings's consistent use of this camera distance is an indication of an ideological stance. The filmmaker points out that a society consists of individuals, but these individuals always live and exist in a context of a social nature. This aesthetic reflection of the social interdependence of individuals is not only apparent in Jennings's use of camera distances. His montage style has the same significance. People and their functions in society are connected in sequences, especially as Jennings uses sound to bind everything together, as when sounds overlap and also anticipate the next image. Jennings's aesthetic expression of the connectedness of Britain through montage is not similar to Eisenstein's dialectical montage, which rather acts intellectually on the audience, almost as *Verfremdung*, and at times in an aggressive manner as in *Strike* (1925) so that the emotions produced in the audience could be fear and disgust. Eisenstein's use of his montage of attractions at least created distancing as an effect with its juxtaposition of images. In a sense he depicted political principles, and the hero of his film were the masses. The main difference between Eisenstein's and Jennings's montages is that Jennings's creates continuity, whereas Eisenstein's creates conflicts through juxtapositions. Jennings's montage technique is more similar to the one used by Pudovkin, though not identical to it. For instance, in *The End of St. Petersburg* (1927) Pudovkin emphasizes the individual and the effects that political principles has in the lives of individuals. In 1928 the French film critic Léon Moussinac compared Pudovkin to Eisenstein as he wrote: 'A film by Eisenstein resembles a shout; a film by Pudovkin evokes a song',[17] and Jim Hillier connects Jennings's use of montage to a poetic statement that has an emotional and not intellectual effect.[18] It is striking that a great number of the people, who have written about Jennings's films, also today, claim that they have been emotionally affected by them, sometimes even brought to tears.

The hope of the future represented by Timothy being baptised seems to continue in the film as the wounded pilot is recovering. How-

---

17 Cited in Richard Taylor, *The Politics of the Soviet Cinema, 1917-1929* (Cambridge: Cambridge UP, 1979), 142.

18 Alan Lovell and J. Hillier, *Studies in Documentary* (London: Secker and Warburg and the BFI, 1972), 87.

ever, the accidents of war are connected to those of peace, as now the mine worker meets with an accident that breaks his arm. In this way Jennings delivers societal critique when he compares war with the working conditions of the miners, when the commentator says: 'It is pretty shocking that this sort of thing should still happen every day, though we have been cutting coal for five hundred years', and he adds, 'Something else for you to think over', and the tone of the film is set for a deliberation of how utopian the post-war world is actually going to be? A heavy note is relieved through a sequence with culture. This is John Gielgud's Hamlet and the gravedigger's scene, but Jennings's choice of this scene is explained as it is cross-cut with a V2 bomb and its devastation. Not only upper-class culture is represented in the film, there are also singing and accordion music in the canteen, life in a pub, and dance bands and beer drinking.

After Christmas 1944 and New Year's celebrations with focus on families with absent friends and kin, the development of the war dominates the sound track of *A Diary for Timothy*. It is not only the voice-over, but also radio news reports about successful Russian offensives that stress that the war has changed decisively for the better. As before in the film, this note of victory is dampened by the challenges of what is to happen after the war is ended. The commentary even claims that life is becoming more dangerous, 'because now we have the power to choose, and the right to criticize and even to grumble. We are free men'. The Welsh miner, Goronwy, expresses doubts about the future when he says: 'One afternoon I was sitting thinking about the past. The last war, the unemployed, broken homes, scattered families. And then I thought, has all this really got to happen again?' The commentator repeats these questions to Timothy lying in his cot with dissolves to victory celebrations and bonfires: 'Will it be like that again? Are you going to have greed for money or power ousting decency from the world as they have in the past? Or are you going to make the world a different place – you and all the other babies?' The very narrative form of *A Diary for Timothy* with its cross-cutting is part of the answer to the question if post-war society will be approaching utopia. Young Timothy as a symbol of hope is another. Yet the question if the class consensus of the war years is a strong enough foundation for a rebirth of British society is never answered in the film, or if an answer is given it is immediately contradicted by the film itself. Is this ambivalence a result of Humphrey Jennings's ideology? In the following, Jennings's attitudes to class and British society will be discussed. The subjects addressed are his combination of left-wing politics and admiration for the working classes with an almost nationalist conservatism, and this combination will be viewed in the light of his immediate historical context and in the light of the social philosophy of Pierre Bourdieu, and Jennings's conservatism will be compared to the conservatism of Edmund Burke. Already here an answer to the question above can be hinted at: it was the immediate context of wartime with the total war effort that acted as a catalyst which fused Jennings's cultural conservatism with his left-wing politics.

IDEOLOGY – THE LONG VIEW

Two approaches offer themselves to explanations of why Humphrey Jennings's ideology as expressed in his films is so cumbersome to identify. One approach is from a long view of British political history, and the other is the short view of the immediate context of the war and post-war years. Many descriptions have been made of Jennings's political and ideological stance. Jennings's biographer Kevin Jackson stresses that he was and remained influenced by his parents' progressive views, which took the form of Guild Socialism. In the spirit of John Ruskin, William Morris and the Arts and Craft Movement this ideology looked back in history to medieval guilds as a system of the socialist idea of workers taking controls of the factories.[19] As we shall see, the concept of using elements of the past to form the future is a cornerstone of Jennings's political thinking. This idea is developed by Robins and Webster in their discussion of Jennings's Pandemonium-project about the Industrial Revolution, which they place in Raymond Williams's 'Culture and Society' tradition with its paradoxical combination of Enlightenment rationalism and Romanticism.[20]

---

19 Jackson, *Humphrey Jennings*, 28–29.

20 Kevin Robins and F. Webster, *Times of Technoculture* (London: Routledge, 1999/2001), 15.

In *The Myth of the Blitz* Angus Calder describes the intellectual history of the image presented of Britain in wartime propaganda. Calder mentions 'Jennings's troubled obsession with finding some interior essence of Britain'.[21] The result of Calder's examination is that in the inter-war period the picture of Britain is basically middle-class. In *Britain Can Take It* Aldgate and Richards see a connection between Jennings and George Orwell, who were both 'articulating a robust Socialist patriotism, a full-blooded love of England and the English centred on an unashamed admiration for the qualities of the common man',[22] and 'Both were middle class left-wing intellectuals who set off deliberately to find the real character of England'.[23] Aldgate and Richards conclude that Jennings's three basic principles were 'admiration of the common people, his instinctive belief in individualism, and his love of English culture',[24] and quite early in *Britain Can Take It* Aldgate and Richards write about 'left-wing tendency' and 'complaints of left-wing bias' in the Film Division of the Ministry of Information.[25] In *Fires Were Started* Brian Winston examines the ideological paradox he finds in Jennings,[26] in whose work he sees an affirmation of fundamental liberal values, a celebration of the working classes and a reaffirmation of 'all the traditional (oppressive) continuities of British, or rather English life', and he mentions Jennings's 'astonishing conservatism'[27] concluding that '[t]he presence of the past is crucial to all of Jennings's films'.[28]

In the following an attempt will be made to explain the paradoxical combination of Jennings's conservatism and his left-wing bias or kind of socialism. The key to an understanding will be the aesthetics of

---

21 Angus Calder, *The Myth of the Blitz* (London: Pimlico, 1991), 181.

22 Anthony Aldgate and J. Richards, *Britain Can Take It. British Cinema in the Second World War* (London: Tauris, 2007), 225.

23 Ibid., 226.

24 Ibid., 228.

25 Ibid., 8–9.

26 Brian Winston, *Fires Were Started* (London: BFI Publishing, 1999), 57.

27 Ibid., 53.

28 Ibid., 52.

his films, which will be analysed in the context of Edmund Burke's concept of continuity and in the context of Pierre Bourdieu's cultural field.

In 1938 Jennings expressed the importance which the past had to him in a radio talk 'The Poet and the Public':

> The idea of extracting an idea of 'what I am' from the past is a thing that the poet does for himself and especially it is a thing that he can do for the community. I mean he can try and tell them who they are. Now he can't tell them who they are unless he does two things: unless he talks about the things that the community knows about, the things that they're interested in, and unless he also looks on the community's past – at the figures, the monuments, the achievements, the defeats or whatever it may be, that have made the community what it is.[29]

Jennings's *Words for Battle* (1941) illustrates how he combined the past and the present, culture and politics. In this film both are represented by compilations. The present is there in contemporary images of Britain, and the visual part of the film is made up of only previously used footage. The past is there also as compilation, but here it is a collection of quotations from literary history read by Laurence Olivier: William Camden, John Milton, William Blake, Robert Browning, and Rudyard Kipling – set to Handel's music. Near the end of the film the quotations leave the literary field and move into the political, as quotes are given from Winston Churchill and Abraham Lincoln's Gettysburg Address.

Ideologically, this kind of sense of the past and the use Jennings continually made of it in his films are comparable to the conservative Edmund Burke, when he expressed his attitude to the importance of the past in his *Reflections on the Revolution in France* (1790). It is aspects of Burke's continuity thinking that are shared between the two, but as we shall see, certainly only aspects. For instance, nothing could be more different from Burke's demophobia than Jennings's deep-seated respect for the ordinary man. In his defence of the maintenance of the

---

29 Winston, *Fires Were Started*, 54

constitution and hereditary monarchy, Burke stresses the authority of the past and the need for historical continuity to preserve a functioning society and also to preserve the societal, organic and basically feudal coherence and unity of the state. Burke argues as a motto for English history that phenomena get politically valuable through having existed for a long time.[30]

In order to compare the use Burke and Jennings made of the past, Pierre Bourdieu's concept of the cultural field will here be introduced. With regard to Jennings's documentary films the particular usefulness of the concept is that in it Bourdieu connects power, politics and aesthetics. He discusses the function of art and artists in society, and to do this he inscribes the artist in a societal structure. As such the autonomous position of art is abandoned, though the crucial point is that artists are 'dominated among the dominant'.[31] The removal of this seeming paradox is explained when art and culture are regarded in a structural light. Pierre Bourdieu's model of society is basically hierarchical and organized in fields. Society as a whole is characterized as the field of class relations. At the top of this there is the dominant pole, at the bottom the dominated pole. Inside the field of class relations and at its very top, the field of power is situated. Again, inside the field of power there is the cultural field containing art and artists; but significantly this cultural field is positioned at the bottom of the field of power. Therefore art and artistic producers may be called 'dominated among the dominant'. This is explained by the fact that they are dominated inside the field of power as they have a low position here, but as the field of power in itself including the cultural field is at the top of the hierarchical societal structure, the cultural field is near the top of the field of class relations or society as a whole. The cultural field is in other words a site of a double hierarchy, and if, hypothetically, the field of power vanished, the cultural field would remain powerful alone at the dominant pole of society. This double hierarchy is the explanation, Bourdieu writes, of the ambivalent ideological stance of artists:

---

30 Edmund Burke, *Reflections on the Revolution in France* (Harmondsworth: Penguin, 1790/1973), 152–153.

31 Pierre Bourdieu, *The Field of Cultural Production* (Cambridge: Polity Press, 1993/2000), 164.

> The structural ambiguity of their position in the field of power leads writers and painters, these 'penniless bourgeois' in Pissarro's words, to maintain an ambivalent relationship with the dominant class within the field of power, those whom they call 'bourgeois', as well as with the dominated, the 'people'.[32]

A combination of Pierre Bourdieu's structural model of the position of the cultural field in society with Edmund Burke's concept of continuity in the power relations of the state can become useful in explaining the contradictory or – to put it more positively – open ideological attitude found in Jennings's documentary propaganda films. The quotation above about the structural ambiguity of the position of the cultural field is just one initial step of this explanation, the more so when one adds the point that cultural producers are actually able to use their position of power, 'especially', as Bourdieu writes, 'in periods of crisis, by their capacity to put forward a critical definition of the social world, to mobilize the potential strength of the dominated classes and to subvert the order prevailing in the field of power'.[33] This idea could be applied to *A Diary for Timothy* with its both implicit and outspoken argumentation for the utopian creation of a welfare state. The next step towards a combination of Bourdieu and Burke in order to explain the primarily conservative tendencies found in Jennings's films would be to identify these tendencies, and here Jennings's reflections of the continuity thinking is exclusively limited to the cultural field, and not to the field of power or to the field of class relations. In many of his films, e.g. *Making Fashion* (1938), *The First Days* (1939), *London Can Take It!* (1940), *Words for Battle* (1941), *Listen to Britain* (1942), *Fires Were Started* (1943), *A Diary for Timothy* (1943), and *Family Portrait* (1951), Jennings repeatedly includes culture and cultural history as arguments for class consensus and for a unified British identity. This stress on his part of the continuity of British culture and society is conservative and Burkian, but here it is as

---

32 Ibid., 164.
33 Ibid., 44.

if the hypothetical removal and annihilation of the field of power had actually taken place. It is the cultural field that remains in Jennings's films at the top of the social hierarchy. So it is the claim and argument of this article that Jennings adopted Edmund Burke's conservative ideology, but with one decisive difference. Burke's conservative continuity thinking, which applies to systems of governments and constitutions, notably the monarchy, is included in Jennings's world view. The crucial point is, however, that Jennings has transferred it from the domain of political power to the domain of the cultural field. As it has been gathered from *A Diary for Timothy*, Jennings is an advocate of social and political change, and this change is based on the class consensus necessitated by the societal effort of the total war. From reports of audiences' reception of Jennings's films it seems that his use of the cultural heritage in connection with the war situation had an emotional appeal. Roger Manvell, Films Officer for the South West and later the North West of England wrote about these qualities of the films:

> I do not exaggerate when I say that the members of audience under the emotional strains of war ... frequently wept as a result of Jennings' direct appeal to the rich cultural heritage going back ... to Shakespeare and the Elizabethans, to Purcell and to Handel. People found themselves being brought suddenly and movingly into touch with what was at stake if indeed the Nazi forces... invaded and took over the conduct of their lives.[34]

IDEOLOGY – THE SHORT VIEW

Humphrey Jennings's film *Welfare of the Workers* (1940) about the working condition and rights of workers during the war production and mobilisation is prophetic of immediate post-war politics with its depiction of factory inspectors from the Ministry of Labour's Welfare Board. Though the country went Labour at the election in 1945, there had also in Conservative circles been tendencies towards a more egalitarian so-

---

34 Aldgate and Richards, *Britain Can Take It*, 223.

cial model. The Beveridge Report's welfare proposals from 1942 were motivated by a sense of national unity and the mood of collectivism and social solidarity during the early war years, and also by the fact that social reform was used as motivation for the total war effort, in which the participation of the working classes in war production was vital and decisive for the outcome of the war. In this sense the war was not only against the Nazi enemy, but also for an improved post-war existence. In Jennings's *A Diary for Timothy* the miner's question, 'The last war, the unemployed, broken homes, scattered families ... has all this really got to happen again?', expresses the mood of this period about post-war reconstruction and social security. The Beveridge Report called for a national minimum income, universal family allowances, a national health service and a Ministry of social security.[35] Add to this that progressive income tax resulted in some redistribution of wealth. The blueprint of the welfare state was produced during the war, and the concept of the welfare state was opposed to the Nazi 'warfare state',[36] and 'Britain's Welfare State of the late 1940s stood out from those of all other industrialised countries'.[37]

The themes of consensus, egalitarianism, and unity in Jennings's films are part of this general mood, shared by film producers, which enabled the transfer of the collective solidarity beyond the war years to peacetime. In *Britain Can Take It* Aldgate and Richards quote David Niven's airman character in *A Matter of Life and Death* for saying: 'Politics ... Conservative by nature, Labour by experience',[38] as indicative of the film makers, and they elaborate on this point by a lengthier quote from Michael Balcon from the Ealing Studios: 'We were middle class people brought up with middle class backgrounds and rather conventional educations. Though we were radical in our points of view, we did not want to tear down institutions ... We were people of an imme-

---

35 John Stevenson, *British Society 1914-45* (Harmondsworth: Penguin, 1984), 452.

36 Arthur Marwick, *Britain in the Century of Total War* (Harmondsworth: Penguin, 1968/1979), 344.

37 Marwick, *Britain in the Century of Total War*, 363.

38 Aldgate and Richards, *Britain Can Take It*, 15.

diate post-war generation, and we voted Labour for the first time after the war; this was our mild revolution'.[39]

CONCLUSION: AESTHETICS AS IDEOLOGY

Through the focus on two of Humphrey Jennings's films, *The Silent Village* and *A Diary for Timothy*, this article has sought to demonstrate how the genres of utopias and dystopias can be found in his documentary propaganda films. This argument is based on reading the films in continuity so that *The Silent Village* represents dystopia, the apocalypse and *Terminus*, and *A Diary for Timothy* a vision of and hope for a possible utopia in the reborn, post-war world after the apocalypse of the war against Nazi barbarism. Jennings did not only use the dystopian barbarism of Nazism as it is depicted in *The Silent Village* as propaganda, he also showed the qualities of Welsh working-class culture in the film, and this positive sociological angle was stressed in *A Diary for Timothy*. In this film, the war is connected to the hopes of creating a utopian post-war British society based on class consensus.

The article initially asked a question about Jennings's ideology, and the answer had to be twofold and viewed in both a long and a short perspective. However, it appeared that the answer could also be looked for in the style or aesthetics of the films with their use of montage, anticipatory soundtracks, and use of the medium-range shot. Jennings's ideological ambivalence was found to be reflected in his narrative film style, featuring narratological rupture, which rather than hampering continuity, connects ideologically disparate elements of British wartime society, such as the questions of class and class conflict.

In the article European utopian novels and films were described as a reversion to the early-bourgeois ideals from the Enlightenment with its stress on democracy, the dignity of all human beings, and human rights. It is obvious that Jennings's propaganda films served democracy in its fight against inhuman Fascism during the Second World War. A close look at the films has shown that they consistently upheld these ideals. Even when it came to the depiction of the enemy, Jennings

---

39 Ibid.

always used understatement, and he was keen to maintain that German culture was not just Nazism, but so much more. We have seen that the enemy was depicted through metonymy, and when it comes to the depiction of the home front, Jennings's idea of the dignity of all human beings is apparent in his depiction of people of all classes performing indispensable functions in a society thrown into total warfare. Here Jennings's hallmark is his use of the medium-range shot that enabled him to present an individual in almost close-up, but always an individual not isolated but in a social context. Jennings and his film editor Stewart McAllister used montage and the soundtrack creatively to tie the films' elements together, and it is here in the montage that both rupture and coherence coexist to create the premise and message of consensus. This consensus is special in the way that that it includes and respects all classes and also class conflicts as seen, for instance, in *The Silent Village*, and Jennings's audience is given a picture of the working classes that was much more nuanced and comprehensive than was usual for the time. In the same sense, the cast of *A Diary for Timothy* with its almost sociological angle is a portrait of British society at the end of the war. Like other intellectuals of the time, for instance George Orwell, Jennings attempted to define the British national character, as his involvement in the Mass Observation Movement bears witness to. To Jennings the value of the continuity of the cultural tradition was the defining element of British identity. This article ties his celebration of historical continuity to Edmund Burke's conservative thinking, but unlike Burke Jennings liberated the concept of continuity from a solely political and institutional context in order to make it into an argument for class consensus. To do this, he had to transfer continuity from the field of power to the cultural field, as these were described by Pierre Bourdieu.

The question of ideology has received the answer during the article that first of all Jennings's ideology was open and inclusive, and that this openness was a necessary condition for his propaganda films and their effect and reception in the British wartime population at large. The approaches to an understanding of this open ideology were twofold. There was the immediate context of the total war that had to include all the social classes in the country, and there was the more theoretical approach of Bourdieu's cultural field, which could explain the strong and pervasive presence of culture and cultural history in practically all of Jennings's films. In this way Jennings's film style of narrative rupture and montage, which he used to create cohesion, is part and parcel of his ideology that consisted of a wide concept of social consensus. The answer to the article research question, 'What Jennings's ideology was like, and if and how this ideology determined the style and aesthetics of his documentary films', is that it was the wartime situation that was the necessary catalyst to unite the contradictions of both ideological and narratological nature stated above. The total war effort had to include all classes so that Britain was not conquered by Nazi barbarism, and this ideal and necessity of class consensus was what was needed to combine Jennings's cultural conservatism with his left-wing politics into the aesthetic expressions of his documentary films. Yet, the consensus ideal is not naively conceived without class conflicts as seen in *The Silent Village*. In *A Diary for Timothy* there is the worried concern whether the welfare state will come into being or not, and the film ends with Jennings' question to Timothy: 'Are you going to make the world a different place – you and all the other babies?'

THE END AND ENDS OF WALKING WITH SPECIAL REFERENCE TO WILL SELF'S PSYCHOGEOGRAPHY

Jens Kirk

'The March of Progress', Rudolf Zallinger's famous illustration of human evolution, figures the birth and history of our race in terms of fifteen nude, able bodied and male representatives of their species walking from left to right.[1] Disregarding the aspects of linearity,[2] ability and gender,[3] what is striking is the decidedly *pedestrian* take on human development favoured by Zallinger. While catching each creature in the act of respectably putting one leg in front of the other permitted Zallinger to solve the problem of representation posed by the private parts of our unclothed forebears, his insistence on ambulation is more than the solution to a problem of decorum. As the title suggests, the activity of walking is central to human evolution. Walking distinguishes us from knuckle-walking apes and, among other things, frees our hands for the use of tools and weapons. In fact, theorists of bipedalism agree in considering walking upright 'to be the Rubicon the evolving

---

1 Zallinger's illustration first appeared in 1965 in F. Clarke Howell's *Early Man* (New York, NY: Time, 1965). *Wikipedia*'s 'March of Progress' entry features the illustration and a discussion of its impact.

2 The linear aspect is critiqued in, for instance, Stephen Jay Gould, *Wonderful Life: The Burgess Shale and the Nature of History* (New York, NY: W.W. Norton and Company, 1990).

3 The gendered aspect of theories of walking and evolution is addressed in Rebecca Solnit, *Wanderlust: A History of Walking* (London & New York, NY: Verso, 2002), 30–44.

species crossed to become hominid, distinct from all other primates and ancestral to human beings'.[4]

Moreover, Zallinger's illustration suggests that walking not only is the cause of humanity as we know it, but remains interminably and intimately connected with Homo sapiens. Man is doomed to be forever walking since it forms the very definition of his manhood. According to the logic of the drawing, the termination of walking would equal the end of mankind. In popular culture, however, we find numerous intertextual references to Zallinger's illustration which distinguish themselves by representing the end of rambling man.[5] While many of the sketches and cartoons agree in imagining the termination of walking, they do so differently. One has man stepping into a void. In another the evolutionary progress of ambulatory man is cut short by a very large drink of Guinness.[6] And, most famously perhaps, a picture has man striding along from ape to a tool (and power tool) wielding incarnation before finally sitting down on an office chair in front of his personal computer.[7] This last example invites a figurative reading of 'sitting down' as a metonymy for other activities such as riding a car, bus, or train.

These intertextual references to and re-fashionings of Zallinger's drawing are fascinating because they seem to agree that the evolutionary point or meaning of taking to our feet in the first place is the termination or cessation of walking and its substitution by something else, for instance, sitting down. We are walking towards a place in evolution where walking has become outmoded. Walking, it appears, is on its last legs. Historians of walking agree with the popular exponents of termi-

---

4 Solnit, *Wanderlust*, 35.

5 Sean Kleefeld has collected a number of the popular takes on Zallinger's illustration on his blog. See Sean Kleefeld, 'The World's Most Famous Comic?', *Kleefeldoncomics.dk* (blog), January 18, 2008, http://kleefeldoncomics.blogspot.dk/2008/01/worlds-most-famous-comic.html

6 For a copy of the illustration, see http://flamingtales.blogspot.dk/2010/04/evolution-of-dungeons-dragons.html.

7 For a copy of the illustration, see http://www.corante.com/loom/archives/004732.html.

nal pedestrianism, but add the crucial notion that walking hasn't disappeared so much as shifted in importance. In his *On Foot: A History of Walking*, Joseph Amato, for instance, outlines how 'walking went from occupying the centre of human life to assuming a much-diminished place in it'.[8] Covering millions of years, he shows how pedestrianism 'passed from the realm of necessity to that of leisure and choice, from the common-place and ordinary to the occasional, eccentric, and symbolic'. Specifically, he argues that walking has lost its aspect of necessity for the large majority of people in the western world during the last couple of centuries. No longer *the* way to get around, it 'has become increasingly segmented, circumscribed, and limited. At the same time, it has become a matter of choice, involving questions of health and recreation, as well as an assertion of individual lifestyle and social philosophy'.[9]

In the history of human evolution, then, it is walking as a necessity that has come to an end for the majority of people in the western world. No longer is pedestrianism the great equaliser among human beings, instead, it is challenged by other and more effective forms of locomotion. Not only is it no longer the only form of human locomotion, it is now also the slowest and most tedious. When walking becomes a choice (and more often than not a choice not taken), it becomes in need of a reason and a motivation. It is precisely at the end of walking as a necessary activity that it becomes an activity in its own right and takes on symbolic potential. When walking becomes a matter of choice, the choice of walking must mean something. Ambulation must have a point, an end, and a purpose. From the key mark of biological difference between human and non-human, walking becomes a mark of social, cultural, and individual distinction.

In the following, before I turn to an examination of the staging of walking in Will Self's writings, I give a brief outline of the development of walking from necessity to choice and its accompanying dependence on writing for meaning.

---

8 Joseph Amato, *On Foot: A History of Walking* (New York, NY: NYU Press, 2004), 16.
9 Ibid., 2.

GOING FISHING: FROM NECESSITY TO CHOICE

To illustrate this development in walking from a basic human necessity to one of choice and distinction, consider the way two classic treaties on the subject of angling thematise pedestrianism. In Izaak Walton's *The Compleat Angler* (1653), three strangers, an angler, a hunter, and a falconer, meet as they are exiting London on foot on a fine spring morning. Catching up with the characters of Venator and Auceps, Piscator exclaims, 'I shall put on a boldness to ask you, sir, whether business or pleasure caused you to be so early up, and walk so fast'.[10] In the middle of the seventeenth century, for a writer of Izaak Walton's class and occupation[11] walking constituted the basic condition of travel for occupational and recreational purposes. No other option existed. Consequently, what strikes Piscator as odd is not the fact that Venator and Auceps *walk*, then, but that they walk *so fast*.[12] For Walton walking is not an activity in itself. It is a necessary means to another end, either business or pleasure. For Walton going fishing actually meant *going* fishing.

Two and a half centuries later, the desire to go fishing remains the same, but the situation has changed beyond recognition. In his *Fly Fishing* originally published 1898, Sir Edward Grey advices the devoted angler who finds himself incarcerated in London by work, that

> [t]he earliest trains leave Waterloo, the usual place of departure for the Itchen or Test, either at or just before six o'clock in the morning. To leave London it is possible once a week, even after late hours, to get up in time for these early trains,

---

10 Izaak Walton, *The Compleat Angler* (London: Wordsworth Classics, 1996), 78.

11 Stephen Greenblatt situates Izaak Walton within a prosperous segment of the merchant middle classes. That a man of not inconsiderable independent means walks the dozen or so miles to his favourite river suggests how basic a condition walking was, but for the very few. See Stephen Greenblatt et al., eds., *The Norton Anthology of English Literature*, 9th ed., vol. B, *The Sixteenth and the Early Seventeenth Century* (New York, NY & London: W. W. Norton, 2012), 1425.

12 In other words, walking is a gesture here signalling urgency. So walking is not completely emptied of meaning as a basic condition.

and if you have no luggage (and you need have none if you go to the same place week after week), you will not find it difficult to get to the station.[13]

The juxtaposition of these two historically distinct discourses on going fishing shows how dramatically walking and the perception of walking changed between the 17th and 19th centuries. In *The Compleat Angler*, walking is an unmarked activity in itself, but walkers distinguish themselves by their relative speed. *Fly Fishing* shows that walking as the A-to-B device of necessity is completely superseded by public transport. Walking, however, is also foregrounded by Sir Edward Grey. But walking is not noteworthy because of its gestural aspects, but because it produces existential side effects. The angler wandering 'alone after sea trout down glens and moors' is revitalized in an extraordinary sense:

> Often after walking a mile or two on the way to the river, at a brisk pace, there comes upon one a feeling of "fitness," of being made of nothing but health and strength so perfect, that life need have no other end but to enjoy them. It is as though till that moment one had breathed with only a part of one's lungs, and as though now for the first time the whole lungs were filling with air. The pure act of breathing at such times seems glorious.[14]

Not only is the angler restored to his own magnificent body, he is also reinstated into a larger whole, into creation or nature.

> People talk of being a child of nature, and moments such as these are the times when it is possible to feel so; to know the full joy of animal life – to desire nothing beyond. There are times when I have stood still for joy of it all, on my way through the wild freedom of a Highland moor, and felt the

---

13 Sir Edward Grey, *Fly Fishing* (Forgotten Books: Classic Reprint Series, nd), 49–50.
14 Grey, *Fly Fishing*, 180.

wind, and looked upon the mountains and water and sky, till I felt conscious only of the strength of a mighty current of life, which swept away all consciousness of self, and made me a part of all I beheld.[15]

Very likely, Sir Edward Grey's celebration of the power of walking to restore the individual to his body and to an innocent sense of nature as all-encompassing would have left Walton gobsmacked. For Walton walking was as basic to human beings as breathing.

WALKING AND WRITING

Historically, somewhere between Walton and Grey writing began systematically to stage walking as meaningful activity in its own right. Walking and discourse are linked etymologically in the Latin *discurrĕre* signifying to run to and fro according to *Oxford English Dictionary* (*OED*). With romanticism, the link between writing and walking becomes explicit.[16] And walking is figured prominently in contemporary British Letters, too. Most notably, walking is foregrounded in the context of psychogeography.[17] According to Robert Macfarlane, walking, under the auspices of psychogeography, is linked with the production of signs, media content, in short, writing:

> Psychogeography: a beginner's guide. Unfold a street map of London, place a glass, rim down, anywhere on the map, and draw round its edge. Pick up the map, go out into the city, and walk the circle, keeping as close as you can to the curve. Record the experience as you go, in whatever medium you favour: film, photograph, manuscript, tape. Catch the textu-

---

15 Grey, *Fly Fishing*, 180–1.

16 See, for instance, Robin Jarvis, *Romantic Writing and Pedestrian Travel* (New York, NY: Palgrave, 1997), and Anne D. Wallace, *Walking, Literature, and English Culture: the Origins and Uses of Peripatetic in the Nineteenth Century* (Oxford: Clarendon Press, 1993).

17 See, for instance, Merlin Coverly, *Psychogeography* (Harpenden, Hertz: Pocket Essentials, 2010).

al run-off of the streets; the graffiti, the branded litter, the snatches of conversation. Cut for sign. Log the data-stream. Be alert to the happenstance of metaphors, watch for visual rhymes, coincidences, analogies, family resemblances, the changing moods of the street. Complete the circle, and the record ends. Walking makes for content; footage for footage.[18]

According to Macfarlane, walking begins and ends with the inscription of signs. First, a circular route on a map is drawn. The point of walking consists in completing that geometrical figure on the map and in recording your experiences as you go along. The amount of ground covered is identical to your content. Walking has an ulterior motive, i.e. the editing, the plotting, and, eventually, the publication of the content recorded during the walk.

In the terminology of this collection of essays, then, walking has reached a *terminus* in the general and metaphorical senses given by the *OED*, 'the point to which motion or action tends, goal, end, finishing-point'. Moreover, *Terminus* is also the point 'from which it starts; starting-point'. In the following, I turn to the staging of walking in examples of Will Self's psychogeography from the 2000s.

FRIVOLOUS, TEDIOUS, AND SERIOUS WALKERS: 'SOUTH DOWNS WAY' (2003)

Originally published in 2003 as one of his *Psychogeography* columns for *The Independent*, 'South Downs Way' is included in the first collection of columns entitled *Psychogeography*. Its opening paragraph contains an early statement of Will Self's reasons for walking:

> I've taken to long-distance walking as a means of dissolving the mechanised matrix which compresses the space-time continuum, and decouples human from physical geography. So this isn't walking for leisure – that would be merely frivolous, or even for exercise – which would be tedious. No, to underscore the seriousness of my project I like a walk

---

18 Quoted in Coverly, *Psychogeography*, 9

which takes me to a meeting or an assignment; that way I can drag other people into my eotechnical world view. 'How was your journey?' they say. 'Not bad,' I reply. 'Take long,' they enquire. 'About ten hours,' I admit. 'I walked here.' My interlocutor goggles at me; if he took ten hours to get here, they're undoubtedly thinking, will the meeting have to go on for twenty? As Emile Durkheim so sagely observed, a society's space-time perceptions are a function of its social rhythm and its territory. So, by walking to the business meeting I have disrupted it just as surely as if I'd appeared stark naked with a peacock's tail fanning out from my buttocks while mouthing Symbolist poetry.[19]

Here Self distinguishes between three kinds of walker: the frivolous walker whose main aim is relaxation, the tedious pedestrian who merely wants to keep fit, and the serious hiker who regards walking as a device or tool with which to undo the socially and culturally determined conception of ourselves and our world. For the serious-minded walker, walking forms a project intended to unsettle the received notions of time and space. If you make the choice of walking for ten hours to get to a meeting or an assignment rather than going there much faster by car, bus, or train, you certainly get a reaction from people. Insisting that walking is a viable A-to-B device in a business context where time is money cannot but create a sense of wonder or amazement in people, who are reduced to staring at the walker in disbelief. The concluding simile, however, suggests that other people are not really dragged into his preindustrial world view. Rather, what is unsettled by the project is not so much other people's received ideas of time and space as their notion of Will Self's mental well-being. At a business meeting, would anyone making an appearance in the nude *and* with a peacock's tail emerging from his backside *and* uttering hermetic poetry unsettle anything but the idea of his own sanity?

---

19 Will Self, 'South Downs Way', in *Psychogeography* (London: Bloomsbury, 2007), 69.

'South Downs Way' concludes in failure and walking misfires miserably. Rather than ambulating proudly into the meeting to the startled disbelief of his business partners, Self merely arrives too late. His dependence on a cab ride to bring him to the beginning of his 22 mile walk across the South Downs National Park in Sussex and Hampshire proves disastrous for his time table. Aiming to earn a half-hour advance on the train, it actually delays him significantly as the cab driver inadvertently drops him off in the wrong place. 'Now, no matter how hard I walked for the rest of the long day, I would still be lagging behind. . . . Machine Matrix 1, Psychogeographers 0. I could hear Durkheim's low and evil laughter in my inner ear. Not a pretty sound'.[20] Defeat is conceded. The very phenomenon he wants to critique deals him an unexpected blow. This suggests dire prospects for his future missions. A project depending on that which it wants to overturn is perhaps doomed to miscarry. Will Self's subsequent three major meditations on walking tend to repeat this structure in terms of an opening theoretical or abstract flamboyant vision, on the one hand, and a walk which always ends in practical and quite concrete failure, on the other, eventually bringing his project and the method of walking into a state of crisis and termination, perhaps.

PEDESTRIAN, AMBITIOUS AND WRITERLY WALKERS: 'WALKING TO NEW YORK' (2007)

Written specifically as an introduction to *Psychogeography* – his first selection of weekly columns from *The Independent* – 'Walking to New York' contains an extended meditation on Self's reasons for walking. In fact, his motives for ambulation are given pride of place and outlined in the first of the five sections, the 'Prologue'. The opening sentence identifies three distinct motives behind his mode of travel: 'I resolved to walk to New York; in the interests of writing about the experience, certainly, yet also with objectives at once more pedestrian and more ambitious'.[21] In this manner, walking is staged as an activity that is propelled by explicit reasons ranging from the commonplace

---

20 Self, 'South Downs', 71.
21 Will Self, 'Introduction: Walking to New York', in *Psychogeography*, 11.

and prosaic to the literary. Thus, walking is presented as in need of an obvious reason, preferably several. This unadorned need of the overt end or point of walking is also echoed in a question asked by his wife on the eve of his departure: 'Remind me again, why is it that you're going to New York?'[22] Moreover, through the character of his wife, Self introduces an important corrective to his own motivations for walking. Not only does she need reminding of his motives, but she is not easily dragged into his eotechnical world view. She regards him with a quizzical look 'as one might regard someone who, whether through disorganisation or ineptitude, had ended up making a journey both senseless and tedious'. Indeed, we're told that she looks at his 'psychogeographical peregrinations as marching along the poorly marked, crinkle-cut frontier between boredom and pretension' yet accepts them since they are beneficial to his mental health and their family. Self, then, gives us his motives for walking and calls attention to the fact that from another point of view walkers are merely incompetent, tedious, and pretentious human beings and walking's only point the maintenance of sanity.

The *pedestrian* reasons for walking to New York concern the fact that he has 'business there',[23] for instance, seeing relatives and promoting his work in the United States. Apart from wanting to go from A to B, Self has reasons that involve less commonplace aims. His *ambitious* reasons include wanting to explore, to heal and condone, and to protest. First of all, he explains:

> I resolved to walk to New York because I wanted to explore. Here was a true Empty Quarter, and, as with other long walks I have taken out of my native city, I had the strong hunch that this would be the first time in the post-industrial era that anyone had ventured across it. . . . I was certain I would be the first person to go the whole way, with only the mute incurious interlude of a club class seat to interfere with the steady,

---

22 Ibid., 12.
23 Ibid., 13.

two-mile-an-hour, metronomic rhythm of my legs, parting and marrying, parting and marrying.[24]

In aiming to become the first human in history to walk from central London to Heathrow, fly to JFK, and walk from the airport to Manhattan, Self turns walking into an act of differentiation distinguishing him from everybody else. But his ambitions are also of a psychological nature, for instance, he aims to heal and unify his divided Anglo-American self and to apologise:

> I hoped to suture up one of the wounds in my own, divided psyche: to sew together my American and My English flesh, my mother's and my father's body bags, sundered by marriage, rived by death. And maybe even, at a more grandiose level (exhibiting what might be termed a Terroristic Personality Disorder), to expiate the sense of weird culpability that had dogged me, ever since 11 September 2001.[25]

Lastly, walking is also invested with political ambitions and the rambler is cast as 'an insurgent against the contemporary world'.[26] Walking becomes a peaceful political act where the pedestrian rebels against the flimsiness of contemporary culture:

> Yes, this was to be a peaceable protest, this discontinuous march from Stockwell in south London to the Lower East Side of Manhattan. If I was assaulting a tyranny it was one of distance and of a form of transportation that decentres and destabilises us, making all of us that can afford it subjects of a ribbon empire that encircles the globe. This is a papery and insubstantial realm, like a sanitary strip wrapped around a toilet bowl.[27]

---

24 Ibid., 13.
25 Ibid., 13–4.
26 Ibid., 15.
27 Ibid., 15–6.

Walking as nonviolent political protest completes Self's set of ambitious motivations. The *writerly* motives he addresses combine elements from the first two sets of reasons and aim at the production of difference and distinction in the field of British Letters. Thus, his journey to New York is to be 'the defining journey so far as my particular brand of psychogeography is concerned'.[28] The walk is to establish a distinctive trademark for Will Self. He acknowledges the legacy from Guy Debord and the French Situationists from the middle of the 20th century and identifies with the desire 'to unpick this conundrum, the manner in which the contemporary world warps the relationship between psyche and place'.[29] But he distinguishes himself from contemporary exponents, for instance, Peter Ackroyd's 'phrenology' and Nick Papadimitriou's 'deep topography'[30] and from the general idea that psychogeographers 'are really only local historians with an attitude problem'.[31] Moreover, the fact that he walks for pedestrian, or A-to-B, reasons allows him to distinguish himself from the psychogeographical methods of walking as 'randomised transit intended to outfox prescribed folkways'[32] available on the Internet or, for instance, Iain Sinclair's 'shamanic attempts' to battle contemporary culture. Lastly, he also seeks to distinguish himself from past exponents of 'writerly journeys in the accepted sense'[33] and writers such as Rousseau, Goethe, Stevenson, and Thesiger.

So it is safe to say that Self invests the notion of walking with a number of points ranging from the unambitious one of getting from A to B, to the more aspiring aims of healing and condoning, and the production of writerly distinction. His act of walking is characterised by failure, however. Rather than feelings of 'elevation'[34] his spirits are plunging in New York, and he realises that his wife's take on his project

---

28 Ibid., 11.
29 Ibid.
30 Ibid., 11-2.
31 Ibid., 12.
32 Ibid., 13.
33 Ibid. 12.
34 Ibid., 57.

was the correct one: '[T]his is just another slog away from commitment and engagement, and towards empty-headedness'.[35] He concludes that it was foolish of him to think that he was capable of healing anything with his feet[36] and that it was a 'dumb idea to walk to New York'. And eventually walking is brought to a complete end. Moreover, when he gives up walking completely he finds that each cab or train he takes drives him 'further and further away from whatever point it had been that [he] was trying to make'.[37]

But some experience of success is expressed as well, particularly the idea that his body has mediated the space between London and New York. But the experience is a personal one which cannot easily be shared with others. When Self asks directions from an elderly man the result is that the New Yorker is left 'painfully disoriented'.[38] Similarly, Self attracts the attention of a group of African Americans in east New York, but only because they are wondering what he is doing in their territory.[39]

OBSESSED AND PSYCHOTIC WALKERS: WALKING TO HOLLYWOOD (2010) AND OBSESSED WITH WALKING (2010)

Walking is figured prominently and problematically in the two texts that emerged from his 2008 walk to Hollywood, his own *Walking to Hollywood* and Australian film maker Rosie Jones's documentary *Obsessed with Walking*. The three 'memoirs'[40] that form *Walking to Hollywood: Memories of Before the Fall* all deal with examples of pedestrianism. 'Very Little' outlines a walk on the Downs[41] and a walk from Toronto Airport into town,[42] for instance. 'Walking to Hollywood' concerns his

---

35 Ibid.
36 Ibid., 61.
37 Ibid., 62.
38 Ibid., 53.
39 Ibid., 55–6.
40 Will Self, *Walking to Hollywood* (London: Bloomsbury, 2010), 431.
41 Ibid., 19–33.
42 Ibid., 48–52.

walk from his home in south London to Heathrow and from LAX to Hollywood. 'Spurn Head' deals with his walk along the Yorkshire coast north of the river Humber. But according to the 'Afterword' each of the 'memoirs' also exemplifies a mental pathology, 'obsessive compulsive disorder for "Very Little", psychosis for "Walking to Hollywood" and Alzheimer's for "Spurn Head"'.[43] In the following, I show how walking is fashioned in the context of mental illness in order to render void the reasons that apparently propelled it in the first place.

'The Consultation', the opening section of 'Walking to Hollywood', is set in the beginning of May 2008 in the office of Dr Shiva Mukti. It outlines how the narrator-protagonist decides 'to take a walking tour of Los Angeles'[44] at the, at least for him, successful conclusion of a series of cognitive behavioural therapy sessions with Dr Shiva Mukti. The psychiatrist, it is specified, '[i]n addition to using all the standard techniques . . . also videoed psychotics during their flamboyant episodes, then showed the films to them when lucid, in order to persuade these patients of the necessity of taking their medication'. The narrator-protagonist, moreover, explains to another of his psychiatrists, Dr Zack Busner, that he has decided to journey on foot to the capital of American cinema in order to '"find out who killed film – for film is definitely dead, toppled from its reign as the pre-eminent narrative medium of the age. I don't know if film was murdered – but I suspect there's a killer out there!"'[45] Also to Busner, Self explains his choice of his particular method and approach, i.e. walking:

> If I want to discover who – or what – did for film I'll be better off walking. Walking is so much slower than film – especially contemporary Hollywood movies, with their stuttering film grammar of split-second shots – and it isn't framed, when you walk you're floating in a fishbowl view of the world. There can't possibly be any editing: no dissolves, no cuts, no fades, no split-screens – and, best of all, no special effects, no

---

43 Ibid., 431-2.
44 Ibid., 109.
45 Ibid., 122.

computer-cheated facsimiles of the world. You see, if I walk to Hollywood I'll be creeping along outside the ambit of the filmic – like a Vietcong insurgent tunnelling through the jungle – and they won't be able to see me coming![46]

'Walking to Hollywood' stages walking in a manner that recalls the earlier texts, then. Walking comes equipped with a series of reasons and purposes, and the concluding simile, moreover, links the walker directly to insurgence. However, in contrast to the earlier texts, this text also *frames* walking. First of all, the notion that we are dealing with a memoir, in the traditional sense of an autobiographical record of the writer's encounters with famous people and places, is compromised in several ways, however. For starters, it clearly fictionalises the experiences we're presented with: Dr Shiva Mukti and Dr Zack Busner are prominent fictional characters familiar to readers of Self's fiction.[47] Moreover, not only is Busner a fictional character, in Self's memoir he is played by Orson Welles (1915–1985) – something the narrator-protagonist realises during his interview with Busner.[48] And later it becomes clear that all the characters encountered on the walking tour of Los Angeles are in fact played by famous actors. The narrator-character himself, for instance, is played alternately by David Thewlis and Pete Postlethwaite. But the extent to which walking is undermined by the text only becomes fully clear at the conclusion of the walking tour of Los Angeles. The opening of the last section of the text, '12: Will Hays and the Fat Boy', returns the narrator-character and the reader to May 2008 and Mukti's office at the beginning of the text: '"And that's what happens to you when you don't take your medication," Shiva Mukti said in the matter-of-fact way psychiatrists affect in order to cope with the extremities of mental delusion'.[49]

---

46 Ibid., 124.

47 Since his debut collection of stories *The Quantity Theory of Insanity* (1991), Busner and Mukti have appeared as key characters on several occasions in, for instance, *Great Apes* (1997) and *Dr Mukti and Other Tales of Woe* (2003).

48 Self, *Hollywood*, 134.

49 Ibid., 324.

The walk to Hollywood, then, is a framed story presented within opening and closing frames that equips the narrator-protagonist with a psychiatric diagnosis and makes clear that the framed narrative outlining his LA walking tour is really a videotape his therapist has made of him in a state of full-blown psychosis. In this manner, walking is discredited as a method of critique and dissent. The narrative of walking is reduced to a case history of Capgras and Fregolis delusion and schizothymia.[50] The reasons for walking are no longer governed by rational choice.

A similar pattern of first staging walking as a significant activity and then questioning it is apparent in Rosie Jones's 2010 documentary *Obsessed with Walking*. Already the title of the documentary suggests a corrective take on the idea of walking as a choice. In her biopic, Jones follows Self on the second leg of his walk, i.e. from LAX to Hollywood. In the beginning of the film, Self outlines his motives for walking. They fall into three familiar groups. First, voicing dissent from and creating a corrective to dominant ways of perceiving space are major points for Self. Walking is styled as 'a way of violently undercutting the fact of intercontinental air travel by walking either side of it for long distances',[51] a way of 'decoupling physical from human geography'.[52] Walking allows you to reclaim urban space and the idea that beauty doesn't automatically exist in in the picturesque. Self makes a particular point of dissenting from Wordsworth and the sense of beauty we have received from the romantics. Secondly, walking is also a privileged 'method of investigating place'.[53] Walking is 'a powerful tool'.[54] It equals 'a biopsy of the reality of LA'[55] and walking equals Peter Ackroyd's idea of 'phrenology'.[56] Lastly, walking has strong personal motives as well for

---

50 Ibid., 325.

51 *Obsessed with Walking*, directed by Rosie Jones (Melbourne, Victoria: Flaming Star Films, 2010), DVD, 01:25-01:30.

52 Ibid., 05:00.

53 Ibid., 02:00.

54 Ibid., 11:00.

55 Ibid., 04:00.

56 Ibid., 16:17.

Self. Having walked with his father as a child, walking is part of his 'patrimony'.[57] Similarly, having grown up in suburbia walking through residential districts in LA means 'constantly recreating coming home',[58] allowing a feeling of being 'at home in the world'.[59]

After Self's outline of his reasons for walking, he challenges his own project by concluding that 'it becomes a little bit obsessive'[60] echoing the title of Jones's documentary. Self's problematisation of his method is immediately developed by Jones who juxtaposes his story to two other walkers whom she regards as 'obsessed with walking' – William Wordsworth and Australian composer Percy Grainger.[61] The former is styled as always pacing 'compulsively up and down his garden path'.[62] The latter is said to have used walking to control 'another compulsion: self-flagellation'.[63]

Casting walking in terms of obsession is a way of questioning its potential as a method of investigation and dissent and its power as a corrective. By turning walking into a compulsion rather than a choice, it is staged as a psychiatric condition, a disorder, rather than a critical stance that you consciously opt for. Suggesting that walking could be a psychological necessity for Self is a way of reducing the seriousness of his overt motives and of suggesting, perhaps, that they are in fact mere rationalisations of a mental pathology.

Jones's problematisation of walking as obsession is followed by an outline of the failure of Self's walk to produce the intended result. In Jones's interview with Self, which concludes her documentary, Self explains: 'When I got back, I realised I couldn't write the book that I had thought was there. So that then I had to undergo a quite profound

---

57 Ibid., 02:40.
58 Ibid., 03:10.
59 Ibid., 03:35.
60 Ibid., 17:15.
61 Ibid., 17:25.
62 Ibid., 17:38.
63 Ibid., 18:00.

re-evaluation of what I was about or how to deal with this material'.[64] The book that did materialise, *Walking to Hollywood*, Self's explains is about 'a kind of investigation into a kind of personal heart of darkness as much as anything else (he laughs)'.[65] He blames the failure on a flaw in his method – 'I didn't talk to enough people'[66] – and on the fact that he has become estranged from the world and from himself: 'I was beginning to feel at once this Will Self person who does this kind of shit and also curiously depersonalised just another ... I'd almost become a passer-by in my own life because all I do is walk across cities so in a way I'm just the guy I see out of the corner of my eye at the stoplight'.[67]

The theme of failure is allowed to end the documentary. Self sums up that not only did walking fail to produce the intended book, but it has been futile on a much larger scale. 'The walking wasn't serving me as a means of escape. I was still exactly where I had been a decade ago in some important senses (laughs)'.[68] Prompted by the interviewer, he admits that walking has reached 'perhaps a crisis of some sort, but I mean, you know, crisis is just part of evolution, isn't it'.[69]

WALKING AS VALEDICTION AND HOMAGE IN 'WALKING TO THE WORLD' (2009)

In the examples from Will Self's writing, walking has so far been the vehicle of protest, healing, penitence, and investigation, among other things. But walking has also been a spectacular failure never really fulfilling its rich promises. The link between walking and mental disorder, moreover, suggest that walking is compulsive and never a matter of choice in the first place. At the moment in history when we walk because we choose to do so for a range of different reasons, Will Self and Rosie Jones suggest that walking, at least for Self, is not the result of a free choice but an uncontrollable mental condition.

---

64 Ibid., 21:15.
65 Ibid., 22:17.
66 Ibid., 22:20.
67 Ibid., 22:50–23:24.
68 Ibid., 25:30.
69 Ibid., 25:50.

What is also clear form Self's texts is the fact that walking and writing need each other and are locked in a relationship of mutual dependence. Writing needs walking for subject matter, and walking needs writing for meaning. Writing invests walking with significance, point, and a clear end (but a significance that it doesn't inherently possess, perhaps). Walking reciprocates by yielding up the stuff of writing, footage. Even when it miscarries and fails to fulfil its many promises, it produces the story of that failure and the end of those promises.

The text concerning the last of the major walks Will Self undertook in the 2000s tries to move beyond the sense of failure that pervades the preceding texts and the impasse of insanity. This is done by reinvesting walking with a new set of meanings. To invest his walk to The World with meaning he refashions his reasons and motives. The point of his walk doesn't concern the serious and ambitious motives apparent in the earlier texts. Rather, the walk is itself turned into particular kinds of discourse. *Psycho Too* (2009), the sequel to *Psychogeography*, also contains an introduction written specifically for the volume. 'Walking to the World' outlines Self's walk to The World, i.e. the property development venture that involves the recreation of the world in the form of several hundreds of small islands of sand off the coast of Dubai. This text also opens in the familiar way with a preamble that stages walking and supplies the reasons for Self's decision 'to walk to the World from J. G. Ballard's house in Shepperton'.[70] This time around, however, instead of a set of motives, a memoir of Ballard forms the introduction. Self outlines his 'Ballardian apprenticeship'[71] and casts Ballard as a visionary:

> Ballard showed the way: the fiction of the twenty-first century, the fiction that would *matter*, was there on the Isle of Grain, there in the interzones, there in the psyches of all of us who appreciated the three-mile sinuous chicane of the Westway flyover, there in our numbed responses to those superfluities of space and time that, together with our own

---

70 Will Self, 'Walking to the World', in *Psycho Too* (London: Bloomsbury, 2009), 11.
71 Ibid., 13.

narcissistic subjectivity, constituted the very essence of what Marc Augé has termed, 'supermodernity'.[72]

Ballard is a writer who mapped out the future of fiction by singling out the interzone, the nonplace, rather than the village, the countryside, or the conurbation as his particular field of interest. The 'Walk to the World' is Will Self's valediction and homage to the dying Ballard.[73] And Self chooses Dubai as his destination because Dubai is the fullest incarnation of Ballard's vision: 'this was the world of Ballard's novels and stories: modular and introverted zones, where social relations had been defined by a CAD-CAM program, and pedestrianism was a leisure activity inseparable from retail opportunities'.[74]

Walking through Downtown Dubai, Self realises that his walk has been successful:

> And then it came – the consummation, although not exactly the one I had so devoutly desired; this was to be no empowering humanisation of the world, nor nostalgic triumph of the eotechnic – I had yoked my psyche to Jim Ballard's visionary gaze, and so the Metro-Centre spake unto Downtown Dubai, a conversation that required no human intermediary. They whispered of their hollowness as they shifted in the wind, feeling the bronchitic pain of their ducts and vents; and they moaned of their ruinations – windows burst, facades cracked, bony girders exposed – and they foresaw their death: a snaggled-toothed row of corpses silhouetted against a bloody sunset.[75]

Next to Ballard, Self's 'Walking to the World' figures another precursor, namely the British travel writer Wilfred Thesiger (1910–2003), who in *Arabian Sands* (1959) tells of his post-World War II journeys across the

---

72 Ibid., 16.
73 Ibid., 28.
74 Ibid., 27.
75 Ibid., 40.

deserts of the Empty Quarter of the Arabian Peninsula and of his encounters with the Bedouin. And next to identifying present day Dubai in terms of a 'very Ballardian, inner space',[76] Self desires to find its contrast and its origin, Thesiger's Empty Quarter, and the peace of the desert and the rich possibilities for contemplation Thesiger experienced there only two generations previously.

Moving beyond the outskirts of Dubai on the way to his desert resort hotel, he eventually strikes out into the empty desert, only, however, to discover initially that it 'wasn't empty at all'.[77] In contrast to Thesiger, Self's gaze is imprisoned by signs of civilisation such as pylons and wrappers for candy bars. This produces a new low in his hike: 'I considered, yet again, jacking it in – whet was the *point*?'[78] But he pushes on and eventually finds himself in 'the desert proper'.[79] This 'primordial world' immediately offers suitable experiences: 'A sand fox, up early, skittered away into a wadi, then, as I reached the top of the next acclivity, six ibex came barrelling along the side of the one beyond. So fast! As fast as *cars*, their front legs punching up high at the air as they bullied their way forward'.[80] The simile suggests, however, that the primeval scenario, or Self's interpretation, already is ineluctably infested with civilisation and 'Ballardian, inner space'. Similarly, Self's experience of the pristine desert is already culturally marked and circumscribed:

> At last I was transported into Thesiger's contemplative space, where a squiggle of dead convolvulus could enthral me for the long minutes it took me to reach it. I bent down to observe the liquid motion of blown sand on the face of the dune; I savoured the contrast between the hard-packed sand on the windward faces and the powder on the sheltered side.

---

76 Ibid., 49.
77 Ibid., 48.
78 Ibid., 49, italics in the original.
79 Ibid., 50.
80 Ibid., 50, italics in the original.

> I went across a rollicking sea of peaks and troughs, soon falling into an easy rhythm: checking my compass bearing on a distant tumulus at the top of each rise, then adjusting my focus to bush after bush, as it was lost from sight.[81]

Not only is the meditative space *already* Thesiger's, the noun *squiggle* suggests representation, and *rollicking sea* is a dead metaphor. Similarly, his response – enthralment and delight – are culturally dictated. After briefly considering sleeping rough, he switches on his mobile (apparently, the primordial world is already equipped with a cellular network) and calls the hotel asking for directions. He finds that his call ruins 'it all: the ibex, the dunes – the desert'.[82] He is jerked back into the world from which he came and he is aware of the signs of civilisation and tourism that now accompany him on the last leg to the hotel. It turns out that today Thesiger's Empty Quarter is just another Ballardian interzone.

At this point Self gives up walking for good, but his realisation of the futility of walking is expressed early in the text:

> What was the point of these rambles anyway? They told me nothing that I didn't know already, or, rather, my method imposed on the raw data of experience a prefabricated narrative: everywhere was the same, everyone was forced to follow the same road/rail/flight path, only I had escaped the man/machine matrix to saunter, barefoot, along the median strip. But wasn't the truth that I was just as determined? ... driven full speed ahead by my ambulatory engine I sat inside the hot, rubbery compartment of my skull, maddened with frustration, staring out through the windscreen of my own eyes.[83]

---

81 Ibid., 50.

82 Ibid., 52.

83 Ibid., 37–8.

Giving up walking does not terminate his visit to Dubai or his text for that matter. Instead he decides to take Dubai on its own terms. The 'Two Fantasias on a Visionary Theme by Sheikh Mohammed bin Raschid Al Maktoum' that conclude his piece show that this method proves just as successful for fulfilling his valedictory and reverential aims. Even though he doesn't walk anymore and has given in to the temporal and spatial dictates of the 21st-century metropolis, he remains fully capable of identifying the correspondences between Ballard's works, e.g. *Millennium People*, *Crash*, *High Rise*, and Dubai.[84] So while it fits walking with a new set of reasons – valediction and homage – 'Walking to the World' nevertheless repeats the established pattern in bringing walking to an end. Moreover, the text not only abandons walking as a method, but goes on to show that the reasons for choosing to walk in the first place – taking your leave from and paying your respects to an important writer – can be fulfilled just as effectively through contemporary and mechanised forms of transportation.

CONCLUSION

Will Self's texts on walking written between 2003 and 2010 concern the end and ends of walking. First, each text is minutely preoccupied with the *reasons* for walking and goes to great length in making its purposes and ends explicit. Walking is staged as an A-to-B device, as a tool that undoes the received conception of us and our world, as a peaceful political act, as an instrument of healing and condoning, as a method of detection, and as a valediction and homage. Secondly, they repeatedly stage walking's *termination* in defeat and failure. Walking doesn't get you from A to B on time, it turns out just to be a laborious way of avoiding commitment, and rather than a conscious political choice it's the act of an obsessive or a psychotic person, yielding nothing more than a prefabricated narrative. An important end for walking remains, nevertheless. At a point in the history of the West where the act of walking is no longer a necessity but a matter of choice, Will Self's texts strike up a vital relationship between walking and writing. While his discourse relies on walking for meaningful content, unnecessary and

---

84 Ibid., 62, 68, 67–73.

pointless walking relies on his discourse for meaning and significance. Writing produces the activity of walking as significant and relevant, and as the site of privileged experience. Walking in turn supplies the stuff of writing and discourse, even if that involves its failure to deliver on the promises it was instilled with in the first place. This seems to be the ultimate point of walking. Walking and writing work together and produce distinction allowing Will Self to differentiate himself from other psychogeographers on the British literary scene. Certainly, it appears that his walks and writings have succeeded in this sense. For instance, the press statement announcing his appointment as Professor of Contemporary Thought at Brunel University mentions that '[h]e has written about his bizarre 'airport walks' in two long essays, 'Walking to New York' and 'Walking to the World', and believes that he may well be the only man to have walked from central London to Heathrow Airport and then taken a flight'.[85] Will Self, I'm sure, relishes the irony that the point or end of his walks in the first decade of the twenty-first century in a sense turned out to be a professorial *chair*.

At the point in history where walking is no longer a necessity, Will Self's texts are symptomatic of the fact that walking must always be staged and created as an activity with a point, or end, or reason. More often than not the reason for walking is the production of a distinct experience in the mind of the pedestrian. For instance, companies now generate a plethora of themed walks around London.[86] Much more spectacularly, The London Millennium Footbridge, which opened in June 2000, offers a particularly fitting image of walking as a heavily staged activity. Linking the City with Bankside, it provides pedestrian access to, among other things, St Paul's Cathedral, the Globe Theatre and Tate Modern. Here walking is inscribed in an experience economy. Not only does it provide easy access to favourite London attractions, the bridge stages walking as an unforgettable affair for the individual.

---

85 Brunel University London, 'Will Self joins Brunel University as Professor of Contemporary Thought', last modified March 12, 2012, http://www.brunel.ac.uk/news-and-events/news/news-items/ne_161686.

86 See, for instance, www.walks.com, www.londonwalks.com, and www.walklondon.org.uk.

Looking north, the pedestrian sees an almost artistically framed image of St Paul's. This is the kind of 'memorable event' that forms the currency of the experience economy according to Joseph Pine and Gilmore.[87] Will Self's investment of walking with a wide range of reasons and motivations and his staging of walking as significant and meaningful speaks ultimately of his identity within an economy that places a premium on experience.

---

87 Joseph B. Pine II and James H. Gilmore, 'Welcome to the Experience Economy', *Harvard Business Review* (July–August 1998): 97–195, esp. 98.

TERMINUS, POLITICS AND THE END OF HISTORY: SOME THOUGHT QUESTIONS ABOUT HUMAN RIGHTS, HISTORY, THE STATE OF GLOBAL CULTURE, AND POLITICAL ENDS

Ben Dorfman

We have many ways to think about *terminus* – the 'end', a boundary, the 'last', or whichever statement about finality one might like to make. Literary scholars find interest in the *terminus* idea in part because, well, books seem to have ends and, as Frank Kermode expressed it, a 'sense of an ending' may be one of the deep connections between literature and life. Life may *be* a kind of literature, as such (evoking literary notions of 'writing the self'). Eschatology likes *terminus* also as the world is supposed to end when the four horsemen of the apocalypse arrive, heralding the final judgment. 'Every mountain and island were moved from their places' the four horsemen came, reads the Book of Revelation, chapter six, and if that does not sound like the end, few things do. Film scholars like endings as films, like books, also seem to have ends. Wise ones, like *Pulp Fiction*, play with senses of endings, making the 'sense of an ending' (via its lack) only more present. Kermode wrote, 'there is a ... need to speak humanly of life's importance in relation to it' – the 'end' (*terminus*). This paper will not focus on Kermode. His sentiment, however, is worth reflecting upon.[1]

One reason for the worth of reflecting upon ends is their political value. That is to say that yes, life might be caught up, or bound up with senses of 'ends'; one might need ends to define oneself. One might find representations of ends in literature or film – potentially, it is also present in the culture-religious imaginations forming so many *mythos*

---

1 Frank Kermode, *The Sense of an Ending* (Oxford: Oxford UP, 2000), 4.

within world societies. However, the 'end' is also a concept binding history and politics – it may be evocative of the issue of political destinies, or where politics should go. It may also evoke what political destinies say about us, or manners, or modes, through which we imagine ourselves. It is a sidebar observation. However, this level of self-reflectivity in political thought, as well as the capacity of political acts and ideas to represent who we are, is one of the modes through which politics becomes cultural, or politics become bound to a 'way of life', as Raymond Williams once defined it.[2] In short shrift, as an expressive form, politics may come into the purview of literature and art.

What I would like to do in this essay is open some questions about 'ends' (*terminus*) and political ideas. Specifically, I would like to do this in relation to perhaps the most famous recent statement about political ends, Francis Fukuyama's *The End of History and the Last Man* (1992). *The End*, as I will refer to the book, was important as it captured a particular geo-political moment; it spoke to modes of the popular imagination of an era, or at least a transformative historical moment. As Fukuyama put it, this concerned the idea that 'a remarkable consensus concerning the legitimacy of liberal democracy as a system of government had emerged throughout the world over the past ... years' (by which he meant largely the 1980s).[3] Moreover, it meant the idea that 'liberal democracy may constitute the 'endpoint of mankind's ideological evolution'.[4] These were big – and controversial – words. However, Fukuyama may have been right. As Eastern Bloc states fell like dominos, and China experienced protest as well (in the years between 1989 and 1991), it appeared that a final discrediting of an idea (Marxism) was taking place. The benefactor was the political-economic liberalism – that which Marxism had always opposed.

This might be true. It is certainly not wrong; how does one argue with the idea that Marxism had a relative though nonetheless drastic crisis of legitimacy in comparison with liberalist politics and econom-

---

2 Raymond Williams, *The Long Revolution* (New York: Broadview Press, 2001), 57.

3 Francis Fukuyama, *The End of History and the Last Man* (New York: Penguin, 1992), xi.

4 Ibid.

ics? How does one doubt liberalism's (and capitalism's) victory? Still, I would like to offer another thought: *human rights* might be as much the benefactor of structures of ideological legitimacy today; those resulting from communism's 'fall', or the 'end of history', as such. In this chapter, I would like to prove this, or at least address it as a question (and if I accomplish that, I will have succeeded [political philosophical points are, after all, hard to 'prove']), via three steps. Firstly, I think it important look at the Fukuyama thesis and assess it – what was it, ultimately, that Fukuyama was trying to say? How did he say it? And was he right? There are many dimensions to the Fukuyama argument – empirical, politicological (or comparative political), and philosophical. Fukuyama's philosophical assertions truly drive the thesis, however – statements about the nature of 'man' and the consequences of that nature. It is on the merits of those assertions that the success of the book really needs to be assessed, or at least approached.

Secondly, I think it important to realize, or at least assert, that a major consequence of *The End* is that it forces us to think about rights. Rights, or their realization and institution, is what Fukuyama advances as the teleology of liberal society – that 'modern liberal democracy 'recognizes' ... human beings .... by granting and protecting their rights'.[5] It is a challenging point because it forces us to think about *human* rights – this is because human rights are the logical extension of the rights idea writ large. The 'rights idea', as such, asserts the absolute inherentness of the human being on an extra-national level – the human being's 'abstract universality'.[6] The *human* rights idea – as opposed to the 'rights' idea – seeks to realize that, and guarantee rights that extend beyond the boundaries of the nation-state, as such.

Lastly, we should make a cultural-critical argument about human rights. In this context, what will be suggested is that, following on the heels of liberalism's victory, it is natural that world society would intensify its use of human rights vocabularies and ideas – even extending their use into advertising, film, video games, and other articles of mass

---

5 Ibid., 202.

6 Lynn Hunt, *Inventing Human Rights: A History* (New York: W.W. Norton, 2007), 153.

consumption. It might also be suggested – and I will suggest – that this has in fact happened. Undoubtedly, this is a massive cultural-analytical point; it will be made insufficiently here as there are simply too many examples to cover. However, by way of invocation of some key examples – simply examples – I would like to show that we 'think' human rights, or maintain them as parts of our 'life-world', in contemporary cultural spaces. This means that in some sort of concatenation of 'global culture', rights are 'present' for us. It means that rights have infiltrated our orders of knowledge, or 'codes of a culture', as Michel Foucault put it, and we 'expect' them to be there. In this way, I would like to suggest that it might be rights as much as liberalism which form our sense of political destiny and hence a political 'end'. 'Political end' means horizons of politics at which it feels natural for us to have arrived, and beyond whose shores it becomes difficult to see.

Of course, Fukuyama's book is an extension of an almost equally famous paper he published in 1989 in *The National Interest*. In that paper, as he summarizes it in *The End*, the point was made that 'a remarkable consensus concerning the legitimacy of liberal democracy as a system of government [was] emerg[ing] throughout the world ... as it conquered rival ideologies like hereditary monarchy, fascism, and ... communism'.[7] It was a bold and prescient statement, though it seemed to get its historical chronologies a bit out of line. This was clear as, at least in a European context, hereditary monarchy as a determined form of rule had largely disappeared by the end of the First World War, and fascism by the end of the Second (regimes in Spain and Portugal [and potentially Greece in the 1960s] being noticeable exceptions). That was a bit beside the point, however, because the context in which Fukuyama wrote – the emergence of popular protest in Eastern Europe, the institution of *Glasnost* and *Perestroika* in the USSR, and Gorbachev's noticeably more open relations with the West – made communism the object of Fukuyama's criticism. Communism might be on its last legs, Fukuyama argued, and indeed it was. By the end of the calendar year

---

7 Fukuyama, *End of History*, xi.

in which Fukuyama wrote – 1989 – most Eastern Bloc regimes would be gone; in fact the Eastern Bloc as a 'bloc' (an ideologically aligned set of states) would be dissolved. *Something* – a historical event of note – had unquestionably happened. The question, of course, was what it was, and what it meant.

What it 'was' had an empirical grounding – a central part of Fukuyama's argumentation. This 'was' was the institution of multiparty elections in states that previously had none (at least under communism), and the styling of those states as openly democratic in ways that were not 'social democratic' or 'popular' democratic (in the sense, for example, that East Germany was the 'German Democratic Republic', Hungary was the 'People's Republic of Hungary', or Romania was the 'Romanian People's Republic' – in other words, socialism claimed its democracy too). The 'was' also involved withdrawal from international defense institutions for pro-Soviet states such as the Warsaw Pact (which was formally dissolved in early 1991). At the time of composing *The End*, during the course of events between 1989 and '91, the processes of popular and state-based self-representation had not yet even reached their completion. The Soviet Union was just dissolving for good as *The End* was published (the Soviet Union's expiration date came on Christmas Day, 1991), and not all Soviet republics had yet declared their independence. Multinational states such as Czechoslovakia still had yet to break into their national constituencies as well. Nonetheless, Fukuyama took empirical stock of the world situation as of 1990. Here, he tallied sixty-three liberal democracies on a global basis – states ranging all the way from liberal democratic stalwarts such as the United States and Great Britain to newly liberalized states such as Czechoslovakia and the Baltic republics (which had become independent) to Central American states which had emerged from long periods as Cold War fighting grounds (for example, Nicaragua and El Salvador) that had turned to socialist governments for periods of time. At the time, sixty-three liberal democracies represented a bit over a third of the world's states in a period when the number of sovereign states was fluctuating greatly. However, Fukuyama's point was the rate of increase from years such as 1960 and 1975. For 1960, Fukuyama counted thirty-six liberal regimes. For 1975, he tallied thirty (as countries such as Greece slipped into junta-like dictatorships for parts of the 1960s). 1989, or 1990 (the precise year of Fukuyama's count), represented seventy-five percent and two hundred and ten percent increases, respectively. This was the hard evidence about what was taking place. Socialism was being displaced. It was being displaced at a near exponential rate in the course of a few short years.

A second dimension to the book, however, concerns politicological comparisons between the systems with which Fukuyama was concerned. These were, again, largely communism and liberal political democracy – and they concerned the nature of the two systems involved.

Very simply – and to streamline a complex argument – Fukuyama discussed what he called the 'weakness of strong states'. Here, while Fukuyama did not exactly take the line that Hannah Arendt offered in *The Origins of Totalitarianism* (1951) – that underneath totalitarian regimes was an absolute willingness to use terror to sustain the authority of the regime. But he did offer that 'totalitarian regimes on both the Right and the Left [from, for example, Franco's pseudo-fascism to Eastern European socialism] sought to use the power of the state to encroach upon the private sphere'.[8] This was not a totally easy argument to make; there was, especially in communism, a liberation theology, or ideal. As Fukuyama wrote, the Marxist realm of freedom 'was the four hour working day'.[9] Marxian freedom represented the reparation of the international division of labor which might break up not only states, but the entire international, or global, community, into blocs of consumers and producers, wherein producers (the international proletariat) were at the beck and call of their paymasters (consumers) and thus suffered a non-recognition of their basic humanity. Marxism did not achieve international revolution – Stalin's doctrine of 'socialism in one country' (i.e., opposed to Trotskyist notions of international revolution) may have forever bound socialism, or at least its practical realization to the state. The point, however, was that 'what was lost in the realm of liberty' (meaning, in essence, the private sphere [thoughts and proper-

---

8 Ibid., 15.
9 Ibid., 132.

ty]) 'was to be regained at the level of national purpose'.[10] Communism supplied national purpose instead of personal freedom.

This resulted in two essentially different governmental systems. One, as Fukuyama indicated in his assessment of the total number of liberal democratic states, involved secret ballot, multi-party elections and universal and equal adult suffrage. The other did not disallow secret ballots or universal and equal adult suffrage (women in Soviet Russia were immediately granted the right to vote in the new system in 1917, where women's suffrage came noticeably later in some Western states [for example, 1920 in the United States, 1945 in France and 1971 in Switzerland]). However, they did disallow multi-party elections. Here, one encountered an ideological split. From the perspective of institutionalized communism, one achieved 'substantive democracy' (in other words, democracy that truly represented a popular interest, and not the discursive power of a ruling elite) by having elected officials only from the people's party (the communists). However, to Fukuyama's mind, this predetermined who the 'people' are and what they want. Thus, 'formal democracy', in which one maintained radically, or at least highly, open democratic procedures (including multi-party ballots [and the acceptance of multi-party results]), was more likely to produce 'substantive' democracy – a true reflection of who the people 'are'.[11]

This assertion, however, gets to the heart of what Fukuyama sought to argue – why political democracy, or liberalism, was the 'end' of political systems (*terminus*), and thus the end of history understood as an ideological contest, or a debate over the nature of what humanity is. This was because political democracy – political liberalism (and to some extent capitalism as the historical accompaniment of liberalism) – accorded with the nature of the human spirit. Indeed, that was perhaps the most fundamental point of *The End*: that humanity *had* (and has) a 'spirit'. Also, the nature of humanity's spirit resonates with its (humanity's) objective history. There are a number of points of reference for this idea, both in Fukuyama (and he uses many of them) and in intellectual

---

10 Ibid., 15.
11 Ibid., 43.

history at large. One is the Platonic notion of *Thymos*, or a kind of animating force to the human soul. In Plato's *Phaedrus*, this is described as needing governance by *Logos*, or the power of rationality.[12] However, *Thymos* was an integral part of the human being – it was that which made he or she come alive, seek recognition and have a sense of presence as an individual. We were *Thymatic* people, Fukuyama asserted. One could not do away with a human essence that sought recognition as an individual. The best political systems, he asserted, met 'man as man' – he or she as who he or she 'is'.[13]

Nonetheless, *Thymos* was not, or at least was not best, conceived of as raw drive – unconquerable thirsts for realist power and domination over others (the sort of 'war of all against all' envisioned by Thomas Hobbes in *Leviathan*, for example). *Thymos* also gave way to the search for *how* one might achieve the recognition one craved, and a cognitive sense of the range of choices one had in that regard. Here, *Thymos*, the human spirit, became rather more like Hegel's *Geist* – a concept of an animating force in human history, yes, but also one which came with, or at least developed, rationality. This came through the uncanniness of existence itself – the fact that we 'were' (or are), but as cognitive beings. Here, we engaged in a reflective process. We learned more about ourselves, asserted Hegel, such that at a certain stage, we might achieve a state of 'absolute knowledge'. Absolute knowledge, of course, did not mean an empirical knowledge of all things – an end to the human discovery process. Absolute knowledge was rather *consciousness* of knowledge of which he spoke; the possibility of science and the possibility of truth – it was the 'movement of carrying forward the form of self-knowledge' one had achieved through time (Hegel's terminology).[14] This was a massively conflicted process – a point very much emphasized by the Russian émigré/French philosopher Alexan-

---

12 *Plato's Phaedrus*, trans. R. Hackforth (Cambridge: Cambridge UP, 1952).

13 Fukuyama, *End of History*, 138.

14 G. W. F. Hegel, *Phenomenology of Spirit*, trans. A. V. Miller (New York: Oxford, 1977), 488.

dre Kojève.[15] However, we had the capacity – *all* of us had the capacity because we were all animated by 'spirit' – to realize those systems which would allow us the greatest freedom for reflection and allow the same for others. These advanced human history to its most conscious and humane stages. It was such a moment of self-consciousness, argued Fukuyama, that we were entering in a political sense with the revolutions of 1989–1991.

Ultimately, this gives us the central argument of *The End* – that liberal democracy 'ended' history because it recognized humanity for what it 'is': *Thymatic* and 'spirited'. Liberal democracy accorded with our desire for recognition, yet also our potential for rationality in creating, or at least recognizing, political systems which might provide that recognition as well as offer us the social contracts through which liberty might be sustained through time. This did not mean historical utopia; far from it. For Fukuyama, democracy involved conflict; it involved the expression of multiple opinions, debates over what best forms it should take, and debates over who should belong to one democratic plurality or another (the terms of state). However, any state or system which ruled through 'tyranny' (control over the individual) was bound to be overthrown. Although based on a liberation idea, which had become the nature of communism, we had reached historico-political *terminus*.

Fukuyama's idea is undoubtedly an interesting one. It is obviously open to attack from a myriad of positions – the Marxist-communist position that defenses of liberalism represent reproductions of bourgeois ideology (in other words, commentators taking Fukuyama's positions use the words 'liberal' and 'democratic' to cover up ongoing economic oppression), deconstructive positions that there really is no such thing as a human 'essence' or 'spirit', and that such things exist in language, discourse, and long-term structures of political control only, or pessimistic existentialist positions that what we built with such concepts of the self was a *techne* by which we lost being's grounding through universalizing it, and forgetting its absolute reaction and relation to its im-

---

15 See Alexandre Kojève, *Introduction to the Reading of Hegel*, trans. Allan Bloom (New York: Basic Books, 1969).

mediate surroundings and to those close communities (read: nationalistically defined) which are the true actors in history.[16] Still, Fukuyama captured something. He captured very much the spirit described by Samuel Huntington, Fukuyama's great intellectual rival in describing the nature of the post-Cold War environment, when he argued that the collapse of the Eastern Bloc 'generated ... the belief that a global democratic revolution was underway and that in short order Western concepts of human rights and Western forms of political democracy would prevail throughout the world'.[17] Huntington saw this as valuable, yes, but culturally relative (ideas of rights and democracy). Fukuyama saw them as universal; within the soul of us all, and realizable on the world stage.[18]

This does, however, lead to a significant question. Was the historical point of arrival (*terminus*) in liberal democracy? Or, was it a deeply connected political form to human nature that, at least in theory, democratic systems and liberalism helped maintain, or realize, in a practical sense? Yes, one might realize *Thymatic* individualism – one might rediscover the age-old Platonic notion of human animation, and provide it with a new rationalistic, potentially modern-scientific impetus. However, was that really what those who overthrew systems that Fukuyama saw as totalitarian, were really looking for? Was it even what Fukuyama himself was looking for? Or are we missing a term – a 'master term' in the global cultural economy, as one commentator has put it – that bridges the individual and democracy, and gives us the 'real' *terminus*, or destination for history?[19] We are missing such a term. The term is rights. It is 'human rights' specifically.

---

16 The position alluded to here is Martin Heidegger's in 'The Age of the World Picture' in *The Question Concerning Technology and Other Essays*, trans. William Lovitt (New York: Harper Torch, 1977), 115–54.

17 Samuel Huntington, *The Clash of Civilizations and the Remaking of the World Order* (New York: Free Press, 1996), 193.

18 This was the nature of the Huntington-Fukuyama debate: the world as breaking into clashing 'civilizations' or the world reaching 'consensus' on the worth of liberal democracy.

19 See Arjun Appadurai, 'Disjuncture and Difference in the Global Cultural Economy', *Theory, Culture & Society* 7 (1990): 299.

Now, the statements about rights could not be clearer in *The End* than they are. Any system of domination – and Soviet-style systems became that, for better or worse – will provide unequal recognition, at least in Fukuyama's eyes. This is a master-slave relationship a relationship between he who decides (dominates) and he who decides not (or is dominated). When such unequal relationships are realized as damaging to the *Thymatic* position of both, however – and the master, despite all his power, sits in a precarious position in a master-slave dialectic (an object of distinct hatred to the slave) – social reform is likely to come. This provides a clear goal for political society: 'universal and reciprocal recognition, where every citizen recognizes the dignity and humanity of every citizen, and where that dignity is recognized in turn through the granting of *rights*' (Fukuyama's italics).[20]

Rights - what, precisely is Fukuyama talking about? And why would we use the term *human* rights, and pose them as more likely the end of history in the political-ideological sense that Fukuyama wants to frame the idea ('end of history') than liberalism itself? Why, in fact, would rights piggyback in on liberalism's global political-ideological success, and attain the variety of discursive-hegemonic position Fukuyama suggests they do? How would *rights* form a limit to visions of history's end, and not a specific political system, like liberalism?

Very simply, the teleology of liberalism *is* rights. It is the sovereignty over the self that rights provide. It is the full modicum of self-realization that is supposed to be a human right and which is supposed to be transportable, or present, over any international boundary – at least according to almost any and all international rights regimes, specifically that provided by the United Nations in the form of the Universal Declaration of Human Rights, or what one scholar has called the international 'fountain-head' of human rights law.[21]

This is an enormously complex topic. It is complex because (a) human rights involve ranges of rights which were introduced by socialist countries and were questioned by many of the liberal democracies

---

20 Fukuyama, *End of History*, xviii.

21 Michael Freeman, *Human Rights: An Interdisciplinary Approach*, 2nd ed. (London: Polity, 2011), 4.

which Fukuyama valorizes. It is complex because (b) human rights and 'rights' are not necessarily the same. 'Rights' might be more founded in nationalistic traditions while *human* rights are founded in a distinctly post-Second World War impetus to internationalism. And the problem of human rights is complex because (c) there is a question of how we construe rights as functioning as a liminal concept in an international environment where the concept or term – its functioning as a referent in our life-world – might be every bit as present if not more so than specific discourses of 'liberalism' or 'democracy' themselves. These issues can be taken apart, however, and we can see liberalism's victory as the road to a subtle hegemony, or cultural presence, of human rights at least at a discursive, or social-ideological, level.

Usually, human rights are broken into two categories: civil and political rights, and economic, social, and cultural rights. Civil and political rights are generally liberal rights – the right to free speech, the right to equality before the law, the right to representation in political systems, the right to due process and the right to freedom of religion, opinion, and assembly. These are sometimes called 'negative rights', and they are, more or less, the right to non-interference. That is non-interference from states themselves. 'Everyone has the right to life, liberty, and security of person' asserts the third article of the Universal Declaration.[22] Civil and political rights encompass this in terms of personal choice and freedom of thought.

Economic, social and cultural rights are the more difficult of the two rights categories because they are more difficult to enforce. This is because they include the right to welfare, housing, healthcare, work, fair compensation for one's work, leisure – a distinctly socialist contribution to the rights catalogue – and the right to national self-determination and development (how, precisely, does one adjudicate about such things?). Historically, these are intensely interesting rights. They drew very clear lines of Cold War ideological battle. Initially, the Soviets and their allies objected to civil and political rights as a non-necessity in states 'where the State and the individual were in harmony', as

---

22 United Nations, 'The Universal Declaration of Human Rights', accessed April 11, 2013, http://www.un.org/en/documents/udhr/index.shtml.

the first Soviet ambassador the UN claimed – and of course, communist states claimed to be exemplary of this.[23] The United States and its allies objected to economic, social, and cultural rights as, first and foremost, unenforceable (again, how does one adjudicate when states provide enough welfare?) and secondly, potentially illiberal themselves. Here, the political-economics of liberalism became present. Freedom involved recognition. However, it also involved self-recognition in the sense of the right to dispose of one's property (or wealth) as one prefers.

How could such seemingly intractably different sets of rights be classifiable and comprehensible as *human* rights – the global extension of the universal rights concepts that Fukuyama sees as the point of liberal systems? This concerns the intricacies of political philosophy. However, utterly essential to understanding human rights is that, in many ways, liberalism – including Fukuyama's claims about it – and socialism are two sides of the same coin. Neither socialists nor liberal democrats (and socialists certainly consider themselves democratic), nor most capitalists for that matter, view themselves as undermining the *Thymatic* individual – the inalienable individual, as most rights declarations, from the American Declaration of Independence and the French Declaration of the Rights of Man and Citizen to the Universal Declaration declare as the subject of rights. This was man in his natural state. This was us – humanity – realizing all the potentials of who we are. In essence, liberal democracy – and capitalism, it must be admitted – maintain that one protects the human individual by allowing him or her to choose. Consequently, liberal democracy allows people to find the best price for their labor, to say what they wish when they wish, to constitute the terms of one's own governance, assemble with whom one would like, remain innocent until proven guilty and dispose of one's property as one wish. Socialism has no quarrel with this. What socialism does wonder about is the moment at which one is able to think clearly – when one is no longer subject to 'false conceptions', as Marx termed them in *The German Ideology*, or 'phantoms of the brain',

---

23 See Johannes Morsink, *The Universal Declaration of Human Rights: Origins, Drafting & Intent* (Philadelphia: University of Pennsylvania Press, 1999), 21.

as he described them in another choice phrase ('false consciousness', it is often called).²⁴ False consciousness can happen when one is forced to demean oneself by accepting unfair wages for 'fair work', if it might be called that. In other words, Marxism maintains that economic exploitation can turn into intellectual exploitation as economic exploitation can lead to a loss of one's sense of one's own intrinsic value. And this value, as Marx asserted – no differently than any liberal (including Fukuyama) – is no more or less than anyone else.

Does this mean that Fukuyama, or anyone advocating positions like his – that history had reached an ideological end because history had finally proved communism wrong – advocates socialist rights (economic, social, and cultural rights) in advocating 'rights'? Clearly not. It does mean, however, that rights follow quickly on the heels of questions of recognition. Any form of rights, whether they have historically socialist or historically liberal roots, engages the question of recognition. It is the means of recognition over which socialism and liberalism debate.

Nonetheless, why *human* rights? Why would human rights sift through to the global environment in a condition of historical 'ends' (*terminus*) as opposed to any other kind of right? Why not national rights? This becomes especially salient because Fukuyama poses rights in terms of states. Liberal democracy, he writes, 'recognizes' all human beings universally because it grants and protects their rights.²⁵ However, that means that 'any human child born on the territory of the United States or France or any of a number of other liberal states is by that very act endowed with certain rights of citizenship?'²⁶ Is it citizenship sufficient for thinking rights? Or do 'citizens' rights appeal to a higher, or more universal, authority – that which grounds human rights, and makes human rights the basis for any supposed rights regime?

The answer is unequivocally yes. Historically, rights unquestionably have their groundings in national contexts. As rights scholar Samu-

---

24 Karl Marx and Friedrich Engels, *The German Ideology*, ed. C. J. Arthur (New York: International, 1993), 37.

25 Fukuyama, *End of History*, 202.

26 Ibid.

el Moyn has noted, rights in their earlier manifestations – in the American Revolution, for instance, or the French Revolution, or those of 1830 (immortalized in Eugène Delacroix's 'Liberty Leading the People'), or 1848 (giving birth to an array of European constitutions) – made their appearance via the attempt of a 'whole people' to incorporate itself 'in the state'.[27] This included (for example) American attempts to break away from imperial power and claim national sovereignty (from Britain) or French attempts to imbue the social body with rights as opposed to the king's rule by divine right (*droit divin*). The appeal was to the mythical origins of rights as exceeding any national boundary, or proprietary to man in his 'natural' state. However, the practical thought was in terms of state citizens – creating 'cosmopolitan individuals' who might contribute to the state. One was seceding from national bodies (for example, in the case of the Americans) or overturning national power structures (in the case of the French – who did so radically with the beheading of Louis XVI) to create rights within a state.

National self-determination is undoubtedly within the purview of human rights. So is citizenship; 'everyone has the right to a nationality', reads the Universal Declaration's fifteenth article.[28] However, human rights represent the essence of rights. Human rights represent the 'right to have rights', as Hannah Arendt so sagely put it.[29] They ensure, or are at least intended to ensure, the universality of the recognition that not only Fukuyama, but any other advocate of rights as well, would hope to maintain. That is simply to say that to think rights is to think human rights. In an era in which the universality of rights is supposed to be more apparent than ever – an era in which a clearly rights-based discourse is supposed to be, and in fact may well be, dominant (namely, that of liberalism) – the victory of a rights-based idea organized around the fundamentals of recognition, and the *Thymicity* of the individual, if it might be called that, make human rights an apparent discourse to

---

27 Samuel Moyn, *The Last Utopia: Human Rights in History* (Cambridge, MA: Harvard Bellknap, 2010), 26.

28 See United Nations, 'The Universal Declaration of Human Rights', note 22.

29 Hannah Arendt, *The Origins of Totalitarianism* (New York: Meridian, 1958), 297.

which one may appeal. Liberalism's victory on the global stage may have blazed a trail for rights discourses. In terms of the, so to speak, 'semantic' import of political ideas, however, this meant that human rights came charging through. Liberalism – liberal democracy, or even liberal capitalism, for that matter – signifies rights. Signifying rights means signifying *human* rights. We thus assume we live in the presence of human rights. At least we assume human rights represent the 'highest moral precepts and political ideals' that we believe can be achieved.[30]

Have rights come 'charging through the door', however; do they occupy the place in our life-world – a configured space of the global cultural environment – that we say they do? Do they stand as the 'highest moral precepts and political ideas' we imagine we can achieve? Are rights a limit to the political imagination – a *terminus* of its possibilities and hence, as the 'referent' of liberalism, as such (even though 'socialist' rights sneak in the backdoor), are rights the end of history, or history's final destination in terms of the political imagination, or senses of 'political value', as it was termed in the introduction (the idea that politics has to do with values, senses of right and wrong, and essential concepts of the human being)?

World mentalities, if such things exist, are extremely difficult to evaluate. Even the most sophisticated theories of cultural globalization – arguments such as Arjun Appadurai's acknowledging the 'deeply perspectival' (and asymmetrical) nature of global cultural experiences or, or Ulrich Beck's, Anthony Giddens's and Scott Lash's – in which globalization is part of 'reflexive modernity', involving a simultaneous unification and fracturing of world experience – cannot claim to capture, in any scientific, or ultimately 'objective', sense, what everyone thinks.[31] Such concepts can only theorize experience, suggest trends, and hope that the descriptions provided by theory resonate with subjective, 'public', experience. Cultural analysis on its broadest scale –

---

30 Moyn, *The Last Utopia*, 1.

31 See Appadurai, 'Disjuncture and Difference in the Global Cultural Economy' and Ulrich Beck, Anthony Giddens and Scott Lasch, *Reflexive Modernization: Politics, Tradition and Aesthetics in the Modern Social Order* (Stanford: Stanford UP, 1994).

that which might address global political mentalities, senses of their limits and the historical imagination – are speculative. They postulate. Such varieties of analysis are what we will make here.

I will make several points. Firstly, on a historical basis, 'human rights' were a small part of American and Soviet foreign policy for the bulk of the Cold War. That is not just a matter of Cold War foreign policies as violating human rights – in Cold War 'hot spots' from Central America to Southeast Asia – but how foreign policy was posed. As Jerome J. Shestack, United Nations diplomat and former president of the American Bar Association, notes, during the Cold War, 'national interest' was the watchword of the two major superpowers.[32] Beyond the initial support for the idea in the late 1940s, contested though it was between major superpowers, 'human rights' *qua* political discourses were largely maintained by grass-roots movements through the bulk of the Cold War years. There were exceptions of course; for example, the Helsinki Accords of 1975, creating modicums of political concord between East and West, brought human rights into the halls of international politics by allowing human rights monitoring in the East. Helsinki was exceptional, however. During the Cold War, political-economic ideologies, capitalism and communism, liberalism and socialism, ruled the day.

That changed by the end of the Cold War, however. Again, liberalism's victory ushered in the age of rights – despite the fact that 'rights' are more than just liberal rights. Presiding over this change, in a sense – at least setting its tone as the leader of the world's remaining superpower – George Bush Sr. posed the upcoming era as ushering in 'a world where the United Nations, freed from cold war stalemate, is poised to fulfill the historic vision of its founders – a world in which freedom and respect for human rights find a home among all nations' (Bush's famous 'New World Order' speech to the US Congress in March 1991). As an American – as one who may have more or less used a Fukuyama-esque interpretation of history (invested in triumphal liberalism) – it may have largely been liberal rights Bush Sr. had in mind. However,

---

32 Jerome J. Shestack, 'Human Rights, the National Interest, and U.S. Foreign Policy', *Annals of the American Academy of Political and Social Sciences* 506 (1989): 17–29.

the point was the intuitive sense of liberalism's – 'democracy's' (and perhaps capitalism's) – victory: it meant rights. It meant permission to think beyond ideologies, and – in terms of the discourse of 'humanity' itself – again 'rights'.

Such ideas manifest themselves in wide ranges of foreign policy – debates over human rights (should rights reflect more liberal protections of free speech, or recognitions of global economic inequality, as third world countries still tend to advance?), or over whether we can expect countries such as China to accept Western human rights standards and, perhaps most significantly, human rights as grounds for military intervention. The latter issue is extremely complex. Often, organizations like NATO, but especially the UN, are hamstrung in their ability to intervene in international humanitarian conflicts – the genocides in Bosnia and Rwanda are perhaps the highest-profile examples of this in the last decade or two. Nonetheless, whether it is in relation to weak interventions, such as those in Bosnia or Rwanda, slightly stronger interventions, such as NATO's in Kosovo in 1999, or decidedly partisan interventions, such as NATO's UN-sanctioned intervention in Libya in 2011, 'human rights' play fundamental roles as at least *justifications* for foreign policy. This is often public justification, made openly in the media and on the world stage. This indicates that at least among significant sectors of the world population, 'human rights' is a recognizable and supposedly legitimate political standard.

Beyond foreign policy, human rights are also difficult to circumvent in entertainment and advertising, however. Indeed, potentially, the ability of human rights to *sell* things, or enter commercial culture, may be the most convincing piece to the puzzle of international, or 'global', acceptance of the idea. Today, we watch human rights movies (e.g., *Blood Diamond* and *The Interpreter*) and buy clothes that explicitly advertise the 'ideology' behind them as rights-oriented. This includes not only fair-trade goods, but wares from mainstream companies like Benetton, who have offered a number of visually striking, rights-based advertising campaigns. Arguably the most striking among them might be the 'Unhate' campaign from 2011 featuring traditional enemies at the heart of international conflicts, such as Benjamin Netanyahu and Mahmoud Abbas, or the leaders of North and South Korea, embracing in a kiss.

Indeed, few major companies, be it McDonald's, Coca-Cola or Ford Motors, present their corporate profile these days without an overture to 'social responsibility', and some description of how they try not to be globally 'unjust', supporting fundamental rights (perusing the 'opinions' section of the Coca-Cola America website, for example, one finds the company apparently highly concerned with the international status of women, republishing an article of Mary Robinson [former UN High Commissioner for human rights] about 'engaging business' in human rights, as well as a commentary from a former US State Department official on 'taking global action to fight hate').[33] Rights organizations such as Amnesty International are experiencing the highest levels of membership they have ever had. Of course, it is a radically unscientific mode of 'proof'. However, any reader is hereby challenged to turn on either the national or international news this evening or over the next several night and note if they do *not* hear the term 'human rights' used at least once. The present ideologically-discursive situation is radically different from the international reality at the height of the Cold War, when the talk was on 'communism', 'socialism', 'democracy', and 'capitalism'.

Are we precisely experiencing a cultural saturation of human rights? Would human rights be avoidable as an ideological referent if we tried to avoid it? It is difficult to say. One could argue, of course, that the prominence of rights discourse in business, advertising, and entertainment is a Western phenomenon – it relies on cultures of development and on levels of 'hyper-capitalist' society where consumers can fool themselves into thinking they support global justice by seeing a movie., It also relies on the world's impoverished and politically oppressed having little time for rights, concerned, as they are, with survival. All this is of course true. Human rights may not figure into

---

33 See Melanne Verveer and Kim Azzarelli, 'At Davos Investing in Women Emerges as a Business Strategy', accessed April 12, 2013, http://www.coca-colacompany.com/opinions/at-davos-investing-in-women-emerges-as-a-business-strategy; Farah Pandith, 'Taking Global Action to Fight Hate', accessed April 12, 2013, http://www.coca-colacompany.com/opinions/taking-global-action-to-fight-hate; and Mary Robinson, 'Engaging Business in Human Rights', accessed April 12, 2013, http://www.coca-colacompany.com/opinions/engaging-business-in-human-rights.

the intellectual or cultural self-conception of all of the world's peoples on an equal basis, or each of the world's people (as individuals) on the same equal basis. 'Rights' may not be the first words out of every person's lips in the morning, and rights organizations may not be viewed favorably by every individual, regime, or global culture. As the recent wave of pro-democracy protests in North Africa and the Middle East shows, however, rights may figure *precisely* into the midst of the discourses of the politically oppressed – human rights are an expectation on an increasingly international basis. Activism takes place in relation to a wide range of culturally-based practices (female genital circumcision, for example). This is activism based not only in the West (the 2013 Berlin Film Festival, for example, was disrupted by protestors concerned with precisely this issue), but also in the communities in which those practices are to be found – from Mali to Niger to Guinea.[34] Undoubtedly, discourses of rights, liberalism, democracy, justice, equality, and social progress are closely connected. It is, however, the universalistic rights imagination, the positing of rights as human – and the idea that there might be a universal recognition, or legitimacy to such an idea – that seems to form the outer limit of contemporary political culture. By political culture, I mean the manifestation of our self-images in a space we might call global culture, or the space of a global 'life-world' itself.

The meanings of history's end – as well as the end of political-ideological battle on the world stage – are debatable. Though they refer predominantly to 'postmodernization', or the rise of a global aesthetic of 'pastiche' and truncated senses of time, or cultural demands for immediacy, brought by changes in technology, labor practices and the end of modern art, the theorization of the irrelevance (or at least increasing irony) of the idea of 'history', has been acknowledged for some time now. We might like to tell a global story, goes the argument, or provide some sense of 'humanity'. However, we do not know how to. The modern idea of progress has been lost.

---

[34] Concerning on-the-ground, local, human rights activism in a range of global locales, see D. Soyini Madison, *Acts of Activism: Human Rights as Radical Performance* (Cambridge: Cambridge UP, 2010).

On the other hand, it can be posited that history has ended because, in fact, the human story has been realized. This might not be in the sense of a historical utopia – in which human rights have been realized, the world's people live in peace and mutual respect, and all peoples are given the political and economic opportunities to realize themselves. However, it might be in terms of the notion that at least we know the meaning of the human story – we know where it *should* go. Fukuyama made a convincing argument in 1992 – one that maintains resonance today. Liberal democracy has attained a kind of victory. Even alternative, outlier regimes from those of Chavez's Venezuela to the Castro brothers' Cuba, have to posit their continued reference to an outmoded ideology – socialism or 'communism' – as a mode of resistance against a globally dominant set of presumptions: that liberalism provides human freedom, and it is within the sinews of liberal politics (liberal democracy) and liberal economics (capitalism) that one finds rights. The irony is that such concepts are not precisely true. Liberalism provides rights. At least it conceives of itself as doing so, and attempts to do so. Its methods of sustaining the 'natural', unalienated individual and his or her 'spiritiual' (*Thymatic*) freedom might be called into doubt. That they attempt to preserve *Thymatic* freedom, precisely as Fukuyama indicates they do, however, is undoubtedly the case.

This, however, is the point. A world in which liberalism has won – in which it constitutes the end of history (*terminus*), even if that end does not designate utopia – is not only, or perhaps not at all, about liberalism, democracy, capitalism, equal opportunity, or justice themselves. It is a world concerned with rights. It is a world in which a set of ideas posited as natural, inalienable, and inseparable from the human being itself are not simply posed as but are *assumed* to be victorious. In this way, the meanings of contemporary politics and historical evolution need to be rethought. *Terminus* does concern a 'consensus' about liberalism after the Cold War. More powerfully, however, it concerns the idea of rights – *human* rights – as outlining our senses of ultimate political possibility. Human rights represent the ultimate point of appeal in terms of what it means to live politically, and the teleology of the construction and development of political systems.

SUBURBAN APOCALYPSE: THE HAUNTED HOUSE OF CAPITALISM

Steen Christiansen

A number of recent horror films have returned to the trope of the haunted house to reveal the anxieties over becoming house-poor; buying into a lifestyle which then disappears. Films such as the *Paranormal Activity* series (2009, 2010, and 2011) insist on the disruption of the hyperhouse as a doomed endeavor, one replete with economic disaster as well as family breakdown. In the *American Horror Story* television series (produced by Ryan Murphy & Brad Falchuk in 2011), we find the most extreme example of a family unable to move out of 'Murder House' because of the downsized economy, and the result is that the wife is raped by a ghost in order to give birth, it seems, to the Antichrist.

    This paper will argue for a re-evaluation of the haunted-house film as one which sees the current economic crisis as an apocalyptic moment, destroying the picture-perfect dreams of the American family with their own house, SUV and 50" plasma TV. 'Moment' should here be understood in Frank Kermode's sense of a cultural environment rife with other themes such as decadence and empire, all brought together in the myth of apocalypse.[1] In the US, this moment can then only be sublimated into the breakdown of the family, much as it happened in the 1970s. 'It is easier to imagine the end of the world than it is to

---

[1] Frank Kermode, *The Sense of an Ending: Studies in the Theory of Fiction with a New Epilogue* (Oxford: Oxford UP, 2000), 28.

imagine the end of capitalism', as Mark Fisher has put it.[2] The dictum becomes the central thesis of his book *Capitalist Realism* in which our current moment is presented as an Eternal Now where there is No Alternative. There is also a sneaking suspicion that maybe, just maybe, the world has in fact already ended because our current crisis has become the norm; we are living in an unexceptional state of exception. There remains, however, an anxiety buried in the normalization of this crisis, something which comes back. This paper extends from the concept of hauntology, a field extending from Jacques Derrida's use in *Specters of Marx* (1996). Rather than focusing on the traumatic, hidden past that has been ignored, such as Jeffrey Weinstock suggests in *Spectral America*,[3] here the emphasis is on the one history which can never be ignored or forgotten: one's credit history.

In this perspective, the household economy becomes an image of society's household economy. Consequently, I am really talking about a social ecology represented on and in a screen ecology – ecology coming from the Greek word *oikos* for home/household and – '*-logy*' meaning 'the study of'. So, I propose to study screen representations of homes in order to understand the US social household. In this way I draw on what Kermode calls consonance between fictional plots and the way we make sense of the world. My paper, then, fits in with a larger tradition of studying the tendency 'of the American suburb to convert the rights and privileges of living there into spiritual, cultural, and political problems of displacement, in which being white and middle class is imagined to have as much or more to do with subjugation as with social dominance'.[4] Different times articulate different concerns of how the house becomes home and vice versa, and the haunted houses dealt with here emphasize economic and financial subjugation of the white middle class.

---

2 Mark Fisher, *Capitalist Realism* (Hampshire: Zero Books, 2009), 2.

3 Jeffrey Andrew Weinstock, *Spectral America: Phantoms and the National Imagination* (Madison, WI: University of Wisconsin Press, 2004), 5.

4 Catherine Jurca, *White Diaspora: The Suburb and the Twentieth-Century American Novel* (Princeton, NJ: Princeton UP, 2001), 4.

The apocalypses that I deal with are therefore not blockbuster spectacles full of fire, brimstone, and CGI such as the *The Core* (2003), *The Day After Tomorrow* (2004), *2012* (2009), or *Battle: Los Angeles* (2011). The end of the ghost films I speak of, however, is always peculiarly bloodless and anti-climactic, rarely visually excessive but instead subdued and subtle. These films are dominated by interior shots, with very few scenes set outside the domestic setting of the house. The apocalyptic end is rather an entropic end of winding down slowly, as well as a lumbering on. The end has always-already happened and remains yet-to-come. As we move into the second decade of the 21st century, it is becoming evident that the apocalypse of our time is not a nuclear bang but a financial whimper. My use of the concept of the end is therefore at once cultural, historical, and economic. I argue that an economic downturn is registering in popular culture and that one way to understand the meaning of this economic downturn, as it registers for people, is to examine these cultural products.

I wish to make a couple of banal observations here about the apocalypse and the end and how they relate to an American household. Banal because how much more can be said about the current economic crisis, which originated in the US but has since rippled all over the world? Is this state of crisis simply the perpetuating logic of capitalism, a crisis created to sustain that favorite capitalist game known as creative destruction? A crisis, as Kermode tells us, is one way of structuring what cannot be structured: in imagining an end for the world we are categorizing a pattern on something which is not ordered – the flow of time – but which is turned into history through this categorization. Such a narrative understanding of the apocalypse provides security and comfort because it controls our perception of time and makes sense of time as something which has a beginning, a middle, and an end. And so the economic apocalypse we are all living through becomes an ordering mechanism for why we must go out and spend in order to postpone the economic collapse waiting for us, right there at the end of our credit limit.

If there is any logic to this scheme of perpetual spending to stave off the apocalypse – and I'm not saying there is – maybe it comes from recognizing that the apocalyptic is not a state of affairs but a mode of thought, as Evan Calder Williams argues in *Combined and Uneven Apocalypse*. In this sense, the financial crisis becomes a way for us to conceive of the world but more insidiously than that, it becomes a misapprehending the world, suggesting that the crisis was inevitable yet unpredictable, no one's fault yet the result of our own choices. Thought of in this way, a crisis is a force that gives us meaning and the apocalyptic mode we find in recent haunted-house films works exactly as a way of thinking about the current economic crisis. Williams's argument is that the late capitalist system has become apocalyptic in itself because it has an inherent state of entropy built into it. I believe that this is revealed by the current financial crisis and is best explained by the going-awry of what George Bataille has called 'the accursed share'.

Bataille defines this phrase as a necessary, wasteful expenditure, enacted to release the pressure in a growing system. He argues that such release is necessary no matter what, because:

> [t]he living organism, in a situation determined by the play of energy on the surface of the globe, ordinarily receives more energy than is necessary for maintaining life; the excess energy (wealth) can be used for the growth of a system (e.g., an organism); if the system can no longer grow, or if the excess cannot be completely absorbed in its growth, it must necessarily be lost without profit; it must be spent, willingly or not, gloriously or catastrophically.[5]

There are two important things in Bataille's definition. The first is that he considers any system which grows as parallel to a living system – hence he implicitly equates capitalism with a living organism. The second interesting aspect of Bataille's definition is that excess wealth must be spent whether or not the system wills it, and it can happen catastrophically. What I believe we are experiencing is that all of a sudden excess wealth is tied up into real estate from which it can no

---

5 Georges Bataille, *The Accursed Share*, vol. 1, *Consumption* (Brooklyn, NY: Zone Books, 1988), 21.

longer be spent, since the housing bubble has burst and the inflated wealth created by credit and loans has disappeared. What happens, then, is that massive amounts of wealth have vanished thereby creating a vacuum.

Bataille describes what occurs when surplus wealth cannot be spent: 'For if we do not have the force to destroy the surplus energy ourselves, it cannot be used, and, like an unbroken animal that cannot be trained, it is this energy that destroys us; it is we who pay the price of the inevitable explosion'.[6] What happens when surplus wealth vanishes in a puff of smoke? I believe it does not explode but implodes instead, creating pockets of devastation in the suburban landscape, pockets which are filled with the lingering traces of that surplus wealth come back to haunt the inhabitants. I will attempt to show how this imploded wealth creates haunted houses before I turn to the question of how this implosion of wealth creates a society which understands its own historical moment as a perpetual crisis.

We have, of course, already seen catastrophic spending occur in the wars on Afghanistan and Iraq, but more than just these conventional wars we have also experienced the occurrence of a new kind of war with the war on terror. The war on terror is a war which cannot be won and instead only generates a perpetual crisis. This wasteful spending has not helped the organism of capitalism grow in the typical manner but rather added to the vacuum of the burst housing bubble, rushing to fill the void with all manners of traumas. While none of the haunted house films explicitly engage with war, it is evident that they are all filled with a fatigue which is not after the orgy but after the war – yet the war lingers. The coming-back of all these terrors creates an unquiet house filled with anxiety and the retreat into magnificent houses seemed like a way to escape and block the uncanny return of the debt crisis. The houses, however, were not vehicles of escape but structures of confinement. The escape from the wasteland of capitalism into McMansions failed precisely because the McMansions constitute the wasteland of capitalism; huge structures built on rickety foundations. The catastrophic war

---

6 Ibid., 24.

spending therefore ends up not releasing the pressure and helping the capitalist organism grow, but is instead implicitly revealed to end up as a cancerous growth on the capitalist ecology.

Houses are interesting constructions filled with what it means to be human, for one of the defining aspects of a house is that it not only houses but also is, in the words of Mark Wigley, 'a mechanism of representation'.[7] What these recent haunted-house films signify is an ongoing attempt to domesticate the house and thereby control the surplus wealth put into them. However, the very fact that the houses are haunted reveals that these houses and the surplus wealth is very much not domesticated and is perfectly happy to bring about the end of life as we know it. As Barry Curtis points out, '[h]ouses are deeply implicated with humanity, and yet they are not human. The tensions arising from that anomaly stress other borders and distinctions in ways that activate acute anxieties'.[8]

The houses we find in these recent ghost films are on the whole hyperhouses, which interestingly means that they have no real history. The ghosts who inevitably haunt them are therefore young restless spirits, tied more to people than places. Interestingly, one thing which unites many haunted-house stories, recent or otherwise, is the idea of illicit ownership and rightful inheritance.[9] As haunted houses always inscribe a relationship between past, present, and future, it is surprisingly clear that the ownership of these hyperhouses is illicit and not only the result of past transgressions but also indicative of future worries and troubles – in this case, the foreboding and inevitably impending capitalist catastrophe. What happens is that the house under capitalist catastrophe 'grows hard', as Benjamin Noys puts it, in the form

---

7 Mark Wigley, *The Architecture of Deconstruction: Derrida's Haunt* (Cambridge, MA: MIT Press, 1995), 163.

8 Curtis, Barry, *Dark Places: The Haunted House in Film* (London: Reaktion Books, 2009), 10–11.

9 Ibid., 34.

of an unpayable mortgage.¹⁰ Not only has value become detached from use but as the equity of these houses dies, we find a terrifying ghost returning as the houses end up possessing the owners, rather than the other way around.

These films are apocalyptic in the way they center on a concrete crisis but the way out is either impossible or can only come about by releasing the surplus wealth. If we try to understand these films in the light of Kermode's typology of apocalyptic fictions – empire, decadence and renovation, progress, and catastrophe – we see that these films are primarily of the catastrophic variety, even when we might think that they might hold a kind of renovation.¹¹ I will return to this idea of problematic renovation, but first look at the catastrophic variety. Here it makes sense to point out the difference between our concepts of crisis, catastrophe, and apocalypse. For most apocalyptic fictions, the crisis event is a revelatory event which carries with it a clarification of things. The crisis is an expected expression of the inevitable apocalypse and as such is only a transitory state. Catastrophe, however, is what Williams calls an 'end without revelation, a historical void, an end of the road that cannot point beyond itself'.¹² It is this catastrophic mode which the recent haunted-house films are placed within. There is no alternative or difference, only the undifferentiated continuation of the world as usual.

The relationship between structure and inhabitant for the couple living in the hyperhouse of *Paranormal Activity* is not simply one of past transgressions (as explored in the third film) but also a living beyond their means. The film opens memorably on a big-screen media center playing a music video of Disgorge's 'Consume the Forsaken' which has suitably demonic lyrics while also tying together consumption and ethical devastation. We find in this opening shot a conflation of the screen

---

10 Benjamin Noys, '"Grey in Grey": Crisis, Critique, Change', *Journal of Critical Globalisation Studies* 1 (2011): 49, accessed October 4, 2012, http://www.doaj.org/doaj?func=abstract&id=743040.

11 Kermode, *The Sense of an Ending*, 29.

12 Evan Calder Williams, *Combined and Uneven Apocalypse* (Hampshire: Zero Books, 2011), 4.

and the demonic, a conflation which I take to be symptomatic both of anxieties of the screen but more specifically of the anxieties of consumption. Right after the opening shot, Micah carries the camera to the front door where his girlfriend arrives home in a cute little convertible. All the signs of comfortable middle-class wealth are established, while at the same time the neighborhood itself is 'established': all the houses look identical, part of the same tract construction project. Conformity and consumption are established immediately before we move indoors and never leave again.

Katie is clearly annoyed with the camera and its size, finding it to be an intrusion on their life. When she insists on being told how much the camera cost, Micah chooses not to answer. The couple's house is awash in all manner of anonymous and bland consumer goods; the big-screen TV, the media center in the den, Micah's work station with multiple monitors and of course the cameras he bought, the tri-pod, the FireWire to connect the camera to his laptop, etc. Everything tells the story of suburban living in all its blandness and sameness; there is no history to the house, nor to the objects they own. There is a strong sense of conspicuous consumption here, in that the couple acquires objects and commodities simply for the objects' own sake, which we can also see as possession in its own right.

We learn early on that Micah is a day trader, which ties the film into the unstable financial flows of network capitalism, since the function of a day trader is to navigate financial flows and ebbs over the course of a day, in order to sell and make money through a fast turnaround. Day traders therefore subsist primarily on bubbles, where there is a constant increase in stocks, bonds, and other investment opportunities. The work of a day trader is precarious and risky and the couple's precarious economic situation is emphasized throughout the film, both jokingly and seriously. When Katie and Micah decide to contact a psychic to help with their troubles, Micah offhandedly asks if maybe the psychic will have any good tips for the stock market. While clearly a simple joke it also reveals something about the unpredictable nature of finance capital and the idea that one needs to be a psychic to do well. More troubling is the deeper correlation between Micah's investments and the supernatural presence in their house. As the demonic presence grows stronger and more dangerous, Micah starts to lose money and while he claims that he will make it all back again, inevitably the demonic presence becomes a parallel to the inherently treacherous investment markets.

The point is that Katie and Micah are established as a typical American couple, a couple who overextend their credit rating, live on risky day trading contingent on bubbles rising through the economy, and are fully enmeshed in this hyper-consumerist lifestyle of tract hyperhouses filled with all the latest gadgets – it is this over-consumptive lifestyle which comes back to haunt them in the form of the demonic presence. The demonic presence is never revealed or explained in this film or the later films so far. Instead, the film ends with Micah being killed, which he must be as punishment for his day trading sins; he is part of the problem of the capitalist catastrophe taking place. This 2007 film thereby anticipates the crash, which everyone saw coming but did nothing about. Tellingly, however, there is no indication that the demonic presence has been vanquished. The film sports several different endings; in one version Katie is evidently possessed by the demon and leaves the house, her whereabouts unknown. In another, Katie is possessed but killed by police officers.

As in so many horror films, evil remains uncontained and free to wreak its havoc in later sequels. Interestingly, although there are three more films in the series and a fifth on its way, the first follow-ups are not chronological sequels but rather prequels of one variety or another. *Paranormal Activity 2* takes place two months before the first film and opens significantly on what appears to be a burglary which will later be revealed to be the demonic presence. Kristi, the sister of Katie, and her husband Daniel install security cameras to catch the burglars but things never pan out in that direction. Here we find another example of how the demonic domestic disturbance is connected to that of wealth. The house intrusion is the origin of the haunting and the time when the house becomes unsafe. What we also see is that the couple is not to blame, the intrusion is wholly external and, unlike the first *Paranormal Activity*, neither have jobs that deserve punishment. Tellingly, Kristie and Daniel are killed by Katie who suddenly rushes into their house and murders them both. Here the violent end is associated with the day trader couple and once again the film ends with Katie on the loose, whereabouts unknown.

Evil remains uncontained in the third film (also a prequel) and the fourth installment carries on the apocalyptic tone of the earlier film, so we may imagine the end of these couples but there is no resolution in terms of the demonic presence, nor is there any kind of attempt of progression or systemic change. These films do suggest that conspicuous consumption, bubble economy, and suburban lifestyle in general are based on problematic foundations where the cracks will come back to haunt the inhabitants, and the problem is considered external to the inhabitants and the houses themselves. The houses end up as mechanisms representing the unstable economic situation and while we do get a distinct sense of catastrophe there is no solution, only an enfolding of an apocalyptic wasteland onto suburbia. Suburbs were originally meant to be utopias, free from the worries of the inner city core – 'perhaps the most radical rethinking of the relation between residence and the city in the history of domestic architecture'.[13] Suburbs are meant to be spaces free of radical otherness, free of society's 'undesirables', as Robert M. Fogelson puts it in *Bourgeois Nightmares*, pointing out that 'it was not what they did, no matter how appropriate, or how they behaved, no matter how respectable, that made them undesirable. It was just who they were'.[14] Historically, this has primarily centered on race, but class divisions have also been part of being undesirable. The irony exposed in *Paranormal Acitivity* is that we are all potentially undesirable in the eyes of capitalism; admitted into a suburban utopia when our credit rating is good, cast out when our credit rating falters.

Turning to a more explicitly apocalyptic case, *American Horror Story* portrays a family which moves into an inexplicably inexpensive house in order to pick up the pieces of their broken family, ironically named the Harmons. As it turns out, the house is massively haunted, with at

---

13 Robert Fishman, *Bourgeois Utopias: The Rise and Fall of Suburbia* (New York, NY: Basic Books, 1987), 3.

14 Robert M. Fogelson, *Bourgeois Nightmares: Suburbia, 1870-1930* (New Haven, CT, and London: Yale UP, 2007), 125.

least one ghost from each decade the house has existed since the 1920s. As such, the house does not exactly tie into the hyperhouse framework, but it does connect to the housing bubble because the previous owners were in the process, before they were murdered, of flipping the house, that is renovating it with an eye to selling it for a large profit. Because of the housing slump they were unable to do so and so the Harmons can buy a house they could otherwise never afford. The accursed share ends up being precisely what haunts the Harmons, as they cannot leave the house once the hauntings become too intense since they have ended up on the edge of foreclosure. The Harmons are able to pay the mortgage but unable to suffer the economic loss that would come from selling the house at a loss.

This fact raises significant issues of ownership; as Curtis points out, haunted houses are both possessed and possessing which is clearly the case once the Harmons find themselves unable to move out of the house.[15] Symbolically, the house now owns them as much as they own it. That the ghostly inhabitants are also part and parcel of this dual ownership becomes obscenely clear in the case of the rape of Vivien (Connie Britton), the wife of the couple, especially as she becomes pregnant with twins – one the child of her husband Ben (Dylan McDermott) and the other that of one of the ghosts of the house, Tate (Evan Peters). Not only does this suggest that Vivien is now somewhat wedded to the house, it is also revealed that Vivien might very well give birth to the Antichrist.

Thus we find the final outcome of the accursed share coming home to roost: the end of the world will come about as a result of the Harmons being unable to leave, which in itself is a result of them being near foreclosure, which again is a result of the previous owners being unable to flip the house. In other words, the accursed share has become inverted and haunting. The excess energy of the house (i.e., capital) cannot be spent because it is tied up in the house. This inability to spend the excess energy is precisely what causes social entropy and chaos and in the case of these ghost stories reveals a terrifying fact: when it becomes impossible for us to expend the excess wealth in the

---

15 Curtis, *Dark Places*, 66.

form of consumption – eating, death, or sex – the ecology of the house will reverse and we are the ones who will be consumed.

Will (Daniel Craig) in *Dream House* is the victim of a house invasion where his family is killed. Despite being suspected of murdering his own family, it is revealed at the end that a burglar was in fact the killer. Although Will fails in his patriarchal duties to protect his family from harm, they forgive him, and so he is absolved of any wrongdoing, going on to write a book about the events and thus profit from his misery. As far as the house goes, we see a picture-perfect hyperhouse with all the latest accessories and a happy family living a happy life. What is revealed is that the house is in ruins, boarded up, and broken down. This dichotomy can only serve to activate the imagery of hundreds of foreclosed houses around the US and the nostalgic past of how this should look. It is the myth of the ideal home revealed to be a tragedy. As Curtis points out:

> 'The Ideal Home' is a complex ecology of past and present, interior and exterior, configuring a resolved relationship between structure and inhabitant. The haunted house is a scenario of confrontation between the narrative of the inhabitants and the house. What haunts it is the symptom of a loss – something excessive and un-resolved in the past that requires an intervention in the present.[16]

But what is required in terms of intervention of the present, is not simply the traumatic events of the murder of Will's family, but a reintegration into financial stability. Will serves as an emblematic image of the man who has lost everything and lives a life on the dregs of society, scraping by only at the mercy of others. He must leave this life behind and reintegrate back into society. On the one hand, then, the tragedy and economic ruin which has befallen Will is clearly marked to not be his fault – instead something terrible from the outside has happened to him making him a victim of circumstances beyond his control. On the

---

16 Ibid., 34.

other, however, the only way to move on – transition, in other words – is to feed back into the game of economic growth: he writes a bestseller. Thus the film reveals a disturbingly reactionary thrust which does not blame the game but instead what might be called a few rotten apples; the only way out isn't to blame the cause for one's misery but to drag oneself up by the bootstraps and get back in the game.

This ending thus seems to promise some form of restoration but it should also be relatively clear that Will does not truly progress but rather returns to his old ways. The restoration which can be said to take place is Will recovering from the trauma of losing his family and getting their forgiveness. Certainly the film wants to present this as a relatively happy ending, whereas my point is that there is no real cultural progression. Will feeds back into the system and manages to get out of his poor conditions by publishing his memoirs. His trauma is thereby commercialized and helps him generate surplus wealth but of a catastrophic variety.

My argument is not that the film necessarily should present an economically progressive agenda although I do claim that its failure to do so is telling. There is no way out, only a way back into the apocalyptic machinery. The solution is not to change the system but to find a new way to generate capital. Here we find a perfect example of Fisher's dictum that there is an alternative, that the world may end and our families die in which case the only resolution is to write a bestseller about it. In other words, experiences only make sense, are only real experiences, if they can be packaged, marketed, and sold for a profit. In this way, no one cares about the experiences of the disenfranchised, since these experiences cannot be capitalized upon. Or more insidiously, the disenfranchised should not complain or desire to overthrow the system; all they have to do is write memoirs of their experiences. If they do this, they will end up like Will, back in a nice house with a nice hardwood floor, forgiven by their families just like Will is, for of course, after all, it was never really Will's fault at all.

These arguments are of course paradoxical and opposing. If Will was never to blame for what happened, if all that befell him truly came from an outside system, this would seem to suggest that the system itself is faulty and should be fixed or thrown out. Yet *Dream House* never even looks in that direction, instead insisting that all Will needs to do is get over his loss, accept that shit happens, and start to feed back into the system. One person might be at fault (Elias Koteas as the home invader) but not the system. The system is not wrong, and in fact Will himself desires to get back into the system, not to reject it. Will's delusional fantasy is that he and his family have just moved into a new, wonderful house. The house is as central to his desires as his family is; Will does not simply want his family back, he wants his house back. He wants his house to forgive him, to accept him back into a lush interior, not the rotten carcass it actually is. Will's house, then, is in fact the monster Will tries to please and we may regard it, significantly, as not just the house that Will built in his mind but in fact the unquiet house of capitalism.

What does it mean to live in a world where the end has already happened? This seems to be the hidden question in these recent films, of which I have only discussed a small sample. It is not that the world in itself seems particularly ravaged or destroyed, but rather that everything is new. The houses lived in are never old – only in *American Horror Story* do they hold any kind of secretive past, but even that past is shallow; the most active ghost is from the 1990s, a murderous pastiche of Kurt Cobain. The most telling fact is that there is no change; the past, the present, and whatever we might think of as the future all blur together in the same suburban routine. Katie and Micah might no longer live in their tract/hyperhouse but someone else will move in and lead a life indistinguishable from theirs. The same goes for *American Horror Story* whose final episode reveals new inhabitants undergoing the same transformation. There is change but it is trivial, it is not a transformation. The system moves toward entropy and reveals the disturbing fact that maybe even our safe suburban zones will turn into what Williams refers to as

> hellish zones of the world, whole populations destroyed in famine and sickness, 'humanitarian' military interventions, the basic and unincorporable fact of class antagonism, closure of access to common resources, the rendering of mass

culture more and more banal, shifting climate patterns and the "natural" disasters they bring about, the abandonment of working populations and those who cannot work in favor of policies determined only to starkly widen wealth gaps.[17]

Many of these events have already occurred, even though the whole point of suburbia was to keep such terrors out. What is interesting about this current historical moment is that there is none of the millennial mysticism to supply and feed our apocalyptic imagination. Rather, we could easily argue that we are at the beginning of an age, the glorious new world of the 21st century, and so, having survived the end of the world in the year 2000 as well as the Y2K bug, we ought to live in a time of restoration and joy. As it turns out, this is not where we are. Instead, we are facing what some have hastily called the end of capitalism, but what seems to be simply another turn of the screw of finance capitalism. As such, it seems that this apocalypse is not an end, nor is it a beginning. None of the films discussed here show any kind of finality or sense of change; they remain more of the same. What they reveal is a concern not about the end of the world but about the end of Western wealth; symbolized by the hyperhouse and imagined as haunted because the foundation is not so quiet as could be wished for. As we see in the other contributions in this collection, the end is usually the beginning of something new. Yet that is simply not the case here.

What really seems to be the apocalypse here is the poverty of these films' imagination. Even after the end of people's personal world (trauma, loss, etc.) the world lingers on with no change to show for it. These films therefore are part of Fisher's basic argument that there is no alternative. What they reveal is the certainty that the terrifying return of the catastrophic accursed share really only creates a permanent state of crisis; an unexceptional state of exception. As Benjamin Noys points out:

---

17 Williams, *Combined and Uneven Apocalypse*, 8.

> While crisis gives traction to critique, and would classically seem to promise the moment of change, the strategic elements that would re-articulate critique with agency are lacking. Instead of a tracing of the opaque stasis of the present, the almost horrifying fact that 'things as they are' remain as such, faith is retained in the old models of dynamism.[18]

The problem for Noys and for the haunted house films that I have discussed here is that there are no alternate concepts with which to critique our perpetuating crisis: 'our supposedly critical concepts of *exit* from capitalism – freedom, difference, excess, the multiple, and flight – all too often lead back *in* to capitalism'.[19] This holds true for the films as well; they have no way out but what is more, most of them do not even wish to find a way out. *Dream House* can only imagine feeding back into the system, while *Paranormal Activity* sees suburbia as a space fraught with dangers, though rather than advocating escape, trading up to bigger and better houses is what it prescribes: escape through conformity. This poverty of the imagination reveals not only the obvious fact that these films in themselves are reactionary but also that our current historical moment is in itself reactionary and incapable of imagining any form of alternative. If even concepts and words such as deceleration, vacuum, withering, and undeath are all subsumed into the same inescapable crisis, then where might our new vocabulary come from which will lead us out of this crisis?

It is not that we should expect mainstream culture to be the place where revolutionary politics emerge but it is interesting that while these films have no problems decoding the predicament we are in, we find no utopian or revelatory moment. In this way, the apocalyptic imagination has failed, the crisis reveals itself to not be a distinguishing moment but rather a situation of permanent catastrophe. Even other films far removed from the haunted-house genre reveals the fact that there is no alternative. *Margin Call* (2011), a film about an investment bank's decision about what to do just at the beginning of the financial crisis,

---

18 Noys, 'Grey in Grey', 55.
19 Ibid, 55, italics in the original.

tells us explicitly what to do in case your choice is either to act morally or take the money: the better option is always to take the money. To the extent that mainstream fictions often end up as faithful manifestations of basic ideological forms, their silence on what comes after capitalist catastrophe is very telling. There is no alternative for these fictions and so all they can do is imagine and represent the end as a state of ongoing, permanent catastrophe. This lack of even an imaginary solution to capitalist catastrophe might prove to be the real end.

THE END: AESTHETIC AND LUDIC TOPOI IN DIGITAL ENTERTAINMENT

Alessandro Canossa and Gordon Calleja

Whether it is the end of humanity, the end of the world or, more ominously, the end of the universe, terminality is one of the most recurring tropes in digital games. Although we are using the term 'trope' here, it is important to note that terminality does not only figure thematically in digital games, but also in the mechanical functions that distinguish them, at least formally, from other media. The end, in games, is not just a theme or a setting for a story, but also a very concrete part of the transaction between players and game: every mistake and every action undertaken could spell the death of the avatar and the end of the play experience. Before dealing with how digital games treat the concept of terminality, it is necessary to clarify some fundamental differences between ludic and traditional entertainment.

According to Espen Aarseth, traditional entertainment exists as a complete artifact in and by itself; the narrative exists a priori, without requiring an audience.[1] The same cannot be said about digital interactive entertainment in general or computer games in particular. Games require in fact an active effort from the player to come into being. Without players, computer games only exist as sets of unrealized potentials in the form of zeroes and ones. Even loading *Super Mario Bros.* on a computer would just cast the Italian plumber in an endless idle loop, unless a player started pressing some buttons. User interaction, the act

---

1 Espen Aarseth, *Cybertext: Perspectives on Ergodic Literature* (Baltimore: Johns Hopkins UP, 1997).

of playing, is necessary in order to actualize the possibilities. This initial premise allows the understanding of games as bi-univocal and asymmetrical sign systems. Frans Mäyrä defined games as sign systems, since they are able to carry meaning on two levels.[2] In fact, games contain both symbolic representations (audiovisual, aesthetic elements) and affordances for gameplay performance (ludic codes).

Games are produced by designers that embed aesthetic and ludic codes in the artifact in order to engender experiences for the players. Defining games as bi-univocal sign systems means that the communication flow 'designer>game>player' is, in fact, reversible. Not only do designers provide ludic and aesthetic codes for players to experience, but players utilize these codes in a personal manner. They express themselves, leaving tangible trails for designers. In fact, every action undertaken by players in a game is potentially traceable and designers often look at these play traces to understand how players experienced a certain game. These play traces take the form of game variables recorded remotely by the system and available to designers for analysis with the purpose of understanding the behavior of players and constantly improving or adapting the game. For example, designers have access to information such as players' favorite areas, preferred characters, action performed most often, etc. The asymmetrical nature of this exchange is due to the very different sets of signs available to players and designers. While designers can conjure almost any aesthetic element (in the form of settings, objects, and characters) and ludic affordance (in the form of possible actions), players are constrained to choose to perform only those actions which are available to them. Designers select the set pieces and prepare the scenario; players make the final choice on how to bring the story to life.

Aesthetic codes consist of those elements that emerge from the sensory-perceptual qualities of the world such as navigation patterns, landscape backdrops, sound cues, and viewing ranges; they describe where the avatar can go, what he/she can hear and see, and as such they are of a spatial-temporal nature (where and when). The aesthetic

---

2 Frans Mäyrä, *An Introduction to Game Studies* (Thousand Oaks: SAGE Publications, 2008).

elements comprise, for example, colors, textures, shapes, lights, ambient sounds, and music; that is, modes of sensory engagement manifest in perception. Perception is here intended in the acceptation posited by Walter Benjamin as *Erlebnis*, one of the two meanings of the term 'experience': a particular sensation that does not create a greater whole but is isolated, categorical, and pre-rational.[3] Perceptions are events that do not prompt cognitive appraisal. Similarly, the effects of aesthetic affordances are mostly unconscious. Just as the soothing effects of relaxing music they affect moods more than emotions.

Ludic codes afford all the actions that players can undertake such as opening doors, re-loading weapons, casting spells, conversing with non-playing characters, and changing clothes. In this way, they define what players can do, and as such they are of a causal-temporal nature (what and when). It is by acting on these elements that players can express interaction attitudes. Interacting with ludic affordances does require conscious activity and eventually leads to the creation of experience in a second acceptation of the term, corresponding to Benjamin's *Erfahrung*: wisdom gained in subsequent reflection on events or interpretation of them. Ludic affordances tend to imply rational, conscious decisions that have an impact on emotions more than moods.

Narration, the story, sits as a beam across the two pillars of ludic and aesthetic affordances. Conversely, from the player's point of view, it is possible to select among the equally optimal arrays of possibilities to express a certain in-game behavior. Players' in-game behavior can be gauged through both qualitative and quantitative methods: game telemetry, metrics, surveys, interviews, think-aloud practices, observation, and videos.

One of the marks of successful game design is the ability to inextricably bind ludic and aesthetic codes so that actions 'belong' to the place where they are performed without necessarily prescribing events that are beyond the players' control and therefore remove agency from players.

---

3 Walter Benjamin. *The Arcades Project* (New York: Belknap Press, 2002).

This indissoluble dyad of aesthetic and ludic codes bears no small resemblance to the much older dyad of form and content. When the meaning of a player-initiated event is perfectly aligned with the aesthetic values and the underlying narration, it is possible to witness the transfiguration of a mere form of entertainment into something else. In the following paragraphs, we will examine how form and content come seamlessly together to turn the ludic object into a work of art.

Terminus, or the end, is the perfect theme for an examination of how actions, spaces, and stories come together in games. And *Terminus* can, in our reading, mean anything from the end of the universe to the end of a player's life. In fact, the end of a player's life is often treated as currency: the eponymous three lives of Mario, the '100% health bar' in action games, and so forth. The terminality of the 'Game Over' sign looms implicitly or explicitly over every interaction, until a coin is inserted, or a button is pressed, and the cycle starts over again. Furthermore, the end of humanity, the end of the world, or the end of the universe are often used as motivational devices to drive players' actions throughout the whole game, but the true nature of these ludic endings is intrinsically cyclical: Every ending is a new beginning. Time, money, and life have been inevitably interlocked in a proto-capitalistic triad ever since games first appeared. Perhaps due to this legacy of the coin, it is rare to find a true 'end' in games. The need to empower players with perceived control of the situation or with the possibility of playing just one more game, leads designers to avoid truly terminal endings. Once dead, the player must be able to insert a new coin or load the last saved state. What player would chose to pay money for a game that promises only one chance to get it right?

From Nietzsche to Kundera, from *Groundhog Day* to *The Matrix*, the eternal return is both prison and redemption for a fallible humanity. Ludic texts have dealt extensively with ending, restarting or interrupting this cycle of death and rebirth throughout their history. We will examine three recently released digital games which feature such a cycle both as an aesthetic theme and as a ludic constraint: *Deus Ex*, which places the player at the center of a casual chain bringing about the end of the human, or more precisely, the shift from the human to the post-human;

Fallout 3, which requires players to give birth to a world turned upside down by apocalyptic conflict; and *Mass Effect*, which makes the player a heroic savior, not only of Earth, but of the universe.

In the game *Deus Ex: Human Renaissance*, the player is required to navigate an uncertain web of fleeting relations between multinational corporations, political oligarchies, and extreme Luddites.[4] These groups will in turn attempt to outsmart and betray each other in a series of conspiracies within conspiracies to finally decide the fate of humanity touched by the cursed blessing of cybernetic augmentations for human enhancement. At the end of the game, the player will have to decide between four possible endings:

1. *Angry God*: This choice will wipe out every single human that has chosen to install cybernetic augmentations on him- or herself, which is the majority of people. It will deny humanity the gift of augmentation technology and return the world to a pre-technological era.

2. *Illuminated Oligarchy:* This choice will allow a small political elite to control the augmentation technology effectively creating a strongly layered society.

3. *New Prometheus:* This choice democratizes the augmentation technology making it available to everyone and radically changing humanity forever.

4. *The Nihilist:* the player can also choose not to choose, commit suicide, and let humanity face its own destiny.

The game affords considerable choice as players are allowed to enact one of four endings. The story is engrossing with believable characters and a deep narrative whilst the environments are 'open' according to Umberto Eco's well-known definition of internally dynamic and inde-

---

4 Eidos Montreal, *Deus Ex: Human Renaissance* (EIDOS, 2012).

terminate fields of meanings.⁵ Nonetheless, none of the four possible end narratives are rooted in the play experience throughout the game. Instead, they are sprung on players at the last moment, thereby disregarding the actions undertaken during the course of the entire game, and paying no heed to previous player choices. Furthermore, throughout the whole game, players are subjected to a constant cognitive strain if they are to keep track of the too-many characters and places that are introduced only to disappear without consequence.

Mass Effect is a trilogy of games, in which players are asked to control Commander Shepard, humanity's herald at the Council of all sentient races in the galaxy.⁶ Shepard's ultimate task will be to end the 'Reaper menace', a breed of machines that cyclically destroy all advanced sentient life in the galaxy every 50,000 years. In order to accomplish this task, Shepard must race against time to rally the advanced races of the galaxy and make one final stand. This is not only to save Earth, but also to break the cycle that has continued for millions of years. The game has garnered overwhelming critical praise for its characters, storyline, voice acting, refined combat system, and overall gameplay, but the most remarkable accomplishment is the sense of freedom and consequence offered to players. In the course of three games and countless hours of game play, players have been taught that choices matter. Decisions of who is to be saved, who is to be killed, and who is to be loved actually change the story in each game. Each decision builds upon the last in a great storytelling snowball effect, so that players are amazed at how the game still recognizes and remembers actions performed dozens of hours earlier. The game keeps track of over one thousand variables in order to customize anything from dialogues with non-playing characters to combat sequences so that the play experience touches a very personal note. For most of the duration of the game, story, actions and spaces are tightly knit in a rich and consistent tapestry that sustains the players' experience.

---

5 Umberto Eco, *The Role of the Reader* (Bloomington, IN: Indiana University Press, 1979).

6 Bioware, *Mass Effect 1, 2, 3* (Microsoft Game Studios, 2007, 2010, and 2012).

Players enjoy this freedom of action and pertinent consequences for most of the game, almost until the end, but when the reckoning with the Reaper God-Mind begins, players are boxed in three pre-defined conclusions: control the Reapers, destroy the Reapers, or merge with the Reapers. The main aesthetic difference in the three scenarios is in the color of the shockwave that destroys the Reapers: blue for control, red for destruction, and green for synthesis. These choices disregard all the numerous variables that the game has kept track of for so many hours of play and completely remove any choice at the end of a game *about* making world-altering choices. Furthermore, no matter how hard players try, no matter how proficient they are, all three endings will spell Commander Shepard's death, irreparably violating the legacy of the coin.

Needless to say, thousands of players around the world have felt let down, if not cheated, not from the type of choices offered, but because the rest of the game had led them to expect that the choices it presented were tough to make and would be tied to narratively important consequences.

Collaborative authorship means that players easily invest hundreds of hours in gameplay across three games to be part of the story; players are trained to expect consequence for their actions, and spaces that dynamically adjust themselves accordingly. This collaborative authorship engenders a sense of entitlement, so much so that, frustrated by the canned endings, a large community of players persuaded Bioware, the game's developer, to release an alternative ending. Unfortunately, rather than keeping into account players' actions and offering customized, personal experiences, the new ending provided more background information, preventing players to truly make a difference and betraying the promises of accountability. In other words, the still had no real connection to the rest of the story.

In the game *Fallout 3* players are tumbled into a post-apocalyptic world, two hundred years after a war has raged over resources ending in nuclear holocaust in 2077.[7] The play arena is set in and around Wash-

---

7 Bethesda Game Studio, *Fallout 3* (ZeniMax Media, 2008).

ington. During the introductory sequence, players witness their own birth and their mother's death in the laboratory where the main character's father carries out important research for the benefit of humanity. A few years later, when players have reached maturity in a secure vault far from the laboratory, the father disappears and players receive their initial task: tracking down their father. In the earlier part of the game, players become accustomed to post-apocalyptic hardships: looming and pervasive radiation poisoning, dangerous mutated organisms, and a wasteland where the few remaining humans fight for the last precious resources, the most important of all being drinking water.

When reaching the middle of the game, players rediscover the location of their father's lab – in the Jefferson Memorial. Players also learn the nature of his research. Project Purity is an attempt to purify all the water in the entire Potomac River with a giant water filter constructed inside the Jefferson Memorial. At this point, players are given the task to finish what their father could not and give new life to a dying world. While exploring the building, players learn for the first time that this was the location where their avatar was born. Scattered around the memorial, players may, for instance, stumble upon a red tricycle. Nowhere does it say that it ever belonged to the main character but it is easy to make that assumption. If the physical player also had a similar tricycle (which he/she is quite likely to have), it triggers an incredibly powerful 'resonant' aesthetic device, a poetic effect which anchors narrative, aesthetic, and ludic elements. It provides background information for the father-son relationship and connotes in a personal manner a location that will play a crucial role in the game. We realize that the player's character was born in the Jefferson Memorial and that it is from this place that a new world order will take its beginning. It is not legitimate to assume that all players can establish such a connection upon seeing the tricycle. Furthermore, it is not necessary in order to understand the story and the mission they have been assigned, but players who are able to do so are rewarded with a personal involvement in the backstory and in the ultimate goal of the game. The game is dense with this type of emotionally resonant devices such as the tricycle and not all of them are supposed to be decoded by all players. For example, an important quest revolves around the American Declaration of Independence, which is intended to resonate predominantly with American audiences. Nevertheless, the redundancy of these devices insures that at least some of them will trigger emotional reactions.

A functional and symbolic analysis of player-triggered events taking place at the Jefferson Memorial returns these co-located occurrences:

- (symbolic) birth of a nation
- birth of the game's hero
- death of the hero's mother during childbirth
- death of the hero's father in order to preserve Project Purity
- re-birth of humanity through clean water
- death of the hero in order to activate the water purifier

All these events revolve around a particular location, the pantheon-like structure, and the physical space of the Jefferson Memorial is unfolded in several paths and levels. For instance, it is initially only possible to explore the underground portion of the memorial, eventually unlocking access to the gift shop and only later gaining entrance to the Rotunda. Actions, spaces, and narration are as tight as possible, yet players are still entirely free to decide how to accomplish different tasks, thereby avoiding the danger of a prescriptive design.

This game, like *Deus Ex* and *Mass Effect*, offers a few multiple choices during the end sequence. These are limited to purifying the water for all living organisms including mutated life forms, or to spread a poison through the waters of the Potomac River that would kill all mutants and preserve only 'genetically pure' organisms. The choices are apparently more limited than in the other two games but there are over two hundred possible permutations of the final cut-scene, all of which are determined by the choices made by players throughout the game. This creates an end narrative that is deeply rooted in the play experience. For example, the scarcity of water is in fact not just a plot device but also a key game mechanic since pure water is used to both heal and cure radiation poisoning.

Game designers often deliberately leverage textual openness; in these open gaps the competence of implied players, actualizing more or less explicit narrative structures, reveals the iconic nature of game aesthetics, providing anchors for affective, narrative, and spatial elements. As seen in the examples above, 'openness' in games can be both aesthetic (player's interpretation of a location or element) and ludic (player's choice of what actions to perform). In this balance between aesthetic/ludic openness and closedness, players can find resonance and reverberation within the elements of the game world, suggested by the examples of the tricycle or the Declaration of Independence. A completely open text would give birth to unlimited semiosis, while a 'closed' text would not permit personal interpretation and the emergence of player-defined masks, trivializing any effort towards a polysemic making sense of things. The right balance, achieved, the authors contend, in *Fallout 3*, presents a perfect equilibrium of form (aesthetic values and spaces), function (actions available to players), and narration.

ABOUT THE CONTRIBUTORS

Alessandro Canossa is associate professor at the College of Arts, Media and Design at Northeastern University. He obtained his Master in Sciences of Communication from the University of Turin in 1999, and in 2009 he received his PhD from The Royal Danish Academy of Fine Arts, School of Design, Architecture and Conservation. His doctoral research was carried out in collaboration with IO Interactive, a Square Enix game development studio. It focused on user-centric design methods and approaches. He has recently edited *Game Analytics – Maximizing the Value of Player Data*, the first ever book on the topic of game analytics (the process of discovering and communicating patterns in game data). He is currently investigating the connections between game behavior, context and personality.

Frances Carey joined the British Museum in 1975, becoming Deputy Keeper of the Department of Prints and Drawings. She was responsible for the exhibition *The Apocalypse and the Shape of Things to Come,* in 1999-2000. From 2003-2011 she was the British Museum's first Head of National Programmes and Senior Consultant for Public Engagement. Outside the British Museum she has served on the research review panel for the Statens Museum for Kunst in Copenhagen, regularly judged print, drawing and watercolour competitions and advised charitable bodies in the museum and heritage field. She now works as a freelance writer and consultant, as well as teaching on a Master's degree programme for the Centre for Enlightenment Studies at King's College London, and chairing the Marie-Louise von Motesiczky Charitable Trust, which is involved in the arts, education and social change.

Jørgen Riber Christensen is associate professor of digital aesthetics at the Institute of Communication, Aalborg University. He has published articles and books as author and co-author within the fields of the media, cultural analysis, aesthetics, and British and American literature and culture. The list of books include *Reklametid* (2003), *Open Windows Remediation Strategies in Global Film Adaptations (ed., 2005), Idé-landet – Kunsten og Virksomheden (2007), Marvellous Fantasy (ed., 2009), Medietid*

2.0 (2009), Fingeraftryk. Studier i krimi og det kriminelle (ed., 2010), and Monstrologi: Frygtens manifestationer (ed. 2012). He is editor-in-chief of the journal *Academic Quarter*.

Steen Christiansen is associate professor of English at Aalborg University, Denmark. His research focuses on visual culture, embodiment and media. He has recently published articles on Darren Aronofsky, zombies, and post-cinema.

Ben Dorfman is associate professor of intellectual and cultural history at Aalborg University. He is the author of a range of articles in cultural theory, intellectual and philosophy of history in journals from *Critical Horizons* to *Culture, Theory & Critique*. He has a forthcoming article on human rights and counter-culture during the Cold War in the volume *Human Rights during the Cold War* (Routledge) and his current book project concerns the relationship between human rights and philosophy of history. Ben is also editor of the journal *Ideas in History*.

Camelia Elias is associate professor of American Studies at Roskilde University. She has published books on the concept of fragment, on the gaze in feminist, queer, and postcolonial films, a monograph on the poet Lynn Emanuel, an introduction to literary theory, and a 'treatise' on creative writing. She has also edited books within cultural studies and poetry. Currently she is working on the poets of the 60s and Tarot, which springs out of her research in esoteric movements and mysticism. She is the president of the largest collection of twentieth-century tarot cards: the 'K. Frank Jensen Collection', at Roskilde University Library.

Joe Goddard is associate professor, teaching American history and politics at the University of Copenhagen in Denmark, and has previously taught at the University of Aalborg and Copenhagen Business School. Goddard's two most recent major works are Contemporary America (fourth edition, with Russell Duncan), published by Palgrave Macmillan in August 2013, and *Being American on the Edge: Penurbia in America*, also published by Palgrave Macmillan in August 2012. Goddard is currently working on projects which chart the history of environmental thought in the U.S. through children's literature and alternative magazines.

Brian Russell Graham is assistant professor of literature, media and culture at Aalborg University. His first monograph, *The Necessary Unity of Opposites*, published by University of Toronto Press in 2011, is a study of Northrop Frye, particularly Frye's dialectical thinking. Graham continues to work with literary and cultural theory, but has also begun original research on English poet William Blake. He also teaches and writes about popular culture.

Jens Kirk is associate professor of English literature and culture at Aalborg University. His special teaching and research interests include contemporary British literature and literary culture. Apart from researching contemporary British writers, he has recently published articles on a range of current issues: the pros and cons of performance-based research funding in the Humanities (together with Jørgen Riber Christensen), digital fan fiction and the idea of transgression, Internet Austen fan culture, and *Flash* in digital fiction. He remains fascinated by the role of psychogeography in contemporary British letters and is currently working on a project entitled representations of M25 across genres and media.

Robert W. Rix is associate professor at the Department of English, Germanic and Romance Studies, University of Copenhagen. He has published widely in several areas relating to the eighteenth century: politics, language, poetry, nationalism, and religion. He is editor of *Romantik: Journal for the Study of Romanticisms.* One focus of his work has been the poet and painter William Blake, who is the subject of the monograph *William Blake and the Cultures of Radical Christianity* (2007). In recent years, Rix has written a number of articles on medieval matters. A book entitled *The Barbarian North in Medieval Imagination* is forthcoming.

Bent Sørensen has a PhD in American Literature from Aalborg University, where he is associate professor of English. He teaches creative writing and twentieth and twenty-first-century literature and cultural studies. He has published books on Edgar Allen Poe and on American literary generations. He has edited volumes on interarts aesthetics and on cultural text studies. Major articles on T.S. Eliot, Nella Larsen, The Beats, Douglas Coupland, Bret Easton Ellis, Cormac McCarthy, Jonathan Lethem, a.m.o. have appeared in *The Explicator, Philament, OASIS, Orbis Litterarum, The Nordic Journal of English Studies, Literary Research, Contemporary Critical Studies* and international collections of essays.